LATIN
IS
FUN

Book I

LATIN IS FUN

Book I

Lively lessons for beginners

John C. Traupman, Ph.D.
St. Joseph's University
Philadelphia

Dedicated to serving our nation's youth

When ordering this book, please specify *either* **R 487 S** *or*
LATIN IS FUN, BOOK I, SOFTBOUND EDITION

AMSCO SCHOOL PUBLICATIONS, INC.
315 Hudson Street / New York, N.Y. 10013

Illustrations by Gerald Smith and Tom O'Sullivan

ISBN 0-87720-550-7

Preface

LATIN IS FUN, BOOK I provides an introductory program that makes language acquisition a natural, personalized, enjoyable, and rewarding experience. The book provides all the elements for a one-year course.

LATIN IS FUN, BOOK I is designed to help students attain an acceptable level of proficiency in four basic skills — reading, writing, listening, and speaking — developed through simple materials in visually focused contexts that students can easily relate to their own experiences. Students are asked easy-to-answer questions that require them to speak about their daily lives, express their opinions, and supply real information.

Along the way, students also enter the world of the Romans and through the medium of the Latin language learn to identify with this *Mundus Romanus* as if it were the still living culture it once was.

LATIN IS FUN, BOOK I consists of six parts. Each part contains four lessons, followed by a *Recognitio* unit, in which structure and vocabulary are recapitulated through various *activitates*. These include games and puzzles as well as more conventional types of exercises. Parts III and VI are followed by an Achievement Test.

Each lesson includes a step-by-step sequence of the following student-directed elements, which are designed to make the materials immediately accessible as well as give students the feeling that they can have fun learning and practicing their Latin.

Vocabulary

Each lesson begins with topically related sets of drawings that convey the meanings of new words in Latin, without recourse to English. This device enables students to make a direct and vivid association between the Latin terms and their meanings. The *activitates* also use pictures to practice and review Latin words and expressions.

To facilitate comprehension, the book uses cognates of English words wherever suitable, especially in the first lessons, which are based largely on Latin words that are identical to or closely resemble their English equivalents. Where the English word is different from the Latin word, pictures simplify identification. Beginning a course in this way shows the students that Latin is not so "ancient" after all and helps them overcome any fears that they may have about the difficulty of learning a "foreign" language.

Structures

LATIN IS FUN, BOOK I uses a simple, straightforward presentation of new structural elements. These elements are introduced in small learning components — one at a time — and are directly followed by appropriate *activitates*, many of them visually cued and personalized. Students thus gain a feeling of accomplishment and success by making their own discoveries and formulating their own conclusions.

Reading

Each lesson contains a short, entertaining narrative or playlet that features the new structural elements and vocabulary and reinforces previously learned grammar and expressions. These passages deal with topics that are either related to everyday experiences or to Roman times. Cognates and near-cognates are used extensively.

Conversation

To encourage students to use Latin for communication and self-expression, the book includes short situational dialogs — sometimes practical, sometimes humorous — in all of the lessons. All conversations are illustrated to provide a sense of realism. Conversations are followed by dialog exercises that serve as springboards for additional personalized conversation.

The Latin Connection

Because more than half of all English words are derived from Latin, simple explanations are given to demonstrate the relationship between Latin and English. Exercises in derivations are designed to improve the students' command of both English and Latin.

Testing

The two Achievement Tests are designed to be simple in order to give *all* students a sense of accomplishment. The tests use a variety of techniques through which mastery of structure and vocabulary may be evaluated. Teachers may use them as they appear in the book or modify them to fit particular needs.

A separate *Teacher's Manual and Key* provides suggestions for teaching all elements in the book, additional testing materials, additional background material to Roman culture, and a complete key to all exercises and puzzles.

J.C.T.

Contents

Pronunciation

Some Latin letters are pronounced more or less the way they are in English. Some, however, are quite different. The letters **b, d, f, k, l, m,** and **n** are pronounced as in English. The letter **w** does not exist in Latin.

VOWELS

LATIN LETTERS	ENGLISH SOUND	EXAMPLES
a	*a* in *a*go	compar**ō**
ā	*a* in f*a*ther	im**ā**gō
e	*e* in p*e*t	prop**e**rō
ē	*a* in l*a*te	l**ē**nis
i	*i in h*i*t*	**i**dem
ī	*ee* in k*ee*n	am**ī**cus
o	*o* in *o*ften	n**o**vus
ō	*o* in h*o*pe	n**ō**men
u	*u* in p*u*t	**u**t
ū	*u* in r*u*de	**ū**tor
y	*y* as in ph*y*sics	ph**y**sicus
ȳ	*ee* as in k*ee*n	perist**ȳ**lium

DIPHTHONGS

ae	*y* in b*y*	C**ae**sar
au	*ow* in n*ow*	n**au**ta
ei	*ey* in gr*ey*	d**ei**nde
eu	*eu* in f*eu*d	Orph**eu**s
oe	*oi* in *oi*l	c**oe**pit
ui	*uey* in gl*uey*	c**ui**

CONSONANTS

c	Always like *c* in *c*an	**c**īvis, **c**entum, **c**antō
g	Always like *g* in *g*o	**g**enus, **g**ula, **g**ingīva
h	Always like *h* in *h*ere	**h**īc, **h**orror
j	*y* in *y*es	**j**ungō, **j**am
p	Unaspirated like *p* in s*p*in	s**p**ongia, **pū**pa
r	Trilled with the tip of the tongue against the ridge behind the upper front teeth	prōve**r**bium, **r**ūmor

1

s	Always like *s* in *s*ing	mi*s*er, mor*s*
t	Unaspirated like *t* in s*t*op	s*t*ola, *tō*tus
u	*w* in *w*ine, when unstressed, preceded by **q,** sometimes by **s,** and sometimes by **g,** and followed by a vowel	q*u*ia, s*u*āvis (but s*u*ōrum), disting*u*ō (but exig*u*us)
v	*w* in *w*ine	*v*īvō
x	*x* in si*x*	e*x*actus
z	*dz* in a*dz*e	*z*ōna

CONSONANT GROUPS

bs	*ps* in a*ps*e	o*bs*ideō, ur*bs*
bt	*pt* in ca*pt*ain	o*bt*inēre
cc	*kk* in boo*kk*eeper	e*cc*e, o*cc*īdo, o*cc*āsum
ch	*ch* in *ch*aotic	mā*ch*ina
gg	*gg* in le*g g*uard	a*gg*er
gu	*gw* in an*gu*ish	lin*gu*a
ph	*p-h* in to*p-h*eavy	*ph*ōca
qu	*kw* in *qu*ick	*qu*ia
sc	*sc* in *sc*ope	*sc*iō, *sc*ūtum
su	See consonant **u**	
th	*t* in *t*ake	*th*eātrum
ti	*ti* in pa*ti*o	nā*ti*ōnēs

STRESS

Words of two syllables are stressed on the first syllable: **o̦mnēs, ta̦ngō, ge̦rit.** Words of more than two syllables are stressed on the next to the last syllable if it is long (that is, if it has a long mark [¯], called a "macron," over the vowel or if it is followed by two consonants): **amī̦cus, regu̦ntur.** If the next to the last syllable is short, the stress falls on the syllable before it: **ma̦china, ge̦ritur.**

Pars
Prima

Latīna et Anglica

Words That Are the Same or Similar in Latin and English; Plural of Nouns; Accusative Case

1 So you're starting to learn Latin. **Splendidum!** You'll have a lot of fun learning the Latin language, and it won't be that hard. Do you know why? Well, there are lots of words that are the same in English and Latin. Over half of all English words come from Latin. These words may be pronounced differently, but many of them are spelled the same way and have exactly the same meaning. There are also Latin words that have a slightly different spelling but can be recognized instantly by anyone who speaks English. You will have fun converting these Latin words into English.

O.K. Let's look at some of them and pronounce them the Latin way. Your teacher will show you how.

Words that are exactly the same in English and Latin:

aliās	insomnia	odor	speculātor
alibī	integer	pauper	splendor
alumnus	inventor	plūs	stadium
bonus	jānitor	radius	status
circus	jūnior	rigor	stimulus
color	labor	rūmor	successor
crātēr	lēgislātor	sagittārius	textile
dictātor	līberātor	senātor	tumor
error	maximum	senior	vacuum
exterior	mīlitia	seriēs	ventilātor
favor	minimum	sinister	victor
gladiātor	minister	speciēs	vigor
honor	murmur	specimen	

2 Here are some Latin words that look almost like English words. Repeat them after your teacher and give the English equivalent:

aggressiō	gravitās	nātūra	positiō
agricultūra	horribilis	nātūrālis	postpōnō
astrologia	imāginātiō	necessitās	praetendō
calamitās	immūnis	nōbilitās	probātiō
caverna	latitūdō	occāsiō	prōgressus
cella	longitūdō	pavīmentum	prōverbium
confirmō	māchina	perfectus	prōvincia
familia	mystērium	portābilis	rapidus

receptiō	rosa	sēnsibilis	suprēmus
religiō	salūtō	solidus	suspīciōsus
removeō	sculptūra	spongia	terribilis
revōcō	sēcrētum	stomachus	testimōnium
rōbustus	sēcūritās	strūctūra	

3 Now you will see how easy it is to convert some Latin words to English words. Latin nouns ending in **-tia** and **-cia** often become English words ending in *-ce*. For example, **dīligen*tia*** becomes *diligence*. If you change the ending **-tia/-cia** to *-ce* in the following Latin words, which English words do you get?

scientia   _____

prōvincia   _____

patientia   _____

malitia   _____

Good! Now you'll be able to understand hundreds of other Latin words like these and immediately give the English form.

Here's another clue. Latin nouns ending in **-ia** sometimes become English words ending in *-y*. For example, **famil*ia*** becomes *family*. If you change the ending **-ia** to *-y* in the following Latin nouns, which English words do you get?

injūria   _____

lūxuria   _____

glōria   _____

historia   _____

There are hundreds of Latin nouns ending in **-ās** that become English words ending in *-y*. For example, **calamitās** becomes *calamity*. If you change the ending **-as** to *-y* in the following Latin nouns, which English words do you get?

necessitās   _____

nōbilitās   _____

quālitās   _____

sēcūritās   _____

Did you notice that in each Latin word ending in **-ās** the preceding two letters were always **-it-?** With a little effort, you can probably think of dozens of English words ending in *-ity*. For each one, there is a Latin word ending in **-itās.** One more thing: each of the four Latin words above are nouns that refer to *qualities* rather than to *things* or *persons*. The same holds true for all words with similar endings.

One more clue. If you look over the long list of Latin words in Section 2 that look almost like English words, you will notice several that end in **-iō**; for example, **aggressiō.** All you have to do is add an *n* and you have the corresponding English noun. Using that method, which English words do you get from the following Latin nouns?

imāginātiō _____

occāsiō _____

positiō _____

receptiō _____

Again, did you notice that the nouns in this group, too, refer to *qualities* or *ideas* rather than to *things* or *persons?* In English, such nouns are called *abstract* nouns. Later on, we will point out that nouns can be masculine, feminine, or neuter. Here is an important lesson: all of these noun groups that we have just been discussing are feminine nouns; and all similar nouns that you can think of are also feminine.

In effect, you have just learned several hundred new Latin words. You know that they are feminine nouns, and you know their English counterparts. You even know that they are all abstract nouns.

4 Here are some Latin words that are somewhat different from English, but you'll have no difficulty figuring out their meanings. Repeat them aloud after your teacher:

medicus

discipulus

asinus

porcus

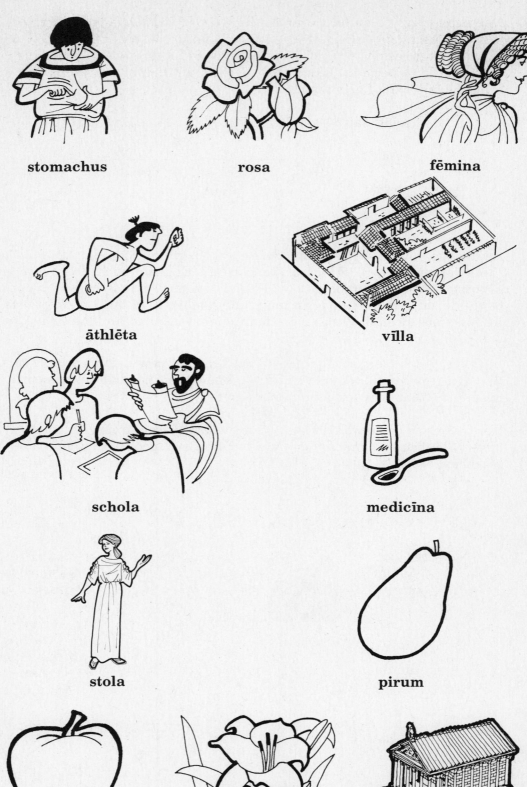

stomachus

rosa

fēmina

āthlēta

vīlla

schola

medicīna

stola

pirum

mālum

līlium

templum

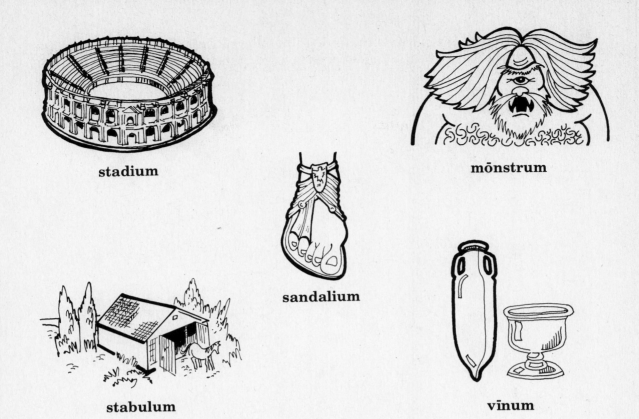

stadium

mōnstrum

sandalium

stabulum

vīnum

In English, we often use the definite article *the* or the indefinite article *a* or *an* before nouns. The Romans used neither. Therefore, **āthlēta** can mean either *the athlete* or *an athlete,* depending on the sentence as a whole in which the word is used.

5 Well, so much for vocabulary. Let's learn some Latin grammar now. Latin nouns can be either masculine, feminine, or neuter. (The Latin word **neuter** simply means *neither.*) The problem is: how do you tell which words are masculine, which are feminine, and which are neuter? It's obvious that **fēmina** (*woman*) and **puella** (*girl*) are feminine, while **pater** (*father*) and **puer** (*boy*) are masculine, and **mālum** (*apple*), **pirum** (*pear*), and **līlium** (*lily*) can be expected to be neuter. But why should **vīlla** (*farmhouse*) be feminine, **lectus** (*bed*) masculine, and **cubiculum** (*bedroom*) neuter? There is no logical reason. We can say that the gender of Latin nouns is either *natural* or *grammatical.*

The ENDINGS of Latin words often give a clue to their gender. For example, nouns ending in **-a,** like **rosa** (*rose*) and **schola** (*school*), are usually feminine, nouns ending in **-us,** like **asinus** (*donkey*) and **medicus** (*doctor*) are usually masculine, and nouns ending in **-um,** like **vīnum** (*wine*) and **stabulum** (*stable*) are usually neuter. We emphasize the word *usually* because **āthlēta** (*athlete*), **agricola** (*farmer*), and **nauta** (*sailor*), even though they end in **-a,** are masculine because they refer to males. Hereafter, the gender of every new noun will be indicated with the letter *m* for masculine nouns, *f* for feminine nouns, and *n* for neuter nouns.

6 Here are some Latin words that are quite different from English and that you must memorize. Note the gender of each word. Repeat aloud after your teacher:

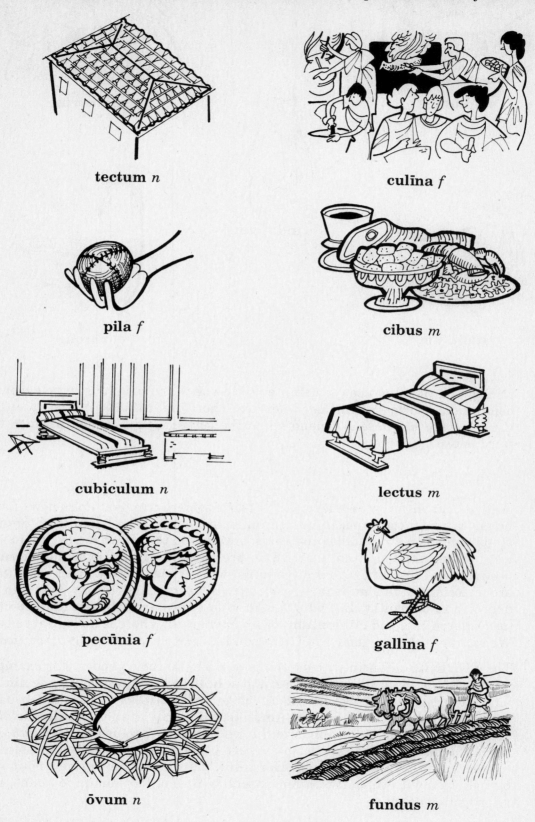

tectum *n*

culīna *f*

pila *f*

cibus *m*

cubiculum *n*

lectus *m*

pecūnia *f*

gallīna *f*

ōvum *n*

fundus *m*

equus *m*

vacca *f*

aqua *f*

caelum *n*

cerasum *n*

tunica *f*

stella *f*

oppidum *n*

puella *f*

balneum *n*

agricola *m*

amīcus *m*

casa *f*

plaustrum *n*

Āctivitātēs

A. Match the following words with the correct pictures:

vīlla	medicus	vīnum
amīcus	schola	fēmina
templum	plaustrum	casa
stadium	rosa	stabulum
pirum	sandalium	pila
discipulus	porcus	āthlēta
mālum	tunica	stola

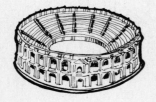

1. _____

3. _____

5. _____

2. _____

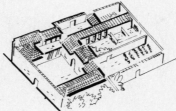

4. _____

6. _____

7. _____

12. _____

17. _____

8. _____

13. _____

18. _____

9. _____

14. _____

19. _____

10. _____

15. _____

20. _____

11. _____

16. _____

21. _____

1. _____

2. _____

3. _____

4. _____

5. _____

6. _____

7. _____

8. _____

9. _____

10. _____

11. _____

12. _____

13. _____

14. _____

15. _____

16.  18. _____ 20. _____

17.  19. _____ 21. _____

7 Now that you have learned some Latin grammar, let's see whether you can figure out the meaning of these sentences:

1. **Discipulus est studiōsus.**

4. **Vīlla est remōta.**

2. **Asinus est obstinātus.**

5. **Mālum est rubrum.**

3. **Porcus est obēsus.**

6. **Stola est longa.**

7. Līlium est pūrum.

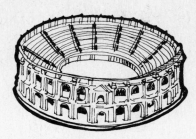

12. Stadium est vacuum.

8. Vīnum est bonum.

13. Āthlēta est rōbustus.

9. Fēmina est modesta.

14. Stabulum est sordidum.

10. Rosa est rubra.

15. Templum est sacrum.

11. Pila est rotunda.

16. Medicīna est amāra.

16   *LECTIO I*

Incrēdibile! Here are some more:

1. Balneum est calidum.

6. Vacca est tarda.

2. Tectum est altum.

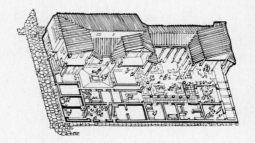

7. Vīlla est spatiōsa.

3. Cibus est bonus.

8. Aqua est frīgida.

4. Pecūnia est rāra.

9. Tunica est sordida.

5. Equus est rapidus.

10. Agricola est ambitiōsus.

11. Puella est laeta.

12. Oppidum est prosperum.

8 How observant are you? Did you notice the *endings* of the adjectives? What is

the ending when the noun is feminine? _____ What is the ending when

the noun is masculine? _____ What is the ending when the noun is neuter?

_____ Feminine nouns ending in **-a** (and, as you saw, a few masculine nouns
ending in **-a**) belong to the same class of nouns, called the FIRST DECLEN-
SION. Masculine nouns ending in **-us** and neuter nouns ending in **-um** belong
to the SECOND DECLENSION. As you will see, there are five declensions in
all.

So far you have used nouns only as subjects of sentences; those nouns are said
to be in the NOMINATIVE (or subjective) case. Notice that the adjective after
the verb **est** (*he/she/it is*) is also in the NOMINATIVE case. When nouns are
used as direct objects in a sentence, those nouns are said to be in the ACCUSA-
TIVE (or objective) case. When nouns like **stella** (*star*), **fundus** (*farm*), or
mālum (*apple*) are used as direct objects in a sentence, the final letter for each
is **m.** The same holds true for adjectives like **bonus, bona, bonum** (*good*).

Let's see whether you can figure out the meaning of the following sentences
containing a direct object (in the accusative case) and using the verb **habet** (*he,
she, it has*). Notice that in a Latin sentence the object comes right after the
subject and the verb normally comes at the end of the sentence. In English, we
can tell from the position of words which is the subject and which is the object.
But Latin is an *inflected* language; that is, Latin *inflects* (changes the endings
of) nouns and adjectives to indicate whether they are the subjects or objects of
sentences.

Repeat the sentences aloud after your teacher:

1. Medicus medicīnam habet.

2. Fēmina stolam habet.

3. Gallīna ōvum habet.

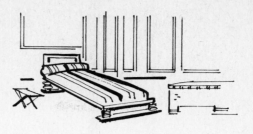

8. Cubiculum lectum habet.

4. Stabulum tectum nōn habet.

9. Agricola fundum habet.

5. Puella pilam habet.

10. Puella mālum et cerasum habet.

6. Agricola equum et vaccam habet.

11. Caelum stellam habet.

7. Āthlēta cibum habet.

12. Discipulus amīcum habet.

Activitās

C. Choose the direct object with the correct accusative ending and write it in the space provided:

1. Puella (pecūnia/pecūniam) habet. _____

2. Agricola (fundus/fundum) habet. _____

3. Fēmina (amīcus/amīcum) habet. _____

4. Medicus (medicīnam/medicīna) habet. _____

5. Casa (culīna/culīnam) habet. _____

6. Discipulus (tunicam/tunica) habet. _____

7. Āthlēta (pila/pilam) habet. _____

8. Agricola (porcum/porcus) habet. _____

9 Since you can now recognize the *singular* form of the nouns you have met, let's look at the *plural* forms. Look carefully at these two groups:

A	B
NOMINATIVE SINGULAR	NOMINATIVE PLURAL
vīll*a*	vīll*ae*
ros*a*	ros*ae*
discipul*us*	discipul*ī*
porc*us*	porc*ī*
ōv*um*	ōv*a*
balne*um*	balne*a*

Group A contains singular nouns; Group B contains the plural forms of those nouns.

What is the plural ending of a feminine noun of the first declension? _____

What is the plural ending of a masculine noun of the second declension? _____

What is the plural ending of a neuter noun of the second declension? _____

Activitātēs

D. Look at the pictures on the next page, choose the correct form of the noun, and write it in the space provided. If there is only one item, choose the singular form; if there are more than one, choose the plural form:

1. rosa   rosae   _____

4. equus   equī   _____

2. fēmina   fēminae _____

5. cerasum   cerasa _____

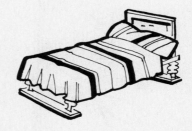

3. stella   stellae   _____

6. lectus   lectī   _____

E. Indicate the gender of the following nouns with the symbol *m*, *f*, or *n*. Then give the plural form:

1. gallīna   _____   _____

2. tectum   _____   _____

3. fundus   _____   _____

4. vacca   _____   _____

5. oppidum   _____   _____

6. āthlēta   _____   _____

7. puella   _____   _____

8. asinus   _____   _____

9. pila _____ _____

10. cubiculum _____ _____

10 When plural nouns, such as **vaccae** (*cows*), **medicī** (*doctors*), and **plaustra** (*wagons*), occur as the direct object in a sentence, the forms **vaccās, medicōs,** and **plaustra** are used to indicate the accusative case. Notice that neuter nouns like **plaustra** always have the same form as subjects and direct objects, that is, the endings of the nominative and the accusative are the same.

Can you figure out the meanings of the following sentences? Repeat them aloud after your teacher:

1. Agricola vaccās habet.

5. Medicus medicīnās habet.

2. Āthlēta mūsculōs habet.

6. Plaustrum equōs nōn habet.

3. Gallīna ōva habet.

7. Discipulus sandalia habet.

4. Puella rosās et līlia habet.

8. Agricola porcōs et gallīnās habet.

22   *LECTIO I*

Āctivitātēs

F. Make the nouns and adjectives plural. Write the correct endings in the spaces provided. Notice that the singular verb **est** becomes plural **sunt** ([*they*] *are*):

1. Rosa est rubra.   Ros____ sunt rubr____.

2. Pila est rotunda.   Pil____ sunt rotund____.

3. Stabulum est vacuum.   Stabul____ sunt vacu____.

4. Pirum est bonum.   Pir____ sunt bon____.

5. Porcus est obēsus.   Porc____ sunt obēs____.

6. Stadium est spatiōsum.   Stadi____ sunt spatiōs____.

7. Equus est rapidus.   Equ____ sunt rapid____.

8. Balneum est calidum.   Balne____ sunt calid____.

G. Make the singular nouns plural. Write the correct endings in the spaces provided. Notice that the singular verb **habet** becomes plural **habent** ([*they*] *have*):

1. Puella pirum habet.   Puell____ pir____ habent.

2. Āthlēta mūsculum habet. Āthlēt____ mūscul____ habent.

3. Agricola vaccam habet.   Agricol____ vacc____ habent.

4. Medicus medicīnam habet. Medic____ medicīn____ habent.

5. Fēmina rosam habet.   Fēmin____ ros____ habent.

6. Gallīna ōvum habet.   Gallīn____ ōv____ habent.

7. Āthlēta pilam habet.   Āthlēt____ pil____ habent.

8. Agricola fundum habet.   Agricol____ fund____ habent.

H. Make the plural nouns singular. Write the correct endings in the spaces provided:

1. Puellae līlia habent.   Puell____ līli____ habet.

2. Fēminae stolās habent.   Fēmin____ stol____ habet.

3. Casae tecta habent.   Cas____ tect____ habet.

4. Scholae discipulōs habent. Schol_____ discipul_____ habet.

5. Caela stellās habent. Cael_____ stell_____ habet.

6. Cubicula lectōs habent. Cubicul_____ lect_____ habet.

7. Discipulī amīcōs habent. Discipul_____ amīc_____ habet.

8. Oppida templa habent. Oppid_____ templ_____ habet.

I. Choose the words from the list that tell others about you:

bona, bonus   modesta, modestus
studiōsa, studiōsus   rōbusta, rōbustus
obstināta, obstinātus sordida, sordidus
obēsa, obēsus   tarda, tardus
pūra, pūrus   rapida, rapidus

Ego sum (*I am*) 1. _____

2. _____

3. _____

4. _____

5. _____

THE LATIN CONNECTION

Write the English word next to the Latin word from which it is derived:

1. sandalium _____   oval
                                        disciple
2. cubiculum _____   pork
                                        stole
3. fēmina   _____   sandal
                                        stable
4. tunica   _____   cubicle
                                        lily
5. stabulum   _____   tunic
                                        feminine
6. ōvum   _____

7. līlium   _____

8. discipulus _____

9. stola   _____

10. porcus   _____

Familia Rōmāna

Plural of Nouns (Continued)

1 Vocābula

avus

avia

pater

māter

frāter (fīlius)

soror (fīlia)

frāterculus

īnfāns

fēlēs

canis

2 Here you have one big, happy family. It's obvious who all the members are. Let's take a closer look:

Familia Seneca est magna. Lūcius est avus et Līvia est avia. Pater est Marcellus. Quis est māter? Claudia est māter. Marcellus et Claudia sunt parentēs. Rūfus est fīlius. Terentius quoque est fīlius. Terentius est minor nātū quam Rūfus. Is est frāterculus. Rūfus et Terentius sunt frātrēs.

quis? *who?*

parentēs *mpl parents*
quoque *too*
minor nātū quam *younger than*
  is *he*
frātrēs *mpl brothers*

Marcella est fīlia. Jūlia quoque est fīlia. Jūlia est minor nātū quam Marcella. Jūlia est īnfāns. Marcella et Jūlia sunt sorōrēs.

sorōrēs *fpl sisters*

Rūfus et Terentius et Marcella et Jūlia sunt līberī. Sunt quattuor līberī in familiā.

līberī *mpl children*
  Sunt *There are*
  quattuor *four*

Sunt octō persōnae in familiā. Sunt etiam

octō *eight*   **persōna** *f person*
etiam *also*

fēlēs et canis. Fēlēs et canis sunt animālia domestica.

Familia Seneca in Ītaliā habitat. Quam splendida familia!

animālia *npl animals*
domesticus -a -um *domestic*
Ītalia *f Italy* **habitat** *lives*
quam *what a*
splendidus -a -um *splendid*

Āctivitātēs

A. Let's get to know the members of the family by name. Look at the pictures and then supply the correct missing name of the person:

1. Lūcius et _____.

4. Marcellus et _____.

2. Claudia et _____.

5. Rūfus et _____.

3. Līvia et _____.

6. Marcellus et _____.

7. Marcella et _____.

10. Lūcius et _____.

8. Marcellus et _____.

11. Rūfus et Marcella et _____.

9. Marcellus et _____.

12. Claudia et _____.

B. Match the words with the pictures:

pater	fēlēs	avus
frāter	frāterculus	īnfāns
parentēs	māter	soror
avia	canis	

1. _____.

2. _____.

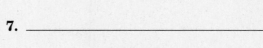

3. _____

7. _____

4. _____

8. _____

5. _____

9. _____

6. _____

10. _____

11. _____

3   Here's something new. All of the words we learned in Lesson 1 that end in **-us** (like **cibus**) are masculine; those that end in **-a** (like **puella**) are feminine, and those that end in **-um** (like **oppidum**) are neuter. In this lesson, we see words that have various endings in the nominative case. But they have a common ending when they are used as the direct object in a sentence.

Look carefully at these two groups. Repeat each set of nouns aloud after your teacher:

A	B
AS SUBJECT	AS OBJECT
pater	pat*rem*
māter	māt*rem*
frāter	frāt*rem*
soror	sorōr*em*
īnfāns	īnfant*em*
parēns	parent*em*
fēlēs	fēl*em*
canis	can*em*
animal	animal

Did you notice that the **e** in **pat*er*, māt*er*,** and **frāt*er*** drops out of the STEM when those nouns are used as direct objects? (The STEM is the part of the word to which the endings are added.) The nominative case often does not show the full stem. For example, the full stem **parent-** exists in the accusative but not in the nominative case, where the **t** is missing. Did you notice that **animal**, like all other neuter nouns, remains the same in the nominative and accusative cases?

We saw in Lesson 1 that the gender of Latin nouns is either *natural* or *grammatical.* Accordingly, what is the gender of **pater** and **frāter?** _____

What is the gender of **māter** and **soror?** _____. What is the gender of **īnfāns, parēns, fēlēs,** and **canis?** _____ Well, if you wrote "masculine (m)" for the first two, you are correct. If you wrote "feminine (f)" for the next two, you are right again. But a baby, parent, dog, and cat can be either male or female, can't they? Therefore, if you wrote "masculine or feminine (m/f)," you can give yourself a pat on the back. You could say the same thing about the word **animal.** But language isn't always logical. The Romans simply decided to make **animal** neuter!

Words like **puer** (*boy*), **magister** (*teacher*), **liber** (*book*), and **vir** (*man*) do not have the masculine ending **-us** as subjects, but they have the regular ending **-um** as direct objects. There are also a few adjectives — like **sacer, sacra,**

sacrum (*holy*), **līber, lībera, līberum** (*free*) — that do not have the masculine ending **-us.** But still they all belong to the second declension.

Now examine the following two groups:

A	B
AS SUBJECT (NOMINATIVE)	AS OBJECT (ACCUSATIVE)

A	B
puer *m*	**puer***um*
vir *m*	**vir***um*
magister *m*	**magistr***um*
liber *m*	**libr***um*
pater *m*	**patr***em*
māter *f*	**mātr***em*
frāter *m*	**frātr***em*

If you look at Group B, you can see that the first four nouns belong to one class of nouns (the second declension) and the last three belong to a different class of nouns (the third declension). Did you notice that the **e** in **magister** and **liber** drops out of the STEM when these nouns are in the accusative case, but the **e** does not drop out of the STEM of **puer?**

The difference between these two declensions will become even clearer when we look at their *plural* forms.

Examine the following two groups. Repeat each set of Latin nouns aloud after your teacher:

A	B
AS SUBJECT (NOMINATIVE)	AS OBJECT (ACCUSATIVE)

A	B
parent*ēs*	**parent***ēs*
patr*ēs*	**patr***ēs*
sorōr*ēs*	**sorōr***ēs*
īnfant*ēs*	**īnfant***ēs*
fēl*ēs*	**fēl***ēs*
can*ēs*	**can***ēs*
animāl*ia*	**animāl***ia*

But:

A	B
av*ī*	**av***ōs*
fīli*ī*	**fīli***ōs*
līber*ī*	**līber***ōs*
frātercul*ī*	**frātercul***ōs*
magistr*ī*	**magistr***ōs*
puer*ī*	**puer***ōs*
vir*ī*	**vir***ōs*
fīli*ae*	**fīli***ās*
avi*ae*	**avi***ās*

Āctivitātēs

C. Match the words with the pictures:

fīlia	avus	frātrēs
sorōrēs	parentēs	avia
fēlēs	fīlius	frāterculus
canēs		

1. _____

5. _____

2. _____

6. _____

3. _____

7. _____

4. _____

8. _____

9. _____   10. _____

D. Vērum aut Falsum. If the statement about the Seneca family is true, write **Vērum** in the space provided. If it is false, write **Falsum** and correct the statement:

1. Lūcius est avus. _____

2. Canis est animal. _____

3. Pater est Marcellus. _____

4. Rūfus est fīlia. _____

5. Claudia est avia. _____

6. Marcellus est parēns. _____

7. Terentius est frāterculus. _____

8. Īnfāns est fīlia. _____

9. Rūfus est puer. _____

10. Jūlia est īnfāns. _____

11. Marcellus et Claudia sunt parentēs. _____

12. Canis et fēlēs sunt animālia domestica. _____

13. Sunt quattuor līberī in familiā. _____

14. Terentius et Rūfus sunt sorōrēs. _____

15. Marcella et Jūlia sunt fīliī. _____

E. Match the descriptions with the pictures:

Pater līberōs dēmōnstrat
  (*points out*).
Frāter frāterculum tenet
  (*is holding*).
Avia īnfantem tenet.
Avus canem tenet.
Canis fēlem tenet.

Sorōrēs frātrēs dēmōnstrant.
Īnfāns mālum tenet.
Frātrēs parentēs dēmōnstrant.
Māter et fīlia animālia tenent.
Soror frāterculum tenet.
Avus et avia animālia tenent.
Parentēs līberōs dēmōnstrant.

1. _____

5. _____

2. _____

6. _____

3. _____

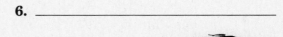

7. _____

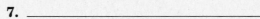

4. _____

8. _____

9. _____

11. _____

10. _____

12. _____

4   There are many Latin nouns of the third declension ending in **-or** that express the doer of an action; for example, **āctor.** Such words are masculine. (Not all Latin words that end in **-or** indicate the doer of an action; for example, **clāmor** *m* means *shout;* **arbor** *f* means *tree.*) The Seneca family will now greet some of them. You should recognize all of them without difficulty. Look at the pictures and repeat the sentences aloud:

1. **Pater senātōrem salūtat** (*greets*).

3. **Marcella gladiātōrem salūtat.**

2. **Māter professōrem salūtat.**

4. **Avus lēgislātōrem salūtat.**

5. Frāterculus vēnditōrem salūtat.

7. Avia āctōrem salūtat.

6. Sorōrēs victōrem salūtant.

8. Gladiātōrēs Marcellam salūtant.

Āctivitātēs

F. Make the following Latin words in the nominative case plural:

1. parēns _____
2. īnfāns _____
3. puer _____
4. vir _____
5. soror _____

6. frāter _____
7. frāterculus _____
8. avia _____
9. animal _____
10. āctor _____

G. Put the following words in the accusative case:

1. avus _____
2. pater _____
3. frāter _____
4. parēns _____
5. vir _____

6. fēlēs _____
7. animal _____
8. canis _____
9. īnfāns _____
10. māter _____

CONVERSĀTIŌ

VOCĀBULA

Salvē *Hello*
Quod nōmen est tibi? *What's your name?*
mihi nōmen est *my name is*
Quid agis? *How do you do?*
Valeō. *I'm fine.*
grātiās *thanks*

tū *you*
ego *I*
quoque *too*
Quid novī? *What's new?*
Nihil novī. *Nothing's new.*
Valē *Good-bye*

COLLOQUIUM

Now you can have some fun filling in the missing words of this conversation. Choose your words from the list below:

grātiās	nihil	Et tibi?
nōmen	Salvē	Valē
Lūcius	Valeō	

THE LATIN CONNECTION

Here you have a chance to show other connections between Latin and English. From which Latin words in this lesson do the following English words come and what do the Latin words mean?

1. paternal _____

2. maternal _____

3. fraternal _____

4. canine _____

5. feline _____

6. infant _____

7. parental _____

8. filial _____

RĒS PERSŌNĀLĒS (*Personal matters*)

The Census Bureau is taking a survey. Fill out the information requested about your family:

Nōmen mihi est _____

Pater: _____

Māter: _____

Frātrēs: _____

Sorōrēs: _____

Avus: _____

Avia: _____

III | Schola

Neuter Nouns; Ablative and Vocative Cases

1   As you can imagine, schools were quite different two thousand years ago. The common Latin word for elementary school was **lūdus,** a word that also meant *fun* and *game!* The more advanced school was called **schola.** School was usually held on an open porch (**pergula**). The pupils sat on a bench (**subsellium**) with their wax tablet (**tabula**) on their laps. They wrote on their tablet with a "pencil" (**stilus**) made of wood, bone, or steel, with a pointed end. Sometimes they were permitted to write on a sheet of expensive paper (**charta**) made of papyrus with a pen (**calamus**) dipped in ink (**ātrāmentum**). The children played on the playground (**ārea**).

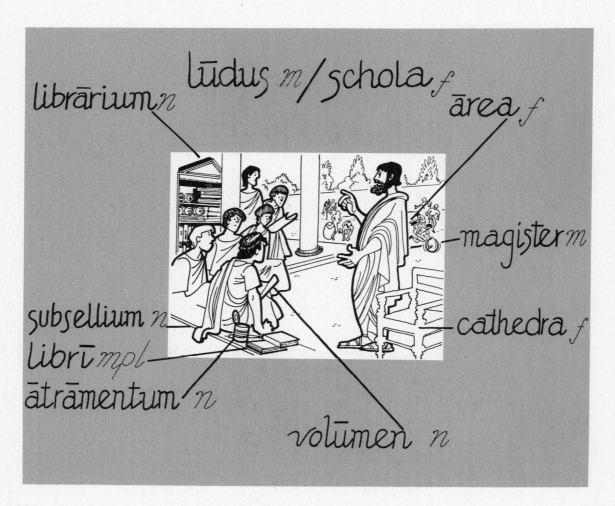

2 Vocābula. Read the words aloud after your teacher:

magister *m*

magistra *f*

liber *m*

discipulus *m*

discipula *f*

charta *f*

schola *f* (or lūdus *m*)

classis *f*

calamus *m*

librārium *n*

volūmen *n*

subsellium *n*

tabula *f*

stilus *m*

ātrāmentum *n*

rēgula *f*

cathedra *f*

fenestra *f*

jānua *f*

Āctivitās

A. Identify the following in Latin and indicate the gender:

1. _____

6. _____

2. _____

7. _____

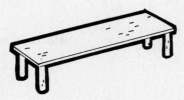

3. _____

8. _____

4. _____

9. _____

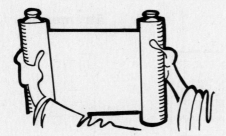

5. _____

10. _____

42   *LECTIO III*

11. _____

14. _____

12. _____

15. _____

13. _____

16. _____

3 Now that you know all of the new words, read the following story and see if you can understand it:

Schola Rōmāna est spatiōsa. Schola fenestram et jānuam nōn habet, sed librārium habet. Magister est persōna intellegēns et populāris. Magister ante classem stat. Classis nōn est magna; est parva sed studiōsa. Sunt trēs discipulī et trēs discipulae. Puerī et puellae in subselliō sedent. Canis et fēlēs nōn in lūdō sunt; sunt in āreā.

Omnis discipulus et omnis discipula habet librum, chartam, calamum, ātrāmentum, rēgulam, stilum, tabulam. Magister volūmen magnum habet.

Magister classem salūtat. Classis magistrum salūtat.

Rōmān_us_ _-a_ _-um_ _Roman_

persōna _-ae_ _f_ _person_

ante (+ _acc_) in _front of_
  stat _stands_
parvus _-a_ _-um_ _small_
  trēs _three_
in _on, in_   **sedent** _sit_

omnis _each_

4 As you read the story, did you notice the preposition **in**? It can mean *on* or *in*. The noun that follows the preposition has a special ending to show that it is not the subject or direct object but the object of the preposition. For example, **ārea** ends in a short **-a** when it is the subject of a sentence. When it is the object of a preposition like **in**, the ending becomes long: **in āreā** (*on the playground*); the noun is in the ABLATIVE CASE.

As you have seen, when the masculine noun **lūdus** (*school*) is the subject of a sentence, it ends in **-us**. When it comes after the Latin preposition **in**, the ending charges to **-ō**: **in lūdō** (*in school*). **Lūdō** is the ABLATIVE CASE.

When the neuter noun **subsellium** is the subject of a sentence, it ends in **-um**. When it comes after the Latin preposition **in**, the ending changes to **-ō**: **in subselliō** (*on a bench*). **Subselliō** is the ABLATIVE case.

Āctivitātēs

B. Complete the sentences about the story you have just read:

1. Schola Rōmāna est _____ .

2. Schola nōn habet fenestram et _____ .

3. Schola habet _____ .

4. Classis nōn est _____ .

5. In lūdō sunt _____ discipulī et _____ discipulae.

6. Puerī et puellae sedent in _____ .

7. Canis et fēlēs nōn sunt in _____ .

8. Canis et fēlēs sunt in _____ .

9. Magister est intellegēns et _____ .

10. Magister stat ante _____ .

11. Magister salūtat _____ .

12. Classis salūtat _____ .

C. If you remember that words like **medicīna** (*medicine*) are feminine, words like **amīcus** (*friend*) and **puer** (*boy*) are masculine, and words like **balneum** (*bath*) are neuter, you should have no trouble marking the gender of the following new nouns. Write *m, f,* or *n* in the space provided. If a noun can be masculine or feminine, write *m/f:*

1. discipulus   _____   2. discipula   _____

3. schola	_____		11. charta	_____
4. lūdus	_____		12. calamus	_____
5. librārium	_____		13. tabula	_____
6. magister	_____		14. stilus	_____
7. ātrāmentum	_____		15. rēgula	_____
8. ārea	_____		16. magistra	_____
9. subsellium	_____		17. jānua	_____
10. liber	_____		18. fenestra	_____

D. Look at each picture. Then choose the correct word that the picture calls for and write it in the space provided:

1. Discipulus _____ habet.
   (calamus/calamum)

4. Magister _____ salūtat.
   (discipulī/discipulōs)

2. Discipula _____ habet.
   (tabula/tabulam)

5. Magister in _____ sedet.
   (cathedra/cathedrā)

3. Magistra _____ habet.
   (librī/librōs)

6. Canis _____ habet.
   (liber/librum)

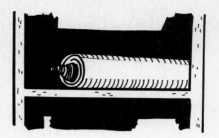

7. Lūdus _____ habet.
(librārium/librāria)

11. Volūmen in _____ est.
(librārium/librāriō)

8. Magister _____ habet.
(chartae/chartās)

12. Canis et fēlēs in _____ sunt.
(āreā/ārea)

9. Discipulae _____ salūtant.
(magistra/magistram)

13. Classis _____ salūtat.
(magistrum/magistrōs)

10. Discipulī in _____ sedent.
(subselliō/subsellium)

14. Magister _____ salūtat.
(classem/classis)

E. Each group contains one word that does not fit in with the group. Write the misfit in the space provided. Be prepared to explain orally the reason for your selection:

1. discipulus, magister, īnfāns, discipula _____

2. liber, calamus, stadium, stilus _____

3. stella, equus, gallīna, vacca   _____

4. rēgula, classis, canis, charta   _____

5. puer, ārea, puella, fīlius, fīlia   _____

6. magistra, fēmina, puella, cathedra   _____

7. asinus, subsellium, fēlēs, canis   _____

8. schola, medicus, magister, agricola   _____

9. templum, lectus, stabulum, vīlla   _____

10. cerasum, pirum, mālum, magistra   _____

11. magistra, balneum, discipula, magister   _____

12. liber, volūmen, ātrāmentum, āthlēta   _____

5 A scroll (**volūmen**) was made of papyrus and consisted of a number of pages (**pāginae**), joined to one another with glue. **Volūmen** is a neuter noun, just like **templum** (*temple*), and it has the same form in the nominative and accusative cases.

Look carefully at these groups:

A	B
SINGULAR	PLURAL
as subject and object	as subject and object
templ*um* (*temple*)	templ*a* (*temples*)
balne*um* (*bath*)	balne*a* (*baths*)
volū*men* (*scroll*)	volū*mina* (*scrolls*)
flū*men* (*river*)	flū*mina* (*rivers*)
nō*men* (*name*)	nō*mina* (*names*)
car*men* (*song*)	car*mina* (*songs*)
forā*men* (*hole*)	forā*mina* (*holes*)

As you can see, the first two words above (**templum** and **balneum**) belong to one class of neuter nouns (the second declension). The rest of the nouns belong to a different class of neuter nouns (the third declension). Did you notice that the **e** in the stem of the third-declension nouns changes to **i**? But no matter which class they belong to, all neuter nouns end in **a** in the plural, both as subjects and direct objects.

Āctivitās

F. Match the sentences with the correct pictures:

Tunica forāmina habet.
Magister volūmina habet.
Liber nōmen habet.

Puella carmen cantat (*is singing*).
Oppidum flūmen habet.
Tectum forāmen habet.

1. _____

4. _____

2. _____

5. _____

3. _____

6. _____

6 Before you practice the next conversation, you need to learn about another Latin noun case, the VOCATIVE CASE. In the English sentence "John, wait for me," the noun "John" is used in direct address. In Latin, direct address is in the VOCATIVE CASE. The VOCATIVE CASE of most Latin nouns is exactly the same as the nominative case. There are two exceptions:

a. A masculine noun ending in **-us** changes to **-e** in the vocative case; for example, **Marc*us*** becomes **Marc*e*, amic*us*** becomes **amic*e*.**

b. A masculine noun ending in **-ius** changes to **-ī** in the vocative case; for example, **Caecīl*ius*** becomes **Caecīl*ī*, fīl*ius*** becomes **fīl*ī*.**

CONVERSĀTIŌ

VOCĀBULA

domina *Miss*	**es** *you are*
ubi? *where?*	**bene parātus -a -um** *well prepared*
tuus -a -um *your*	**magnificus -a -um** *fantastic*
hīc *here*	**tū** *you*
meus -a -um *my*	

COLLOQUIUM

Complete this dialog by writing the pupil's replies, choosing from the following list:

Grātiās, magistra. Schola est magnifica!
Hīc est liber meus.
Salvē, Domina Cornēlia.
Hīc est calamus meus et ātrāmentum et volūmen.

RĒS PERSŌNĀLĒS

The school year has just begun, and you are writing—in Latin, of course—a shopping list of some school supplies that you will need from the stationery store (**taberna chartāria**). What would you include in your list? Be sure to write the Latin names so that the man in the stationery store (**chartārius**) will understand you:

1. _____   4. _____

2. _____   5. _____

3. _____   6. _____

Dēscriptiō

Agreement of Adjectives

1 The new words that follow are all adjectives. They describe the people or objects in the pictures. See whether you can guess their meanings:

gravis

pinguis

ēnormis

ferōx

ēlegāns

mollis

dulcis

dīves

amābilis

vetus

fēlīx

tristis

Āctivitās

A. Here is a list of adjectives that are similar to English adjectives. How many English derivatives can you fill in?

1. difficilis _____

2. excellēns _____

3. familiāris _____

4. fragilis _____

5. impatiēns _____

6. incrēdibilis _____

7. intellegēns _____

8. irrītābilis _____

9. memorābilis _____

10. nōbilis _____

11. obēdiēns _____

12. populāris _____

13. prūdens _____

14. simplex _____

15. terribilis _____

16. ūtilis _____

2 Now see whether you can read and understand these descriptions of characters. (Notice that in Latin the adjectives generally come after the nouns they describe.)

Antōnius est discipulus studiōsus. Est obēdiēns et intellegēns. Est etiam justus et polītus. Itaque est populāris. Antōnius multōs amīcōs excellentēs in classe habet. Sed interdum est irrītābilis et impatiēns. Est imperfectus sed tamen est amābilis et prūdēns.

etiam *also*
polīt*us -a -um* *polite*
  itaque *therefore*
mult*ī -ae -a* *many*
sed *but*   interdum *sometimes*
tamen *still*

Valeria est puella bella. Est discipula ambitiōsa in classe Latīnā. Est obēdiēns et intellegēns. Est etiam honesta et bona.

bell*us -a -um* *pretty*

Itaque est populāris. Valeria multās amīcās excellentēs in classe habet. Sed interdum est irrītābilis et impatiēns. Tamen est amābilis et prūdēns.

amīca *f girlfriend*

Activitās

B. From the above character sketches, list in the first column all of the Latin adjectives that describe Antonius. In the second column, list all of the Latin adjectives that describe Valeria. List all adjectives in the order in which they occur and be sure not to miss any:

A	B
1. _____	1. _____
2. _____	2. _____
3. _____	3. _____
4. _____	4. _____
5. _____	5. _____
6. _____	6. _____
7. _____	7. _____
8. _____	8. _____
9. _____	9. _____
10. _____	10. _____
11. _____	11. _____

3 Now draw lines from one column to the other, connecting only those adjectives that Antonius and Valeria share in common. Although **Antōnius** is a masculine noun and **Valeria** is a feminine noun, are the endings of the adjectives that you

connected the same or different? _____. Now look at the Latin adjectives that **Antonius** and **Valeria** do not share in common. Are those

endings the same or different? _____. All the new adjectives listed earlier in this lesson have the same endings when they describe masculine and feminine nouns. Did you notice that many of those adjectives end in **-is?** But when such adjectives describe neuter nouns, they end in **-e.** Observe the following examples:

liber ūtilis *useful book* **vīlla ūtilis** *useful farmhouse* **tectum ūtile** *useful roof*

All the other new adjectives not ending in **-is** keep the same ending when they describe masculine, feminine, or neuter nouns. For example:

vir vetus	*old man*	**fēmina vetus**	*old woman*	**oppidum vetus**	*old town*
puer dīves	*rich boy*	**puella dīves**	*rich girl*	**oppidum dīves**	*rich town*
vir prūdēns	*prudent man*	**fīlia prūdēns**	*prudent daughter*	**animal prūdēns**	*prudent animal*

Note that **vetus** is not an adjective of the first and second declension like **bon*us* -*a* -*um*** but an adjective of the third declension.

Āctivitātēs

C. Choose the adjective with the correct ending and write it in the space provided:

1. Antōnius est _____. (irrītābilis, irrītābile)

2. Elephantus est _____. (ēnormis, ēnorme)

3. Liber est _____. (difficilis, difficile)

4. Valeria est _____. (incrēdibilis, incrēdibile)

5. Magister est _____. (populāris, populāre)

6. Mālum est _____. (dulcis, dulce)

7. Subsellium est _____. (fragilis, fragile)

8. Discipula est _____. (familiāris, familiāre)

D. Complete the sentences with the proper adjective with the correct ending, chosen from the following list:

fragilis, fragile	**nōbilis, nōbile**
ēnormis, ēnorme	**amābilis, amābile**
difficilis, difficile	**pinguis, pingue**

1. Schola est _____.

2. Senātor est _____.

3. Amīcus est _____.

4. Porcus est _____.

5. Ōvum est _____.

6. Elephantus est _____.

Select the proper adjective for each picture:

vetus   tristis
ēlegāns   difficilis
nōbilis   irrītābilis
ferōx   fēlīx

1. Mōnstrum est _____.

5. Īnfāns est _____.

2. Vir est _____.

6. Fēmina est _____.

3. Senātor est _____.

7. Puella est _____.

4. Liber est _____.

8. Discipulus est _____.

4 You learned earlier that **m** is the typical ending of a noun in the accusative case, singular. For example, **pater, patre*m*; īnfāns, īnfante*m*; canis, cane*m*.** The same is true of adjectives of the third declension. For example:

Amīcus meus est populāris.
My friend is popular.

Ego amīcu*m* populāre*m* habeō.
I have a popular friend.

Pater meus est dīves.
My father is rich.

Ego patre*m* dīvite*m* habeō.
I have a rich father.

But, as usual, neuter adjectives remain the same in the nominative and accusative cases. For example:

Oppidum est vetus.
The town is old.

Ego oppidum vetus vīsitō.
I am visiting an old town.

Activitās

F. Match the sentences with the correct pictures:

Puer fēlem ferōcem habet.
Īnfāns mālum ēnorme habet.
Agricola porcum pinguem habet.

Puella mātrem dīvitem habet.
Fēmina stolam ēlegantem habet.
Discipulī magistrum impatientem habent.

1. _____

4. _____

2. _____

5. _____

3. _____

6. _____

5 There is still more to learn about the use of these adjectives. So far, we have seen how they describe a single person or object. In addition to the singular form, we need to know the plural form, just as we did when we learned about adjectives that end in **-us, -a, -um.** Note carefully the change in the endings of the following adjectives from the singular to the plural. Repeat the sentences aloud after your teacher:

Māter est amābil*is*	Mātrēs sunt amābil*ēs.*
Amīcus est familiār*is.*	Amīcī sunt familiār*ēs.*
Subsellium est grav*e.*	Subsellia sunt grav*ia.*
Oppidum est memorābil*e.*	Oppida sunt memorābil*ia.*
Ōvum est fragil*e.*	Ōva sunt fragil*ia.*

Latin adjectives agree in gender and number with the person or thing they are describing. Think carefully. What is the plural form of an adjective if the

singular form ends in **-is?** _____. Did you notice that adjectives with this ending can describe a masculine or feminine noun?

What is the plural form of an adjective if the singular form ends in **-e?** _____ Did you notice that adjectives with this ending describe neuter nouns?

6 If you look over the new adjectives of the third declension in this lesson, you will notice that not all of them end in **-is;** for example, **excellēns, vetus, fēlīx, ferōx, dīves.** These adjectives do not show the complete stem in the nominative case, singular. Notice how the endings of these adjectives change from the singular to the plural in the following sentences. Read the sentences aloud after your teacher:

Vir est fēlīx.	Virī et fēminae sunt fēlīc*ēs.*
Valeria est ēlegāns.	Valeria et Claudia sunt ēlegant*ēs.*
Pater est intellegēns.	Pater et māter sunt intellegent*ēs.*
Animal est obēdiēns.	Animālia sunt obēdient*ia.*
Oppidum est vetus.	Oppida sunt vet*era.*
Fēmina est dīves.	Fēminae sunt dīv*itēs.*

By comparing the forms of the adjectives in the two columns, you will see that the *complete* stem of **fēlīx** is **fēlīc-.** What is the complete stem of **ēlegāns?**

_____; of **intellegēns?** _____; of **obēdiēns?**

_____; of **vetus?** _____.

Āctivitātēs

G. Complete the following sentences with the correct form of the adjective. Don't forget to check whether the noun in each sentence is singular or plural and whether it is masculine, feminine, or neuter:

1. Avia est _____. (amābilis, amābilēs)

2. Senātōrēs sunt _____. (nōbilis, nōbilēs)

3. Valeria est _____. (pinguis, pinguēs)

4. Discipulī sunt _____. (familiāris, familiārēs)

5. Canis est _____. (obēdiēns, obēdientēs)

6. Monstrum est _____. (ferōx, ferōcēs)

7. Cerasa sunt _____. (dulce, dulcia)

8. Liber est _____. (gravis, grave)

9. Volūmina sunt _____. (gravēs, gravia)

10. Oppidum est _____. (memorābilis, memorābile)

11. Oppida sunt _____. (memorābilēs, memorābilia)

12. Rōmānī sunt _____. (dīves, dīvitēs)

13. Valeria est _____. (prūdēns, prūdentēs)

14. Parentēs sunt _____. (intellegēns, intellegentēs)

15. Animal est _____. (obēdiēns, obēdientia)

16. Animālia sunt _____. (terribilēs, terribilia)

17. Pecūnia est _____. (ūtilis, ūtilēs, ūtile, ūtilia)

18. Lectī sunt _____. (mollis, mollēs, molle, mollia)

19. Īnfāns est _____. (irrītābilis, irrītābilēs, irrītābile, irrītābilia)

20. Oppida sunt _____. (vetus, veterēs, vetera)

H. Now let's see whether you can supply the correct plural forms of the adjectives:

1. Fundus est vetus.   Fundī sunt _____.

2. Amīcus est familiāris.   Amīcī sunt _____.

3. Discipula est intellegēns. Discipulae sunt _____.

4. Vir est fēlix.   Virī sunt _____.

5. Fēlēs est amābilis.   Fēlēs sunt _____.

6. Ōvum est fragile. Ōva sunt _____.

7. Volūmen est ūtile. Volūmina sunt _____.

8. Animal est ēnorme. Animālia sunt _____.

8 Now that you have some experience with Latin adjectives, you can see that there are two groups of adjectives according to their *endings:*

First and second declensions: Adjectives that end in **-us, -a, -um: bon*us*, bon*a*, bon*um.***

Third declension: (a) Adjectives that have the masculine and feminine ending **-is** and the neuter ending **-e: moll*is*, moll*is*, moll*e.*** (b) Adjectives that have the same ending for masculine, feminine, and neuter: **dīves, fēlīx, vetus.** Because these adjectives do not show the complete stem, the genitive form will be given: **dīves; dīvitis.**

Activitātēs

I. Here are some more adjectives of the first and second declensions. How many can you recognize? First write their English meanings and then the Latin feminine and neuter forms:

LATIN ADJECTIVE	ENGLISH ADJECTIVE	FEMININE FORM	NEUTER FORM
1. altus	high; deep	alta	altum
2. crūdus	_____	_____	_____
3. fāmōsus	_____	_____	_____
4. fortūnātus	_____	_____	_____
5. frīgidus	_____	_____	_____
6. hūmidus	_____	_____	_____
7. nūdus	_____	_____	_____
8. pūrus	_____	_____	_____
9. rārus	_____	_____	_____
10. rīdiculus	_____	_____	_____

11. sevērus _____ _____ _____

12. sincērus _____ _____ _____

13. sordidus _____ _____ _____

14. spatiōsus _____ _____ _____

15. splendidus _____ _____ _____

16. tacitus _____ _____ _____

17. timidus _____ _____ _____

18. tōtus _____ _____ _____

J. One good way of easily learning new adjectives is by studying opposites. For example, you will easily recognize all the adjectives in the first column. Now try to figure out the meanings of their opposites in the second column, and then write the meaning of that opposite in the space provided:

1. bonus   malus   _____ bad _____

2. difficilis   facilis   _____

3. dīves   pauper   _____

4. dulcis   amārus   _____

5. ferōx   mītis   _____

6. frīgidus   calidus   _____

7. gravis   levis   _____

8. intellegēns   stupidus   _____

9. magnus   parvus   _____

10. mollis   dūrus   _____

11. pinguis   macer   _____

12. pulcher   dēfōrmis   _____

13. rōbustus   infīrmus   _____

14. vetus   novus   _____

K. Look at the pictures of opposites. Then write the appropriate Latin adjective below the picture:

1. magnus _____

2. mollis _____

3. intellegēns _____

4. vetus _____

5. difficilis _____

6. pinguis _____

7. gravis _____

8. frīgidus _____

9. pulchra _____

10. robustus _____

11. dulcis _____

12. dīves _____

13. ferōx _____

14. bonus _____

CONVERSĀTIŌ

VOCĀBULA

hodiē *today*
habēsne? *do you have?*
sānē, habeō *yes, I do (have)*

habeō *I have*
minimē *no, not at all*
fidēlis *faithful*

COLLOQUIUM

Complete this conversation by writing Octavia's replies, choosing from the following list:

Minimē! Sed est obēdiēns et amābilis et timidus.
Valeō, grātiās. Quid agis tū, Caecilī?
Valē, Caecilī.
Estne canis tuus ferōx?
Sānē, habeō. Canis meus est parvus et mītis. Habēsne canem?

RĒS PERSŌNĀLĒS

You are the casting director for a movie studio. Your job is to find the ideal actor and actress. List at least four qualities that you are looking for. After supplying a good Latin name for your actor and actress, write the Latin adjectives in the spaces. Don't forget to give the adjectives the correct endings:

ĀCTOR

Nōmen: _____

1. _____

2. _____

3. _____

4. _____

ĀCTRIX

Nōmen: _____

1. _____

2. _____

3. _____

4. _____

Recōgnitiō I (Lectiōnēs I-IV)

Latin has no definite article (*the*) or indefinite article (*a, an*).

Latin nouns are either masculine, feminine, or neuter.

The gender of Latin nouns is either natural or grammatical.

First-declension nouns end in **-a.** Such nouns are generally feminine.

Second-declension nouns end in **-us** or **-um.** Nouns ending in **-us** are generally masculine; nouns ending in **-um** are generally neuter.

Synopsis of Endings of Nouns and Adjectives of the First and Second Declensions

		MASCULINE	FEMININE	NEUTER
Singular	as subject (nominative)	**-us**	**-a**	**-um**
	as direct object (accusative)	**-um**	**-am**	**-um**
Plural	as subject (nominative)	**-ī**	**-ae**	**-a**
	as direct object (accusative)	**-ōs**	**-ās**	**-a**

Synopsis of Endings of Nouns of the Third Declension

		MASCULINE	FEMININE	NEUTER
Singular	as subject (nominative)	various	various	various
	as direct object (accusative)	**-em**	**-em**	same as subject
Plural	as subject (nominative)	**-ēs**	**-ēs**	**-(i)a***
	as direct object (accusative)	**-ēs**	**-ēs**	**-(i)a***

---

*Some neuter nouns end in **-a,** others in **-ia.**

66

Synopsis of Endings of Adjectives of the Third Declension

		MASCULINE	FEMININE	NEUTER
Singular	describing subject (nominative)	-is*	-is*	-e*
	describing direct object (accusative)	-em	-em	-e
Plural	describing subject (nominative)	-ēs	-ēs	-ia
	describing direct object (accusative)	-ēs	-ēs	-ia

Āctivitātēs

A. Using the clues on the left, write the Latin words that begin with the letters in the word **GLADIĀTOR**:

1. chicken

2. school

3. donkey

4. schoolboy

5. baby

6. athlete

7. tablet

8. obedient

9. rapid

---

*While most adjectives of the third declension have **-is** as the masculine and feminine ending (**trist***is*) and **-e** as the neuter ending (**trist***e*), some adjectives of the third declension have the same ending for masculine, feminine, and neuter (**fēlix, vetus, dīves, excellēns**).

B. Fill in the Latin words suggested by the pictures. Then read down the boxed column to find the Latin word for someone who enters a competition:

1. ___ ___ ___ ___ ___ ___ ___

2. ___ ___ ___ ___ ___

3. ___ ___ ___ ___

4. ___ ___ ___ ___ ___ ___ ___ ___

5. ___ ___ ___

6. ___ ___ ___ ___ ___

7. ___ ___ ___ ___ ___

8. ___ ___ ___ ___

9. ___ ___ ___

10. ___ ___ ___ ___

C. Word-search puzzle. Search for the Latin equivalents of the English words listed below. You will find them all in the letter maze. Circle each word as you find it and write it next to the English word. The words may be read from left to right or down:

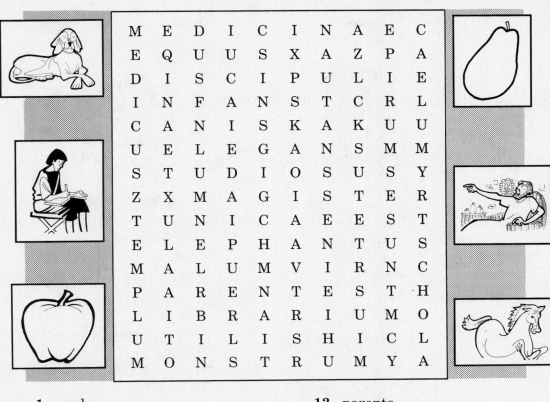

```
M E D I C I N A E C
E Q U U S X A Z P A
D I S C I P U L I E
I N F A N S T C R L
C A N I S K A K U U
U E L E G A N S M M
S T U D I O S U S Y
Z X M A G I S T E R
T U N I C A E E S T
E L E P H A N T U S
M A L U M V I R N C
P A R E N T E S T H
L I B R A R I U M O
U T I L I S H I C L
M O N S T R U M Y A
```

1. apple _____
2. teacher _____
3. tunics _____
4. bookcase _____
5. pupils _____
6. temple _____
7. useful _____
8. sky _____
9. school _____
10. pear _____
11. (he) is _____
12. horse _____

13. parents _____
14. elephant _____
15. studious _____
16. dog _____
17. doctor _____
18. monster _____
19. (they) are _____
20. here _____
21. man _____
22. elegant _____
23. medicines _____
24. baby _____

D. Picture Story. Can you read this story? Much of it is in picture form. Whenever you come to a picture, read it as if it were a Latin word:

Antōnius est ⬭ Romānus. Antōnius in ⬭ habitat. In magnā habitat. Ejus ⬭ nōminātur Claudia. Ejus ⬭ nōminātur Caecilius. Ejus ⬭ nōminātur Caecilia. Pater ejus est ⬭. Māter ejus est ⬭. Antōnius est ⬭ studiōsus. In scholā Antōnius in ⬭ sedet. ⬭ sunt intellegentēs et obēdientēs. In scholā sunt multae rēs: ⬭, ⬭, ⬭, ⬭, ⬭, ⬭, ⬭. ⬭ est bonus sed sevērus. Magister in ⬭ sedet. Antōnius in ⬭ Latīnē loquitur. Antōnius ⬭ fidēlem habet. ⬭ est bonus et intellegēns sed Latīnē nōn loquitur.

VOCĀBULA

ejus *his*	**multae rēs** *many things*
nōminātur *is called*	**Latīnē loquitur** *speaks Latin*

Pars
Secunda

V Verba

How to Express Actions; -ĀRE Verbs

1   The new words that follow are all verbs. They describe actions. See whether you can guess their meanings:

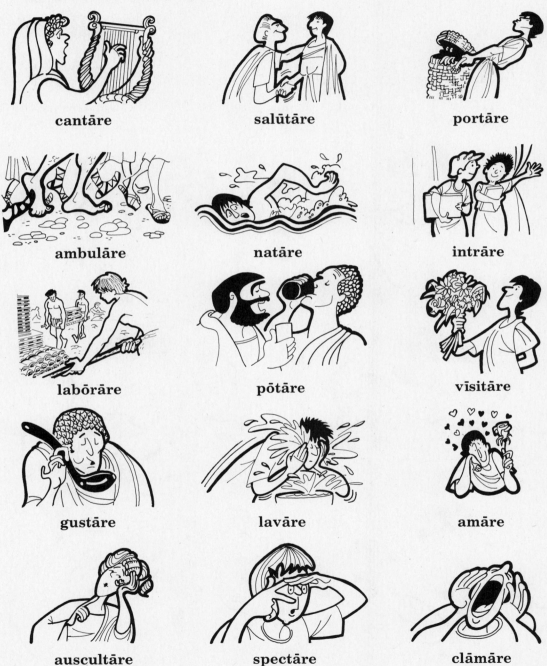

cantāre   salūtāre   portāre

ambulāre   natāre   intrāre

labōrāre   pōtāre   vīsitāre

gustāre   lavāre   amāre

auscultāre   spectāre   clāmāre

Āctīvitās

A. Match the verb with the noun that could be used with it and write your answers in the spaces provided:

1. cantāre _____

2. gustāre _____

3. pōtāre _____

4. intrāre _____

5. portāre _____

6. auscultāre _____

vīllam
īnfantem
carmen
mūsicam
cibum
aquam

2 Many people will be involved in the story you are about to read. Who are they?

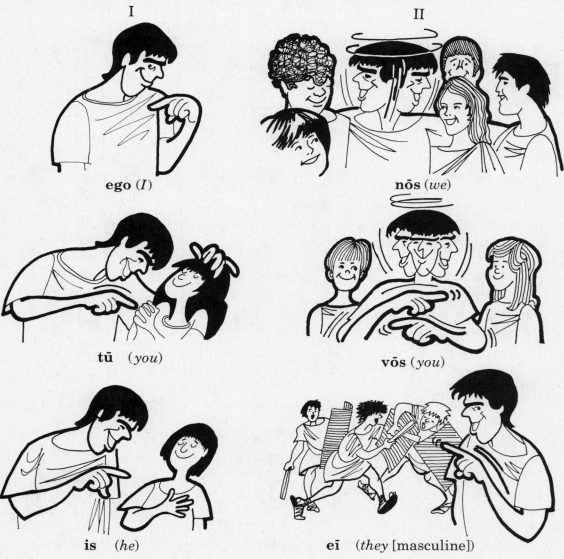

I
ego (*I*)

II
nōs (*we*)

tū (*you*)

vōs (*you*)

is (*he*)

eī (*they* [masculine])

ea (*she)*

eae (*they* [feminine])

id (*it)*

ea (*they* [neuter])

These words are called subject pronouns. How many people does each subject

pronoun in Group I refer to? _____ How many people does each subject

pronoun in Group II refer to? _____ Notice that **tū** and **vōs** both mean

you. When do you use **tū?** _____

When do you use **vōs?** _____

3 Which pronoun would you use if you were referring to **Cornēlius?** _____

Which pronoun would you use if you were referring to **Cornēlia?** _____

To **Cornēlia** and **Drūsilla?** _____ To **medicī?** _____

To **līlium?** _____

The pronoun **is** means *he,* and **ea** means *she.* But remember that in Latin things
can be masculine, feminine, or neuter. Therefore, the pronouns must agree with
them. For example, **liber** (*book*) is masculine, and so the pronoun referring to
liber is the pronoun **is,** here meaning *it.* **Īnsula** (*island*) is feminine, and so the
pronoun referring to **īnsula** is **ea,** here also meaning *it.* **Plaustrum** (*wagon*) is
neuter, and so the pronoun referring to **plaustrum** is **id.**

Āctivitās

B. Write the pronoun you would use in referring to each person or thing:

1. magister	_____	6. lūdus		_____
2. medicīna	_____	7. ōvum		_____
3. puerī	_____	8. vīlla		_____
4. pirum	_____	9. Cornēlia et soror		_____
5. stellae	_____	10. templa		_____

4   At the beginning of this lesson, we learned 15 important "action words" or verbs. Notice that they all end in **-āre,** and they all express some kind of action — to do something; **cantāre** means *to sing;* **amāre** means *to love,* **clāmāre** means *to shout,* **spectāre** means *to look at,* and so on.

If we want to use these verbs to express someone's actions, we must make some changes. In English, for example, we can say "I sing, you sing, she sings." Did you notice that the *ending* of the English verb changed in the third example? We added an *s* to *sing.* In Latin, the verb changes its ending much more frequently than in English. Here are the endings that go with the different subjects:

I	**-ō**
you	**-ās**
he, she, it	**-at**
we	**-āmus**
you	**-ātis**
they	**-ant**

Let's see how these endings work. Take, for example, the **-āre** verb **cantāre.** We remove the infinitive ending **-āre** and add the proper ending for each verb form:

cantāre

cantō	*I sing, I am singing*
cantās	*you sing, you are singing*
cantat	*he, she, it sings; he, she, it is singing*
cantāmus	*we sing, we are singing*
cantātis	*you sing, you are singing*
cantant	*they sing, they are singing*

NOTE:

1. In Latin, the pronoun is generally omitted because the verb indicates the subject. When the pronoun is expressed, it is used for emphasis:

   Pater meus in agrō labōrat; *ego* **in āreā lūdō.**
   My father works in the field; I play on the playground.

2. Each verb form has two meanings. For example, **clāmō** means *I shout* or *I am shouting.* The first meaning expresses a general action; the second meaning expresses an action that is going on right now.

The characteristic vowel in the ending of all these verbs is **a**. All these verbs, therefore, belong to the same class, or conjugation. We say that all these verbs belong to the FIRST CONJUGATION.

Activitās

C. Write the verb forms that go with the pronouns.

	cantāre	natāre	clāmāre	amāre
ego	_____	_____	_____	_____
tū	_____	_____	_____	_____
is, ea, id	_____	_____	_____	_____
nōs	_____	_____	_____	_____
vōs	_____	_____	_____	_____
eī, eae, ea	_____	_____	_____	_____

Activitās

D. Match the descriptions with the pictures they describe:

Discipulus librōs portat.
Puellae magistrum salūtant.
Ego amīcum vīsitō.
Vōs aquam pōtātis.
Parentēs fīliam amant.
Cūr tū nōn labōrās?

Scholam intrāmus.
Cornēlia carmen cantat.
Tū canem lavās.
Ego et Claudia mūsicam
  auscultāmus.

1. _____

3. _____

2. _____

4. _____

5. _____

8. _____

6. _____

9. _____

7. _____

10. _____

5 Here's a story using some of the words you have just learned:

Diēs est calidus et hūmidus. Discipulī in scholā dīligenter labōrant.

diēs *m day*
dīligenter *hard*

"Magister," clāmat Claudius, "ego nōn labōrāre optō. Natāre optō." Discipulī sūdant. Etiam magister sūdat. Omnēs sūdant.

optāre *to want, wish*
sūdāre *to sweat* **etiam** *even*
omnēs *all*

"Et ego in flūmine natāre optō," clāmat Sextus. "Ego sūdō."

"Est perīculōsum in flūmine natāre," dicit magister. "Aqua est alta et frīgida."

perīculōsus -a -um *dangerous*
dicit (*he*) *says*
altus -a -um *deep*

Post scholam Claudius et Sextus ad flūmen ambulant. Puerī tunicās et sandalia exuunt et flūmen laetē intrant. Sed flūmen est nimis altum.

post *after*   **ad** *to*
exuunt *(they) take off*
laetē *happily*
   nimis *too*

"Auxilium!" clāmat Claudius. "Auxilium!" clāmat Sextus.

auxilium! *help!*

Tunc maximē magister ad flūmen pervenit, clāmōrēs auscultat, flūmen intrat, et discipulōs servat.

tunc maximē *just then*
  pervenit *(he) arrives*
clāmōrēs *shouts*
servāre *to save*

Āctivitātēs

E. **Vērum aut Falsum** Write **Vērum** in the space provided if the statement is true. Write **Falsum** if the statement is false and correct the statement:

1. Diēs est frīgidus. _____

2. Magister et discipulī sūdant. _____

3. Discipulī in scholā dīligenter labōrant. _____

4. Claudius natāre optat. _____

5. Claudius et Sextus in scholā natant. _____

6. Flūmen est perīculōsum. _____

7. Aqua in flūmine est nimis alta. _____

8. Magister flūmen intrat et natat. _____

F. Choose the verb with the correct ending and write it in the space provided.

1. Discipulī in scholā dīligenter (labōrat; labōrant). _____

2. Discipulī et magister (sūdat; sūdant). _____

3. Sexte, cūr semper (clāmās; clāmātis)? _____

4. Tū et Cornēlius Rōmam (vīsitās; vīsitātis). _____

5. Ego et Claudius in flūmine (natō; natāmus). _____

6. Parentēs mūsicam (auscultat; auscultant).

_____

7. Ego fēlēs et canēs (amō; amāmus).

_____

8. Māter īnfantem (lavat; lavant).

_____

G. Match the descriptions with the correct pictures:

Mūsicam auscultāmus.   Ea scholam intrat.
Carmen cantās.   Is gladiātōrem spectat.
Eī clāmant.   Ea in flūmine natat.
Aquam pōtō.   Eae cerasa gustant.

1. _____

4. _____

2. _____

5. _____

3. _____

6. _____

7. _____   **8.** _____

H. Now make complete Latin sentences by adding the correct verb forms:

1. (swim)   Puerī et puellae in flūmine _____.

2. (shout)   Cūr īnfantēs semper _____?

3. (enter)   Magister pergulam _____.

4. (carry)   Rūsticus porcum _____.

5. (taste)   Cūr vōs cibum nōn _____?

6. (visit)   Avus et avia familiam _____.

7. (look at)   Tū animālia domestica _____.

8. (love)   Pater et māter fīlium _____.

9. (taste)   Frāterculus medicīnam _____.

10. (wash)   Māter īnfantem_____.

QUAESTIŌNĒS PERSŌNĀLĒS

Notice that **-ne** attached to the first word in the sentence indicates a question in Latin calling for a "yes" or "no" answer:

1. Amāsne canēs et fēlēs?

   _____

2. Natāsne in flūmine?

   _____

3. Auscultāsne mūsicam classicam?

   _____

4. Labōrāsne valdē in scholā?

   _____

5. Cantāsne carmina moderna?

   _____

6. Ambulāsne ad scholam?

   _____

7. Vīsitāsne avum et aviam?

   _____

8. Salutāsne magistrōs et magistrās in scholā?

   _____

CONVERSĀTIŌ

VOCĀBULA

quia *because*   **eāmus** *let's go*

COLLOQUIUM

Complete the dialog with expressions chosen from the following list:

sūdās salvē frīgida est
natāre calidum quoque
perīculōsum alta flūmen
amō   eāmus flūmine

VI Ubi est?

Prepositions With the Accusative and Ablative

1 The phrases below the pictures all consist of a preposition and an object. Latin prepositions are generally very short words just like the English prepositions *of, on, upon, in, over, through.* Look at the pictures and see whether you can guess the meanings of the words below them:

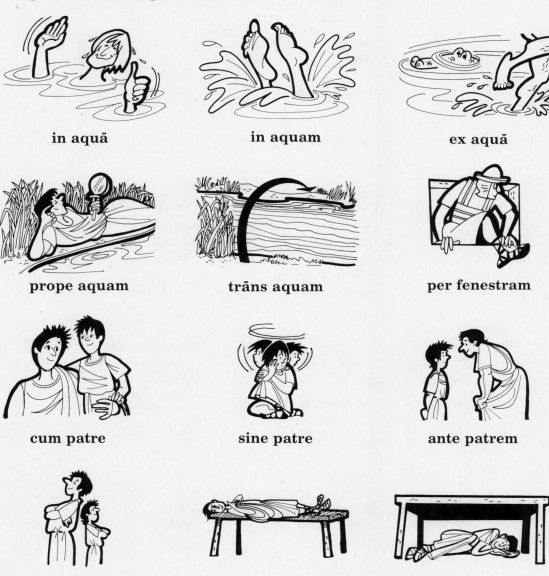

in aquā

in aquam

ex aquā

prope aquam

trāns aquam

per fenestram

cum patre

sine patre

ante patrem

post patrem

in mēnsā

sub mēnsā

dē mēnsā

circum casam

inter casās

ad casam

ā casā

super casam

2   Now let's see how these prepositions are used in the following story:

Tīberius et Claudius in oppidō parvō habitant. Tīberius in casā prope Claudiī casam habitat. Est via angusta inter casās, ubi puerī saepe lūdunt, dum avus et avia in subselliō sedent. Est alia via ante casās. Via est lāta et longa. Hodiē est equus cum plaustrō in viā. In plaustrō sunt multa pōma: māla, cerasa, ūvae, pira. Sed ubi est pōmārius? Est in forō.

Claudiī *Claudius'*
angust*us -a -um* *narrow*
saepe *often*
  lūdunt *play*   **dum** *while*
sedent *(they) sit*
  ali*us- -a -ud* * *another*
lāt*us -a -um* *broad, wide*
multa pōma *much fruit*
ūva *f grape*
pōmārius *m fruit seller*
  forum *n marketplace, forum*
veniunt *(they) come*

Tīberius et Claudius ē casā veniunt et trāns viam ad equum et plaustrum ambulant. Deinde Tīberius in plaustrum cōnscendit et ūnum cerasum gustat. "Cerasum est suāve!" exclāmat Tīberius, et dē plaustrō salit.

deinde *then*
  cōnscendit *(he) climbs*
suāv*is -is -e* *delicious*
salit *(he) jumps*

Tunc maximē pōmārius ē forō ad plaustrum ambulat et clāmat: "Puerī, puerī, sī vōs pōma in forum prō mē portābitis, māla vōbīs dabō." "Grātiās," clāmant puerī. Deinde puerī pōma in forum prō pōmāriō portant.

sī *if*
prō mē *for me*
  portābitis *(you) will carry*
  vōbīs dabō *I'll give you*

---

*Note the neuter ending **-ud** instead of **-um**.

Āctivitās

A. The following questions are based on the story that you have just read. Answer each question with a preposition and its object(s):

1. Ubi Tīberius et Claudius habitant?

_____

2. Ubi est casa Tīberiī?

_____

3. Ubi est via angusta?

_____

4. Ubi est via lāta et longa?

_____

5. Ubi puerī saepe lūdunt?

_____

6. Ubi sunt avus et avia?

_____

7. Ubi est equus?

_____

8. Ubi sunt multa pōma?

_____

9. Ubi est pōmārius?

---

3 Some Latin prepositions take the accusative case; some take a special form called the ABLATIVE CASE. The table below shows you how to form the ablative case of the various classes of nouns. For review, the nominative and accusative cases are listed first:

SINGULAR						
	FIRST DECLENSION	SECOND DECLENSION		THIRD DECLENSION		
NOMINATIVE	ros*a*	am*ī*c*us*	plaustr*um*	pater	can*is*	animal
ACCUSATIVE	ros*am*	am*ī*c*um*	plaustr*um*	patr*em*	can*em*	animal
ABLATIVE	ros*ā*	am*ī*c*ō*	plaustr*ō*	patr*e*	can*e*	anim*ālī*

PLURAL						
	FIRST DECLENSION	SECOND DECLENSION		THIRD DECLENSION		
NOMINATIVE	ros*ae*	am*ī*c*ī*	plaustr*a*	patr*ēs*	can*ēs*	anim*ālia*
ACCUSATIVE	ros*ās*	am*ī*c*ōs*	plaustr*a*	patr*ēs*	can*ēs*	anim*ālia*
ABLATIVE	ros*īs*	am*ī*c*īs*	plaustr*īs*	patr*ibus*	can*ibus*	anim*ālibus*

Activitātēs

B. Here are some sentences with prepositions that always take the accusative case. Match the sentences with the pictures they describe:

Fabius circum stadium ambulat.
Fabius est ante jānuam.
Fabius est post sorōrem.
Fēlēs est prope Fabium.

Fabius trāns āream ambulat.
Fabius ad equum ambulat.
Fabius per jānuam ambulat.
Fabius inter gallīnās est.

1. _____

3. _____

2. _____

4. _____

5. _____

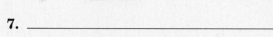

7. _____

6. _____

8. _____

C. Here are some more pictures. Look at them carefully, and then complete the sentence below each picture with the correct preposition. Choose from the list below, but use each preposition only once:

ad	**circum**	**per**	**prope**
ante	**inter**	**post**	**trāns**

1. Magister _____ discipulōs stat.

3. Canis _____ virum ambulat.

2. Equus est _____ plaustrum.

4. Cornēlia _____ līlia ambulat.

5. Fabius _____ flūmen natat.

7. Vacca _____ stabulum ambulat.

6. Fēlēs _____ aviam est.

8. Pōmārius pira _____ forum portat.

D. The following sentences contain prepositions that always take the ablative case. Match the sentences with the pictures:

Medicīnam prō stomachō pōtō.   Discipula ē scholā venit.
Vacca ā stabulō venit.   Pōmārius dē plaustrō salit.
Gallīna est sine pennīs (_feathers_).   Fabius cum cane ambulat.

1. _____

3. _____

2. _____

4. _____

5. _____ **6.** _____

E. Look carefully at the pictures and then insert the most suitable preposition in the sentence. Choose from the list below, but use each preposition only once. These prepositions always take a noun in the ablative case:

ā(b)	**dē**	**prō**
cum	**ē(x)**	**sine**

1. Puer est _____ pecūniā. **4.** Pater _____ familiā labōrat.

2. Fēlēs _____ mēnsā salit. **5.** Āthlēta _____ stadiō venit.

3. Marcella _____ sorōre cantat. **6.** Agricola _____ agrīs venit.

4 Did you notice that the prepositions **ā(b)** and **ē(x)** were listed with parentheses around the second letter. The forms **ab** and **ex** are used if the next word begins with a vowel or an **h,** just as in English we use the form *an* instead of *a* if the next word begins with a vowel (*an* apple, *a* pear, *an* hour). Now look at the following Latin sentences and note the forms of the prepositions:

Senātor *ā* forō venit.
The senator is coming from the forum.

Agicola *ab* agrō venit.
The farmer is coming from the field.

Porcus *ē* stabulō venit.
The pig is coming out of the stable.

Puer *ex* aquā venit.
The boy is coming out of the water.

5 The following prepositions may be used with either the accusative or the ablative case, but in somewhat different circumstances:

in   sub   super

Compare the sentences in Column I with the sentences in Column II. Notice that the three sentences in Column I contain prepositions used with the ABLATIVE CASE, while the three sentences in Column II contain prepositions used with the ACCUSATIVE CASE.

I   II

Puer in aqu*ā* est.
The boy is in the water.

Puer in aqu*am* salit.
The boy is jumping into the water.

Avis est super stabul*ō*.
The bird is on top of the stable.

Avis super stabul*um* volat.
The bird is flying over the stable.

Canis est sub lect*ō*.
The dog is under the bed.

Canis sub lect*um* currit.
The dog is running under the bed.

In Column I, the prepositions take the ablative case to indicate "location" or "position"; in Column II, the prepositions take the accusative case to express "motion" or "direction."

Activitās

F. In the following sentences, decide whether the preposition indicates "location" or "direction." Then choose either the noun in the accusative or ablative case and write your choice in the space provided:

1. Puerī in _____ natant.
(flūmine / flūmen)

2. Magistra in _____ currit.
(scholā / scholam)

3. Īnfāns sub _____ sedet.
   (mēnsā / mēnsam)

4. Āthlēta in _____ salit.
   (aquā / aquam)

5. Avēs super _____ volant.
   (vīllā / vīllam)

6. Ego librōs in _____ portō.
   (scholā / scholam)

7. Cūr canis sub _____ currit?
   (lectō / lectum)

8. Fenestra super _____ est.
   (jānuā / jānuam)

6 Some of the prepositions have several meanings. We can determine the meaning in each situation from the sentence as a whole. Here are several meanings of the preposition **in**: *in, on, to, into.* See how the following sentences demonstrate these different meanings:

Fēlēs *in hortō* sedet.
The cat is sitting in the garden.

Fēlēs *in hortum* currit.
The cat is running into the garden.

Fēlēs *in mūrō* sedet.
The cat is sitting on the wall.

Senatōrēs *in Hispāniam* nāvigant.
The senators are sailing to Spain.

The preposition **ad** may mean *to, toward* or *at:*

Vir *ad oppidum* ambulat.
The man is walking to town.

Quis est *ad jānuam?*
Who is at the door?

The preposition **dē** has two different meanings:

Rūsticī *dē monte* dēscendunt.
The peasants are coming down from the mountain.

Parentēs fābulās *dē līberīs* saepe nārrant.
Parents often tell stories about their children.

Āctivitās

G. Choose the correct preposition and write it in the space provided:

1. Vacca _____ stabulum ambulat.
   (ad / dē)

2. Avus et avia _____ jānuam sunt.
(ad / in)

3. Vir _____ elephantō salit.
(ad / dē)

4. Magistra multās fābulās _____ Rōmā nārrat.
(dē / ad)

5. Āthlēta _____ stadium currit.
(dē / in)

6. Discipulae _____ jānuam sunt.
(in / ad)

QUAESTIŌNĒS PERSŌNĀLĒS

1. Ubi habitās?

_____

2. Estne casa tua in oppidō?

_____

3. Estne casa tua prope scholam?

_____

4. Habitāsne cum avō et aviā?

_____

5. Laborāsne post scholam?

_____

6. Estne via ante casam lāta aut angusta?

_____

VOCĀBULA

Venī mēcum. *Come with me.*   **Libenter.** *Gladly.*

COLLOQUIUM

Fill in what the first person in this dialog would say. Choose from the following list:

In casā parvā prope forum.
Cum amīcīs lūdit.
Salvē, Flāvia. Quid novī est?
In āreā post scholam.

Est in forō.
Bene. Ego quoque cum cane ad forum ambulō.
  Venī mēcum.
Soror est cum avō et aviā.

Plūs verbōrum

How to Ask Questions and Say "Yes" or "No" in Latin; -ĒRE Verbs

1   Here are more action words. These verbs belong to the **-ēre** family, also called the SECOND CONJUGATION. Can you guess their meanings?

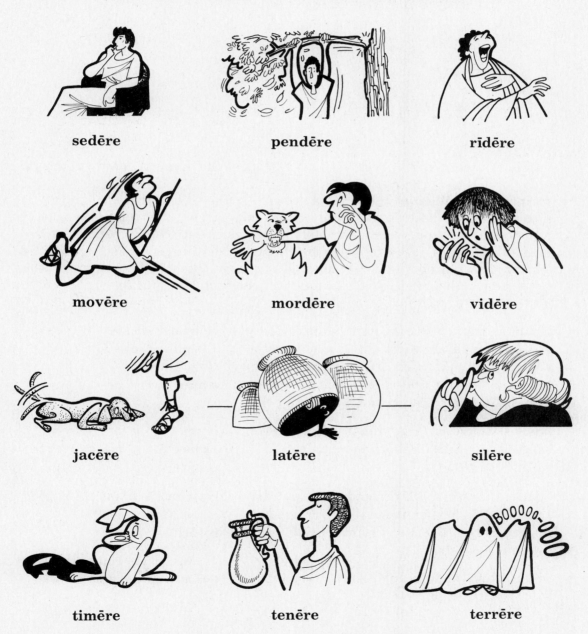

sedēre   pendēre   rīdēre

movēre   mordēre   vidēre

jacēre   latēre   silēre

timēre   tenēre   terrēre

Activitās

A. Match the verb with the word or phrase that could be used with it and write your answer in the space provided:

1. sedēre   _____

2. latēre   _____

3. jacēre   _____

4. mordēre   _____

5. tenēre   _____

6. rīdēre   _____

7. pendēre   _____

8. timēre   _____

dē arbore
mōnstrum
in subselliō
īnfantem
in lectō
pirum
ad jocum (*at the joke*)
post arborem

2 Did you notice that these new verbs do not belong to the **-āre** family? Each family of verbs has its "typical vowel." What is the "typical vowel" of the **-āre**

verbs? _____ What is the "typical vowel" of the **-ēre** verbs? _____ Did you also notice that these new verbs all have a long mark (called a macron) over the next-to-last syllable, which, therefore, receives the stress? Remember how we made changes in the **-āre** verbs by dropping the infinitive ending **-āre** and adding personal endings? We must do the same thing with these new verbs. Let's see what happens. Read the following story and look for the endings of the **-ēre** verbs:

Hodiē Lucrētia per viās Rōmae ambulat et ad Claudiae casam venit. Claudia ad jānuam **sed**et**.** Ubi Lucrētia Claudiam **vid**et**,** Lucrētia statim **rīd**et et dīcit, "Salvē, Claudia. Cūr ad jānuam **sed**ēs**?"**

Rōmae *of Rome*
Claudiae *Claudia's*
ubi *when*
statim *immediately*

"Salvē, Lucrētia. Ego hīc sed**eō** quia tē exspectō. Optāsne **vid**ēre hortum meum?" rogat Claudia.

tē *you*
exspectāre *to wait for*
rogāre *to ask*

"Sānē, hortum **vid**ēre optō," **respond**et Lucrētia. "In hortō **hab**ēs arborēs magnās et rosāria cum rosīs albīs et rubrīs. Et pōma dē arboribus **pend**ent**."**

respondēre *to answer, respond*
arbor *f tree*
rosārium *n rosebed*
  albus **-a -um** *white*
  ruber rubra **rubr**um *red*

"Sub arbore **sed**ēre aut **jac**ēre possumus,"

aut *or*   **possumus** *we can*

clāmat Claudia cum gaudiō. "Ego sub arbore saepe sed*eō.*"

gaudium *n joy*

Puellae hortum intrant. Tunc maximē frāterculus Claudiae, nōmine Jūlius, ē culīnā venit et clāmat: "Claudia! Lucrētia! Vōsne in hortō sed*ētis?*"

culīna *f kitchen*

Jūlius hortum intrat sed puellās nōn vid*et,* quia sil*ent* et post rosārium lat*ent.*

"Frāterculus meus tam molestus est," susurrat Claudia. "Sī hīc man*ēmus* et nōn respond*ēmus,* Jūlius nōs nōn comperiet." Puellae subrīd*ent.*

tam molestus *such a pest*
susurrāre *to whisper*
  manēre *to stay*
nōn comperiet *will not find*
subrīdēre *to smile*

Activitās

B. **Vērum aut Falsum.** If a sentence is true, write **Vērum** in the space provided. If it is false, write **Falsum** and correct the sentence:

1. Hodiē Claudia Lucrētiam vīsitat. _____

2. Claudia et Lucrētia in culīnā sedent. _____

3. Sunt rosāria cum albīs et rubrīs rosīs in hortō. _____

4. Jūlius est Claudiae pater. _____

5. Jūlius cum Claudiā et Lucrētiā sub arbore sedet. _____

3 Now see whether you can apply the correct endings to the verb **sedēre** below. Look carefully over the story and find an example of every ending that you need.

To form the present tense of **-ēre** verbs, drop _____ and add the endings:

ego   _____

tū   _____

is, ea, id   _____

nōs   _____

vōs   _____

eī, eae, ea _____

Āctivitātēs

C. Now let's practice with other important **-ēre** verbs. Fill in all the forms:

	habēre (*to have*)	**manēre** (*to stay*)	**jubēre** (*to order*)	**docēre** (*to teach*)
ego	_____	_____	_____	_____
tū	_____	_____	_____	_____
is, ea, id	_____	_____	_____	_____
nōs	_____	_____	_____	_____
vōs	_____	_____	_____	_____
eī, eae, ea	_____	_____	_____	_____

D. Complete with the correct forms of the verbs. Be sure to drop all infinitive endings (**-ēre**) before starting:

1. (tenēre)   Māter īnfantem _____.

2. (docēre)   Magistra multōs discipulōs _____.

3. (habēre)   Nōs rosārium in hortō _____.

4. (manēre)   Cūr tū in oppidō magnō _____?

5. (rīdēre)   Ego ad jocum tuum _____.

6. (jacēre)   Fēlēs sub mēnsā in culīnā _____.

7. (mordēre)   Canēs līberōs in āreā _____.

8. (pendēre)   Jūlius dē arbore _____.

9. (silēre)   Ubi magister docet, discipulae in scholā _____.

10. (movēre)   Cūr tū mēnsam ad fenestram _____?

11. (timēre)   Ego et Caecilius medicum _____.

12. (terrēre)   Mōnstrum nōs nōn _____.

13. (respondēre)   Cūr tū et amīcus tuus nōn _____?

14. (jubēre)   Pater _____ fīlium in casā manēre.

15. (latēre)   Discipulī malī post scholam _____.

4 Now you are ready to learn how to ask questions in Latin. As in English, certain words are used to introduce questions in Latin. Here are some examples:

Cūr silēs? *Why are you silent?*
Ubi manētis? *Where are you staying?*
Quō cibum portās? *(To) Where are you taking the food?*
Quandō animālia domestica ē stabulō ambulant? *When do the domestic animals come out of the stable?*
Quōmodō gladiātōrēs in stadiō vidēre possumus? *How can we see the gladiators in the stadium?*
Quot puellae in hortō latent? *How many girls are hiding in the garden?*
Quis in lectō meō jacet? *Who is lying in my bed?*
Quid tē noctū terret? *What frightens you at night?*

Suppose you don't have a special word to introduce the question. Then there are three ways in Latin to ask a question:

a. If you expect the answer to be "yes," introduce the question with the word **nōnne:**

> **Nōnne lūnam et stellās vidēs?** *You see the moon and the stars, don't you?*

b. If you expect the answer to be "no," introduce the question with the word **num:**

> **Num magistrum veterem timēs?** *You're not afraid of the old teacher, are you?*
> **Num frātrēs et sorōrēs habēs?** *You don't have brothers and sisters, do you?*

c. If the answer may be either "yes" or "no," add **-ne** to the key word, usually the verb, at the beginning of the question:

> **Sedentne spectātōrēs in theātrō?** *Are the spectators sitting in the theater?*
> **Terretne tē aqua?** *Does water frighten you?*

5 Strangely enough, the Romans did not have just one word for "yes." The answer "yes" is expressed by **ita, sānē, vērō,** or by repeating the verb in the question:

> **Habetne puer pecūniam? — *Sānē / Ita / Vērō.*** *Does the boy have money? — Yes.*
> **Mordetne canis? — Mordet.** *Does the dog bite? — He does.*

Āctivitātēs

E. Change the following statements to questions expecting the answer "yes." Then give the English meanings of the questions:

1. Māter pōma in culīnā lavat.

_____

_____

2. Puer in aquā sine parentibus natat.

_____

_____

3. Fēlēs sub subselliō jacet.

_____

_____

4. Senātōrēs in forō vidēs.

_____

_____

F. Change the following statements to questions expecting the answer "no." Then give the English meanings of the questions:

1. Cerasa et pira amās.

_____

_____

2. Gallīna canem timet.

_____

_____

3. Vīnum in mēnsā est.

_____

_____

4. Līberī in scholā silent.

_____

_____

6 The Romans had several ways of saying "no." They might say **nōn, minimē, minimē vērō,** or they would repeat the verb of the question with a negative:

Rīdēsne? — Nōn / Minimē / Minimē vērō. _Are you laughing? — No._
Num rīdēs? — Nōn rīdeō. _You're not laughing, are you? — No, I'm not._

Activitās

G. Answer the following questions with a Latin "yes" or "no." Try to use a different form of the Latin "yes" or "no" each time:

1. Suntne cerasa rubra? _____

2. Num pōmārius in forō est? _____

3. Timentne puerī mōnstrum? _____

4. Nōnne māter īnfantem amat? _____

5. Docetne magistra Latīnē? _____

6. Nōnne āthlētae mūsculōs magnōs habent? _____

7. Estne rosārium in hortō tuō? _____

8. Num canis fēlem terret? _____

9. Pater, habēsne pecūniam prō mē? _____

10. Num sumus semper fēlīcēs in lūdō? _____

11. Nōnne medicus medicīnam habet? _____

12. Amantne Rōmānī Rōmam? _____

7 Now listen in on an interview between a snobbish Roman senator and clever young Lucius:

SENĀTOR PUPIĒNUS: Salvē, puer. Quod nōmen est tibi?

LŪCIUS: Ego sum Lūcius, fīlius Marcellī.

sum *I am*
  Marcellī *of Marcellus*

SENĀTOR: Paterne est lēgislātor hīc in urbe?

hīc *here*
urbs *f city*

LŪCIUS: Minimē. Est vēnditor in forō.

vēnditor *m vendor*

SENĀTOR: Oooo? Quid pater vēnditat?

vēnditāre *to sell*

LŪCIUS: Pōma . . . cerasa, ūvās, et cētera.

et cētera *and so on*

SENĀTOR: Videō. Hmmm . . . nōn est senātor?

LŪCIUS: Ita. Nōn est senātor. Est agricola.

SENĀTOR: Cūr lūdum nōn frequentās? Num lūdum amās?

frequentāre *to attend*

LŪCIUS: Lūdum valdē amō!

valdē *a lot*

SENĀTOR: Sed quōmodō est id possibile?
Cūr autem nōn in lūdum vādis?
LŪCIUS: Ego vērō in lūdum vādō.

SENĀTOR: Sed quōmodō est id possibile?
LŪCIUS: Est simplissimum, senātor. Lūdus
est prope arēnam. Ego in lūdum gladiātōrium vādō, ubi gladiātōrēs sē exercent.
Valē, senātor!

cūr autem *why then*
vādis *you go*
vērō vādō *I am going*

simplissimum *very simple*
gladiātōrius -a -um
gladiatorial
sē exercēre *to practice*

Activitās

H. Answer the following questions based on the interview:

1. Quis est Luciī pater?

_____

2. Quid est patris occūpatiō?

_____

3. Ubi est Lūcius hodiē?

_____

4. Estne Lūciī pater lēgislātor?

_____

5. Num Lūciī pater senātor est?

_____

6. Ubi est Lūciī pater?

_____

7. Quid pater vēnditat?

_____

8. Amatne Lūcius lūdum?

_____

9. Amatne Lūcius lūdum gladiātōrium?

_____

10. Ubi est lūdus gladiātōrius?

_____

CONVERSĀTIŌ

VOCĀBULA

nōn jam *no longer*
adulēscentulus *m young man*
merēre *to éarn*

aliquandō *someday*
erō *I'll be*
esse *to be*

COLLOQUIUM

Complete the dialog with responses chosen from the following list:

Vērum est. Nōn jam scholam amō.
Per labōrem.
Senātōrēs multam pecūniam merent.

Nihil novī est.
Ad urbem vādō.
Pecūniam merēre optō.

THE LATIN CONNECTION

Look over the list of Latin words and then the list of English words (called derivatives) that come from the Latin words. Write the English word in the space next to the Latin word that is connected with it in meaning:

1. movēre _____

2. silēre _____

3. urbs _____

4. timēre _____

5. vidēre _____

6. rīdēre _____

7. jacēre _____

8. pendēre _____

9. manēre _____

10. suburbium _____

remain
suburb
pending
silent
ridiculous
adjacent
movement
urban
timid
videotape

QUAESTIŌNĒS PERSŌNĀLĒS

1. Habitāsne in urbe aut in suburbiō? _____

2. Amāsne rosās aut līlia? _____

3. Habēsne arborēs circum casam tuam? _____

4. Lūdisne in viā aut in āreā? _____

5. Lūdisne cum amīcīs aut cum frātribus et sorōribus? _____

6. Frequentāsne lūdum in urbe aut in suburbiō? _____

7. Estne pater tuus lēgislātor aut āthlēta aut medicus aut vēnditor? _____

8. Habēsne multōs amīcōs aut amīcās in lūdō? _____

9. Ambulāsne ad scholam? _____

10. Estne rosārium in hortō post casam tuam? _____

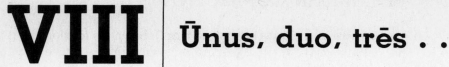

VIII Ūnus, duo, trēs . . .

How to Count in Latin; Numbers I to XXX

1 Repeat the numbers aloud after your teacher:

1	I	ūnus, ūna, ūnum	16	XVI	sēdecim
2	II	duo, duae, duo	17	XVII	septendecim
3	III	trēs, trēs, tria	18	XVIII	duodēvīgintī
4	IV	quattuor	19	XIX	ūndēvīgintī
5	V	quīnque	20	XX	vīgintī
6	VI	sex	21	XXI	vīgintī ūnus
7	VII	septem	22	XXII	vīgintī duo
8	VIII	octō	23	XXIII	vīgintī trēs
9	IX	novem	24	XXIV	vīgintī quattuor
10	X	decem	25	XXV	vīgintī quīnque
11	XI	ūndecim	26	XXVI	vīgintī sex
12	XII	duodecim	27	XXVII	vīgintī septem
13	XIII	trēdecim	28	XXVIII	duodētrīgintā
14	XIV	quattuordecim	29	XXIX	ūndētrīgintā
15	XV	quīndecim	30	XXX	trīgintā

The numerals that we use today (Arabic numerals) were not introduced into Europe until about a thousand years after the time of Julius Caesar. Until this time, Europe used Roman numerals. We still see them used today. In the Roman system, the placement of vertical lines *after* a numeral indicated *addition;* for example, VII means 5 + 2, XIII means 10 + 3. The placement of vertical lines *before* a numeral indicated *subtraction;* for example, IV means 5 − 1, IX means 10 − 1.

NOTE: The declension of **duo** is irregular:

duo	duae	duo
duorum	duarum	duorum
duos	duas	duo
duobus	duabus	duobus
duobus	duabus	duobus

Āctivitātēs

A. Match the Latin number with the Roman numeral and write it in the space provided:

1. octō _____

2. decem _____

3. ūndēvīgintī _____

4. quattuor _____

5. sēdecim _____

6. duo _____

7. vīgintī septem _____

8. novem _____

9. quattuordecim _____

10. trēs _____

11. vīgintī ūnus _____

12. septendecim _____

13. quīndecim _____

14. sex _____

15. quīnque _____

XVI
IV
XXI
VI
XIV
III
XVII
V
IX
VIII
XV
XIX
II
X
XXVII

B. Write out these numbers in Latin:

VII _____

III _____

XIV _____

V _____

X _____

XX _____

IV _____

I   _____

XXV   _____

XIII   _____

VIII   _____

XXX   _____

2   Here's a story in which you have to know your numbers:

Marius et soror sua, Aurēlia, tabernam crūstulāriam intrant. Crūstula optant.

CRŪSTULĀRIUS: Salvēte. Quid optās, Marī?

MARIUS: Crūstula optāmus. Quantī cōnstat ūnum crūstulum?

CRŪSTULĀRIUS: Ūnum cōnstat vīgintī nummīs.

MARIUS: Vīgintī? Est cārissimum.

CRŪSTULĀRIUS: Crūstulum vērō magnum est.

MARIUS: Tot nummōs nōn habeō.

CRŪSTULĀRIUS: Quot nummōs habēs, Marī?

MARIUS: Tantummodo decem nummōs.

CRŪSTULĀRIUS: Mē paenitet, nōn satis est.

AURĒLIA: Ego aliquot nummōs habeō.

CRŪSTULĀRIUS: Quot nummōs habēs, Aurēlia?

AURĒLIA: Eōs ēnumerābō: ūnus, duo, trēs, quattuor, quīnque, sex, septem. Ego septem nummōs habeō.

CRŪSTULĀRIUS: Mē paenitet, nōn jam satis est. Pretium est vīgintī nummī.

MARIUS: Ō, trēs nummōs ultrā in sacculō habeō.

CRŪSTULĀRIUS: Id satis est. Hīc est crūstulum.

MARIUS: Et hīc sunt vīgintī nummī.
CRŪSTULĀRIUS: Grātiās. Valēte.

MARIUS ET AURĒLIA: Valē.

Marius et soror sua ā tabernā ad casam ambulant. Prīmum Marius crūstulum gustat; deinde Aurēlia. Vērum est: pecūniam nōn habent sed crūstulum suāve habent. Itaque fēlīcēs sunt.

---

suus -a -um *his*
  taberna *f shop*
crūstulārius -a -um *pastry*
  crūstulum *n cookie*
crūstulārius *m pastry baker*
  salvēte *hello*
quantī cōnstat *how much is*
  (*costs*)
nummus *m cent*

cārissimus -a -um *very expensive*
vērō *but*

tot *that many*

quot *how many*

tantummodo *only*

mē paenitet *I'm sorry*
  satis *enough*
aliquot *some*

Eōs ēnumerābō *I'll count them*

nōn jam *still not*
pretium *n price*

ultrā *more*
  sacculum *n wallet*

valēte *good-bye*

prīmum *first*

suāvis -is -e *delicious*
  itaque *and so*

Āctivitātēs

C. Answer the following questions based on the story:

1. Ubi sunt Marius et Aurēlia?

   _____

2. Quid vēnditat crūstulārius in tabernā?

   _____

3. Quid Marius et Aurēlia optant?

   _____

4. Quantī cōnstat ūnum crūstulum?

   _____

5. Quot nummōs habet Marius?

   _____

6. Estne id satis?

   _____

7. Quot nummōs habet Aurēlia?

   _____

8. Estne id satis?

   _____

9. Quot nummōs Marius in sacculō habet?

   _____

10. Estne crūstulum parvum aut magnum?

    _____

11. Quō Marius et Aurēlia ambulant?

    _____

12. Suntne fēlīcēs aut tristēs?

    _____

D. Imagine yourself sitting on a bench in a school in ancient Rome, learning arithmetic. See whether you can get the answers before the rest of the Roman girls and boys:

EXAMPLE: Quot sunt ūnus et duo? **Ūnus et duo sunt trēs.**

1. Quot sunt duo et duo?

_____

2. Quot sunt trēs et quattuor?

_____

3. Quot sunt sex et sex?

_____

4. Quot sunt decem et decem?

_____

5. Quot sunt octō et decem?

_____

6. Quot sunt sex et septem?

_____

7. Quot sunt novem et quattuor?

_____

8. Quot sunt trēdecim et duo?

_____

9. Quot sunt quīnque et vīgintī ūnus?

_____

10. Quot sunt decem et vīgintī?

_____

E. Very good. You deserve a **crūstulum.** Now that you're getting used to the numerals, try your skill at some problems in subtraction:

EXAMPLE: Quot sunt ūnus dē tribus? **Ūnus dē tribus sunt duo.**

1. Quot sunt duo dē decem?

_____

2. Quot sunt decem dē vīgintī?

_____

3. Quot sunt trēs dē quattuordecim?

_____

4. Quot sunt septem dē vīgintī?

_____

5. Quot sunt octō dē sēdecim?

_____

6. Quot sunt quīnque dē quīndecim?

_____

7. Quot sunt octō dē septendecim?

_____

8. Quot sunt trēs dē trīgintā?

_____

9. Quot sunt trēs dē vīgintī duōbus?

_____

10. Quot sunt trēs dē duodētrīgintā?

_____

F. Now that you are practically an expert in addition and subtraction in Latin, here are some math problems for you to solve. Read the Latin carefully and then give your answer in a complete Latin sentence:

    1. Aurēlia decem crūstula habet, et Marius tria crūstula habet. Quot crūstula habent Aurēlia et Marius?

_____

2. Marius trīgintā nummōs habet. Tabernam chartāriam intrat. Liber constat tribus nummīs. Rēgula cōnstat ūnō nummō, et charta cōnstat quīnque nummīs. Quot nummōs Marius nunc habet?

_____

3. Rūfus est agricola; animālia in fundō habet. Habet trēs vaccās, decem gallīnas, duōs equōs, duōs canēs et duās fēlēs. Quot animālia habet Rūfus?

_____

4. Māter flōrēs (*flowers*) amat et multōs flōrēs in hortō habet. Decem rosās et vīgintī quattuor līlia habet. Quot flōrēs māter in hortō habet?

_____

5. Terentius agrōs procul ab (*far from*) urbe vīsitat, ubi varia animālia videt. Decem vaccās et duōs equōs et quīnque porcōs et decem gallīnās videt. Quot animālia Terentius in agrīs videt?

_____

6. Multī Rōmānī hodiē ante templum stant. Sunt trēs senātōrēs, sex magistrī, duo āthlētae, ūnus agricola, ūnus nauta, ūnus crūstulārius et duo medicī. Quot Rōmānī ante templum hodiē stant?

_____

7. Magister in oppidō parvō est semper populāris. Multōs amīcōs habet. Trēs sunt professōrēs, quīnque sunt gladiātōrēs, et quīndecim sunt senātōrēs. Quot amīcōs habet magister?

_____

8. Drūsilla ad forum ambulat, quia pōma prō mātre optat. Cerasa cōnstant quīnque nummīs. Pira cōnstant vīgintī nummīs, et ūvae cōnstant quīnque nummīs. Quantī cōnstant pōma?

_____

9. Sunt multae persōnae in familiā Senecā. Sunt parentēs, avus et avia, duo fīliī et duae fīliae. Quot persōnae in familiā Senecā sunt?

_____

10. In vīllā meā sunt multae fēlēs. Ūna est sub subselliō, duae sunt in mēnsā, ūna est prope jānuam, ūna est inter lectōs et ūna est super tectō. Quot fēlēs in vīllā meā habeō?

_____

G. Look at the pictures below. Count the number of objects or persons in each picture and write out the number of objects or persons below the picture. For example, if you see three elephants in the picture, write **trēs elephantī.** Be sure that both noun and adjective have the correct singular or plural form:

1. _____

2. _____

3. _____

4. _____

5. _____

6. _____

7. _____

8. _____

9. _____

11. _____

10. _____

12. _____

3 The numbers we have been using so far are called CARDINAL numbers. There are also ORDINAL numbers. The Romans sometimes used these ORDINAL numbers as the names of their children. A boy might be named **Quīntus** and a girl **Quīnta.** All of these ORDINAL numbers have masculine, feminine, and neuter forms, just like all other adjectives (**bonus, bona, bonum**). Here are the first ten ORDINAL numbers:

prīmus *-a -um*	*first*
secundus *-a -um*	*second*
tertius *-a -um*	*third*
quārtus *-a -um*	*fourth*
quīntus *-a -um*	*fifth*
sextus *-a -um*	*sixth*
septimus *-a -um*	*seventh*
octāvus *-a -um*	*eighth*
nōnus *-a -um*	*ninth*
decimus *-a -um*	*tenth*

Āctivitās

H. Write the ordinal numbers corresponding to the following cardinal numbers:

1. septem _____

2. quattuor _____

3. sex _____

4. decem _____

5. ūnus _____

6. octō _____

7. duo _____

8. quīnque _____

9. trēs _____

10. novem _____

4 Now read this story about the Scipio family:

Familia Scīpiō octō membra habet. Pater, nōmine Publius, quadrāgintā annōs nātus est. Pater in agrīs cum fīliīs labōrat. Māter, nōmine Cornēlia, trīgintā septem annōs nāta est. Māter in vīllā labōrat, praecipuē in culīnā. Prīmus fīlius, nōmine Quīntus, quattuordecim annōs nātus est. Fīlius secundus, nōmine Cornēlius, duodecim annōs nātus est. Duo fīliī scholam in oppidō frequentant. Post scholam in agrīs cum patre labōrant. Sunt intellegentēs et rōbustī.

Fīlia prīma, nōmine Octāvia, decem annōs nāta est. Fīlia secunda, nōmine Tīberia, octō annōs nāta est. Duae fīliae in vīllā labōrant aut in hortō lūdunt, quia in oppidō parvō puellae scholam nōn frequentant; māter est eārum magistra; māter puellās docet.

Familia etiam animālia domestica habet: ūnum canem et ūnam fēlem et ūnam avem. In tōtō sunt sex membra in familiā: sex persōnae et tria animālia. Avus et avia cum familiā nōn habitant; in fundō procul ab oppidō in casā rūsticā habitant. Familia avum et aviam rūrī saepe vīsitant.

membrum *n member*
quadrāgintā *forty*
  annōs nātus *-a -um years old*

praecipuē *especially*

eārum *their*

avis *f bird*
in tōtō *in all*
procul (ab) *far (from)*
**rūsticus *-a -um* rustic*
rūrī *in the country*
  saepe *often*

CONVERSĀTIŌ

VOCABULA

Quid est tēcum? *What's the matter with you.*
perītus -a -um *good, skillful*

mathēmātica -ae *f mathematics*
fascia -ae *f bandage*
computāre *to count, do figures*

COLLOQUIUM

You are asking all the questions today. Complete the dialog, choosing from the following list:

Quot sunt septem et novem?   Quot sunt octō de sēdecim?
Quid est tēcum hodiē?   Quot sunt decem et quīnque?

QUAESTIŌNĒS PERSŌNĀLĒS

1. Quot annōs nātus (nāta) es tū?

_____

2. Quot annōs nāta est māter tua?

_____

3. Quot annōs nātus est pater tuus?

_____

4. Quot frātrēs habēs?

_____

5. Quot sorōrēs habēs?

_____

6. Habēsne canem?

_____

7. Habēsne fēlem?

_____

8. Habēsne avem?

_____

9. Habitatne avus cum familiā tuā?

_____

10. Habitatne avia cum familiā tuā?

_____

Lectiō V

a. Subject pronouns:

ego	*I*	**nōs**	*we*
tū	*you*	**vōs**	*you*
is	*he*	**eī**	*they* (masculine)
ea	*she*	**eae**	*they* (feminine)
id	*it*	**ea**	*they* (neuter)

b. To conjugate an **-āre** verb, drop **-āre** from the infinitive and add the proper endings:

EXAMPLE: **cant*āre***

If the subject is **ego**   add **ō**   to the remaining stem: ego cant*ō*

tū	**ās**	tū cant*ās*
is, ea, id	**at**	is, ea, id cant*at*
nōs	**āmus**	nōs cant*āmus*
vōs	**ātis**	vōs cant*ātis*
eī, eae, ea	**ant**	eī, eae, ea cant*ant*

In Latin, the personal pronouns are not generally used except for emphasis or clarity, since the endings of the verbs indicate the pronoun subjects.

c. Verbs of the **-āre** family:

amāre	*to love*	**lavāre**	*to wash*
ambulāre	*to walk*	**natāre**	*to swim*
auscultāre	*to listen to*	**optāre**	*to want, wish*
cantāre	*to sing*	**portāre**	*to carry*
clāmāre	*to shout*	**pōtāre**	*to drink*
cōnstāre	*to cost*	**rogāre**	*to ask*
dare	*to give*	**salūtāre**	*to greet*
dēmonstrāre	*to point out*	**servāre**	*to save*
ēnumerāre	*to count up*	**spectāre**	*to watch, look at*
gustāre	*to taste*	**stāre**	*to stand*
habitāre	*to live*	**sūdāre**	*to sweat*
intrāre	*to enter*	**vēnditāre**	*to sell*
labōrāre	*to work*	**vīsitāre**	*to visit*

Lectiō VI

a. The ABLATIVE case:

	FIRST DECLENSION	SECOND DECLENSION		THIRD DECLENSION		
			SINGULAR			
NOMINATIVE	**ros***a*	**amīc***us*	**plaustr***um*	**pater**	**can***is*	**animal**
ACCUSATIVE	**ros***am*	**amīc***um*	**plaustr***um*	**patr***em*	**can***em*	**animal**
ABLATIVE	**ros***ā*	**amīc***ō*	**plaustr***ō*	**patr***e*	**can***e*	**animāl***ī*

	FIRST DECLENSION	SECOND DECLENSION		THIRD DECLENSION		
			PLURAL			
NOMINATIVE	**ros***ae*	**amīc***ī*	**plaustr***a*	**patr***ēs*	**can***ēs*	**animāl***ia*
ACCUSATIVE	**ros***ās*	**amīc***ōs*	**plaustr***a*	**patr***ēs*	**can***ēs*	**animāl***ia*
ABLATIVE	**ros***īs*	**amīc***īs*	**plaustr***īs*	**patr***ibus*	**can***ibus*	**animāl***ibus*

b. Prepositions that always take the accusative case:

ad	*to, toward; at*	**per**	*through*
ante	*in front of, before*	**post**	*after, behind*
circum	*around*	**prope**	*near*
inter	*between, among*	**trāns**	*across*

c. Prepositions that always take the ablative case:

ā, ab	*from, away from; by*	**ē, ex**	*out of*
cum	*with*	**prō**	*for; in front of*
dē	*from, down from; about*	**sine**	*without*

d. Prepositions that take the accusative case to express "motion" or "direction" and the ablative case to express "location" or "position":

in	(position) *in, on;* (direction) *into*
sub	*under*
super	*over, above*

Lectiō VII

a. To conjugate an **-ēre** verb, drop **-ēre** from the infinitive and add the proper endings:

EXAMPLE: **sedēre**

If the subject is **ego**   add **eō**   to the remaining stem: **ego sed***eō*
           tū   **ēs**   **tū sed***ēs*
           is, ea, id   **et**   **is, ea, id sed***et*
           nōs   **ēmus**   **nōs sed***ēmus*
           vōs   **ētis**   **vōs sed***ētis*
           eī, eae, ea **ent**   **eī, eae, ea sed***ent*

b. Verbs of the -**ēre** family:

docēre	*to teach*	pendēre	*to hang*
(sē) exercēre	*to exercise, practice*	respondēre	*to answer*
habēre	*to have*	rīdēre	*to laugh*
jacēre	*to lie*	sedēre	*to sit*
jubēre	*to order*	silēre	*to be silent*
latēre	*to hide, be hidden*	subrīdēre	*to smile*
manēre	*to remain, stay*	tenēre	*to hold*
mordēre	*to bite*	terrēre	*to frighten, scare*
movēre	*to move*	timēre	*to fear, be afraid of*
(sē) paenitēre	*to be sorry*	vidēre	*to see*

c. Questions may be introduced by a specific word:

cūr	*why*	quō	*where(to)*
quandō	*when*	quōmodō	*how*
quid	*what*	quot	*how many*
quis	*who*	ubi	*where; when*

d. If there is no specific word to introduce a question and

(1) you expect the answer to be "yes," use **nōnne** to introduce the question:

> *Nōnne* **Fabius lūdum frequentat?** *Fabius attends school, doesn't he?*

(2) you expect the answer to be "no," use **num** to introduce the question:

> *Num* **canis īnfantem terret?** *The dog doesn't scare the baby, does it?*

(3) you are simply asking for information and the answer may be either "yes" or "no," use **-ne** attached to an important word at the beginning of the question:

> **Habēs***ne* **pecūniam prō crūstulō?** *Do you have money for a cookie?*

e. "Yes" may be expressed by **ita, sānē, vērō,** or by repeating the verb. "No" may be expressed by **nōn, minimē, minimē vērō,** or by repeating the verb with **nōn.**

Lectiō VIII

a. Cardinal numbers:

1	I	ūnus, ūna, ūnum	11	XI	ūndecim
2	II	duo, duae, duo	12	XII	duodecim
3	III	trēs, trēs, tria	13	XIII	trēdecim
4	IV	quattuor	14	XIV	quattuordecim
5	V	quīnque	15	XV	quīndecim
6	VI	sex	16	XVI	sēdecim
7	VII	septem	17	XVII	septendecim
8	VIII	octō	18	XVIII	duodēvīgintī
9	IX	novem	19	XIX	ūndēvīgintī
10	X	decem	20	XX	vīgintī

21	XXI	vīgintī ūnus		26	XXVI	vīgintī sex
22	XXII	vīgintī duo		27	XXVII	vīgintī septem
23	XXIII	vīgintī trēs		28	XXVIII	duodētrīgintā
24	XXIV	vīgintī quattuor		29	XXIX	ūndētrīgintā
25	XXV	vīgintī quīnque		30	XXX	trīgintā

b. Ordinal numbers:

prīmus	*first*	**sextus**	*sixth*
secundus	*second*	**septimus**	*seventh*
tertius	*third*	**octāvus**	*eighth*
quārtus	*fourth*	**nōnus**	*ninth*
quīntus	*fifth*	**decimus**	*tenth*

Activitātēs

A. Verb Game. Here are some pictures of people doing things. Describe each picture using the correct form of one of the following verbs:

auscultāre	**natāre**	**portāre**	**tenēre**
labōrāre	**pōtāre**	**rīdēre**	**vēnditāre**

1. Puerī in flūmine _____ .

3. Frāterculus fēlem _____ .

2. Discipulus magistrum _____ .

4. Māter in culīnā _____ .

5. Vēnditor pōma _____.

7. Nōs in lūdō _____.

6. Drūsilla aquam _____.

8. Asinus līberōs _____.

B. First write the Latin word next to the English word. Then circle the Latin word in the puzzle on page 127:

1. to look at _____	**13.** to see _____
2. to shout _____	**14.** 26 _____
3. to save _____	**15.** 8 _____
4. to sweat _____	**16.** 19 _____
5. to drink _____	**17.** 9 _____
6. to want _____	**18.** 13 _____
7. to stand _____	**19.** 4 _____
8. to laugh _____	**20.** 30 _____
9. to stay, remain _____	**21.** first _____
10. to hold _____	**22.** tenth _____
11. to hang _____	**23.** fourth _____
12. to hide _____	**24.** ninth _____

V	I	G	I	N	T	I	S	E	X	P	N
I	S	O	Q	O	P	L	P	Z	D	E	O
D	Q	P	X	V	O	A	E	Q	E	N	N
E	Z	T	L	E	C	T	C	P	C	D	U
R	Y	A	P	M	T	E	T	O	I	E	S
E	R	R	K	Y	O	R	A	T	M	R	Z
K	T	E	N	E	R	A	R	A	U	E	K
Y	S	E	R	V	A	R	E	R	S	P	T
Q	U	A	T	T	U	O	R	E	X	R	R
U	N	D	E	V	I	G	I	N	T	I	I
A	C	L	A	M	A	R	E	X	K	M	G
R	I	D	E	R	E	X	W	Q	W	U	I
T	R	E	D	E	C	I	M	S	S	S	N
U	Y	K	M	A	N	E	R	E	Z	Y	T
S	U	D	A	R	E	S	T	A	R	E	A

C. Cruciverbilūsus:

HORIZONTĀLE

  1. father
  2. baby
  5. friend
  6. another
  7. senators
11. to
12. you (*acc.*)
13. rose
15. I
17. medicine
18. through
20. yes
21. cherry

PERPENDICULĀRE

  1. wagon
  2. on
  3. cat
  4. sailors
  8. we
  9. you
10. queens
14. grandmothers
16. pear
19. she

D. The Latin Connection. Dozens of words that you use everyday come from Latin. If you know the Latin origin, you will be able to understand the word better. Here are some of them. Write the English derivative next to the Latin word from which it is derived:

1. crūstulum _____

2. ruber _____

3. lūna _____

4. servāre _____

5. manēre _____

6. spectāre _____

7. portāre _____

8. taberna _____

9. jocus _____

10. suburbium _____

11. movēre _____

12. ūnus _____

13. adulēscentulus _____

14. octō _____

15. respondēre _____

16. salūtāre _____

17. duo _____

18. urbs _____

duet
import
octave
unit
crust
tavern
respond
ruby
joke
lunatic
suburb
remain
urban
adolescent
remove
inspect
preserve
salute

Wouldn't you like to know your future? Follow these simple rules to see what the cards have in store for you. Choose a number from two to eight. Starting in the upper left corner, and moving from left to right, write down all the letters that appear under the number in Latin:

sex M	septem B	trēs F	octō S	quattuor V	duo V	quīnque M	octō U
octō C	trēs A	quattuor I	duo I	quīnque U	septem O	octō C	sex U
septem N	quattuor T	trēs M	duo T	quīnque L	sex L	trēs I	octō E
sex T	quattuor A	quīnque T	trēs L	septem A	duo A	octō S	sex A
septem F	octō S	duo L	trēs I	sex P	quīnque I	septem O	quattuor F
septem R	trēs A	quīnque A	septem T	duo O	sex E	octō U	quīnque M
sex C	quattuor E	quīnque I	septem U	trēs M	sex U	quattuor L	octō S
septem N	trēs A	duo N	quattuor I	quīnque C	sex N	septem A	trēs G
sex I	trēs N	quattuor X	duo G	sex A	trēs A	quīnque I	duo A

F. All of the following people are saying some numbers. What are they?

1. _____

4. _____

2. Casae numerus est _____

5. _____

3. Numerus est _____

6. _____

G. Picture Story. Can you read this story? Much of it is in picture form. Whenever you come to a picture, read it as if it were a Latin word (with the correct endings!):

Hodiē est diēs fortunātus, est diēs festus. Quia diēs festus est, nōn est [schola] hodiē. Lūcia est [fēmina] duodecim annōs nāta. In [urbe] magnā habitat. Sed hodiē Lūcia cum [puerō] et [virō] et [puellā] fundum visitat ubi [avus] et [avia] habitant. Villa est antiqua sed commoda, et [lectī] sunt antiquī et commodī. Prope [villam] est flūmen cum [rīpā] frīgidā. Post villam est hortus cum [arbore] magnā. In arbore sunt [pōma] rubra. In culīnā [fēmina] suāvia torret. [Avus] pōma suāvia ex hortō ad [mēnsam] in culīnā portat. Frāterculus per agrōs cum [cane] ambulāre amat. Lūcia sub [arbore] magnā sedēre amat. Tunc Lūcia [rīdet] quia contenta est. Etiam [puer] contentus est. Vita in fundō est admīrābilis. Nōnne tū in fundō sub arbore sedēre optās magis quam in [schola]?

VOCĀBULA

diēs festus *holiday*		**tunc** *then*	
commodus -a -um *comfortable*		**admīrābilis** *wonderful*	
torrēre *to bake*		**magis quam** *rather than*	

Pars
Tertia

Plūs et plūs verbōrum!

-ĔRE Verbs

1 These new action words are all verbs that belong to the **-ĕre** family, also called the THIRD CONJUGATION. See whether you can guess their meaning:

currĕre

scrībĕre

legĕre

emĕre

vēndĕre

dīcĕre

lūdĕre

dūcĕre

vincĕre

cadĕre

edĕre

frangĕre

quaerĕre

vādĕre

gerĕre

You have probably noticed that these 15 verbs do not belong to the **-āre** or **-ēre** families. To which family do these verbs belong? _____ You remember that in the **-ēre** family of verbs the first ē has a "long" mark (macron) over it to show that the ē is long. Since the ē is the next-to-last syllable and is long, it receives the stress. But in the **-ĕre** family, the first ĕ is marked with a curved line (breve) to show that it is short and, therefore, does not receive the stress.

2   Just as we made changes in the **-āre** verbs by dropping the **-āre** and in the **-ēre** verbs by dropping the **-ēre** from the infinitive and adding certain endings, we must do the same with **-ĕre** verbs. The endings, however, are different. Read the following story and see whether you can spot the endings of the **-ĕre** verbs:

Hodiē Cornēlius et Claudia cum patre in urbem ad Circum **vād***unt*. Ad portam sunt vēnditōrēs quī crūstula et dulcia **vēnd***unt*. Pater duo crūstula prō Cornēliō et Claudiā **em***it*. Per portam pater et līberī Circum intrant et multōs equōs pulchrōs vident. Cornēlius equōs **dīlig***it;* Claudia quoque equōs valdē **dīlig***it*. Octō equī in quōque cursū **curr***unt*.

> **Circus** *m racetrack*
> **porta** *f gate*
> **quī** *who*   **dulcia** *npl candy*

> **dīligĕre** *to like*
> **valdē** *a lot*
> **in quōque cursū** *in each race*

"Pater," **quaer***it* Cornēlius, "quem equum maximē **dīlig***is?*"

> **quem** *which*
> **maximē** *most*

"In opīniōne meā," respondet pater, "ille equus badius est vēlōcissimus. In equō badiō ego **pōnō***.*"

> **ill***e* **-a -ud** *that*
> **badi***us* **-a -um** *chestnut*
>   **vēlōcissim***us* **-a -um** *fastest*
> **pōnĕre** *to bet*

"Claudia, quem equum tū **dīlig***is?*" **quaer***it* Cornēlius ut crūstulum mordet.

> **ut** *as*

"Ego quoque equum badium **dīlig***ō,*" **dīc***it* Claudia ut patrem spectat et subrīdet.

"Bene," **dīc***it* pater. "Vōs equum badium **dīlig***itis*. Ego quoque. Nōs equum badium **dīlig***imus*.*"

"Ego duo crūstula in equō badiō **pōnō***!*" **dic***it* Claudia. Cornelius et pater subrīdent.

Nunc equī parātī sunt **currĕre**. Omnēs spectātōrēs in Circō clāmant. Octō equī ē carceribus volant. Equus albus prīmus **curr***it;* equus cānus **curr***it* secundus. Sed ad fīnem equus badius **vinc***it*. Claudia et Cornēlius et pater cum gaudiō domum vādunt.

> **parā***tus* **-a -um** *prepared*
> **ē carceribus** *out of the starting gate*
>   **volāre** *to fly, come flying*
>   **alb***us* **-a -um** *white*
> **cān***us* **-a -um** *grey*
> **fīnis** *m finish (line)*
> **domum** *home*

Activitās

A. **Vērum aut Falsum.** If the sentence is true, write **Vērum**. If it is false, write **Falsum** and correct the sentence:

1. Claudia et Cornēlius cum patre ad Circum vādunt.

_____

2. Vēnditōrēs crūstula et dulcia ad portam vendunt.

_____

3. Pater dulcia prō Claudiā et Cornēliō emit.

_____

4. Pater equum album dīligit, sed fīlius et fīlia equum badium dīligunt.

_____

5. Equus albus ad fīnem vincit.

_____

3 Now see whether you can apply the correct endings to the verb **dīligĕre** (_to like_). Look carefully through the story and find an example of every ending that you need. To form the present tense of **-ĕre** verbs, drop _____ and add the endings:

ego _____

tū _____

is, ea, id _____

nōs _____

vōs _____

eī, eae, ea _____

Āctivitātēs

B. Match the sentences with the pictures they describe:

Āthlēta currit.
Agricola equum dūcit.
Pōmārius ūvās vēndit.
Māter pōma emit.

Avia librum legit.
Discipulī scrībunt.
Puer dē arbore cadit.
Puella stolam gerit.

1. _____

5. _____

2. _____

6. _____

3. _____

7. _____

4. _____

8. _____

C. Now let's practice important **-ĕre** verbs. Fill in all the forms:

	dīcĕre	**gerĕre**	**quaerĕre**	**vādĕre**
ego	_____	_____	_____	_____
tu	_____	_____	_____	_____
is, ea, id	_____	_____	_____	_____
nōs	_____	_____	_____	_____
vōs	_____	_____	_____	_____
eī, eae, ea	_____	_____	_____	_____

D. Complete each sentence with the correct form of the verb:

1. (currĕre) Equus badius in Circō _____.

2. (vēndĕre) Pōmārius pōma in forō _____.

3. (gerĕre) Senātōrēs Rōmānī togās albās _____.

4. (lūdĕre) Ego et Claudia in āreā prope lūdum _____.

5. (cadĕre) Pira dē arbore _____.

6. (edĕre) Nōnne tū cerasa rubra _____?

7. (emĕre) Diāna crūstula in tabernā crūstulāriā _____.

8. (dīligĕre) Nōs omnēs mūsicam _____.

9. (dīcĕre) Quid magistra dē vitā in urbe _____?

10. (dūcĕre) Agricola equum badium in stabulum _____.

11. (vādĕre) Quōmodō puella parva per urbem sine parentibus _____?

12. (vincĕre) Prīmus equus semper _____.

13. (frangĕre) Īnfāns ōvum _____.

14. (quaerĕre) Cūr magister dē frātre meō _____?

E. Here are some -**ĕre** verbs. Match them with the English meanings. Write the matching letter in the space provided:

1. tū vēndis _____

2. ea edit _____

3. nōs scrībimus _____

4. eae dīligunt _____

5. ea gerit _____

6. vincimus _____

7. ego emō _____

8. vōs caditis _____

a. I buy
b. we are winning
c. she is eating
d. you are falling
e. she is wearing
f. they like
g. we are writing
h. you sell

4 English words are often made up of two Latin words. For example, the English verb *invade* comes from the Latin prefix **in-** and the Latin root (or base) **vādĕre**. The short Latin word **in-** is called a *prefix* because it is placed *before* the root. We can describe the process as follows:

PREFIX + ROOT =   LITERAL ENGLISH MEANING   ENGLISH DERIVATIVE

in- + **vādĕre** = **invādĕre**   *to go into*   *invade*

By this method, our vocabulary will grow by leaps and bounds. But first we must learn some Latin prefixes. Many of them exist as independent Latin prepositions, some of which we have already met:

ā or **ab-**	*from, away*
ad-	*to, toward*
circum-	*around*
con- or **com-**	*with; together; completely, up* (**comedĕre** *to eat up*)
contrā-	*against*
dē-	*down; away from*
ē- or **ex-**	*out of, from*
in- or **im-**	*in, into*
inter-	*between*
intrō-	*in, inward*
per-	*completely, through*
post-	*after, behind*
prae-	*before, ahead*
prō-	*forward, forth*
re-	*back; again*
sub- or **suc-**	*under, beneath; from beneath, up; after*
trāns-	*across*

Activitās

F. Now let's see how it works. Consult the list of prefixes above. Let's take Latin verbs and add various prefixes according to the example below, and give the literal meaning and English derivative:

PREFIX + ROOT			LITERAL MEANING	ENGLISH DERIVATIVE
con-	+ cēdĕre	= concēdĕre	*to go (along) with*	*concede*
ex-	+ cēdĕre	= _____	_____	_____
inter-	+ cēdĕre	= _____	_____	_____
prae-	+ cēdĕre	= _____	_____	_____
prō-	+ cēdĕre	= _____	_____	_____
re-	+ cēdĕre	= _____	_____	_____
suc-	+ cēdĕre	= _____	_____	_____
in-	+ dūcĕre	= _____	_____	_____
intrō-	+ dūcĕre	= _____	_____	_____
prō-	+ dūcĕre	= _____	_____	_____
re-	+ dūcĕre	= _____	_____	_____
dē-	+ portāre	= _____	_____	_____
ex-	+ portāre	= _____	_____	_____
im-	+ portāre	= _____	_____	_____
re-	+ portāre	= _____	_____	_____
trāns-	+ portāre	= _____	_____	_____
in-	+ habitāre	= _____	_____	_____
dē-	+ pendĕre	= _____	_____	_____

CONVERSĀTIŌ

VOCĀBULA

cibus fēlīnus *cat food*
mūs *m mouse*
eum *him*
captāre *to catch*
mūrēs *mpl mice*

quaerit (*she*) *looks for*
tāle . . . quālis *such . . . as*
quantī? *how much?*
mīlle dēnāriīs *a thousand dollars*

COLLOQUIUM

What would the second person say in this dialog? Circle your answers from the choices provided:

RĒS PERSŌNĀLĒS

Complete these five sentences by writing something original about yourself:

1. Dīligō _____ .

2. Lūdō _____ .

3. Vādō _____ .

4. Legō _____ .

5. Emō _____ .

Esse aut nōn esse

The Verbs **esse** *and* **posse;** *Professions and Trades*

1   Vocābula

vēnditor *m*

mūsicus *m* / **mūsica** *f*

cantor *m* / **cantrix** *f*

āctor *m* / **āctrix** *f*

medicus *m*

tōnsor *m* / **tōnstrix** *f*

servus *m* / **serva** *f*

sartor *m* / **sartrix** *f*

146

pugil *m*

pictor *m*

āthlēta *m*

lanius *m*

pīstor *m*

faber tignārius *m*

sculptor *m*

coquus *m* / **coqua** *f*

advocātus *m*

mīles *m*

senātor *m*

Āctivitātēs

A. Match the following occupations with the related pictures:

sculptor   pugil
āthlēta   mīles
mūsica   coqua
vēnditor   lanius
āctrix   serva

1. _____

5. _____

2. _____

6. _____

3. _____

7. _____

4. _____

8. _____

9. _____

10. _____

B. Now identify these pictures:

1. _____

5. _____

2. _____

6. _____

3. _____

7. _____

4. _____

8. _____

C. Each of the following sentences indicates where the person works. In the spaces provided, write the name of the place in the nominative case with the gender and then give the English meaning. You should be able to figure out the name of the place from the occupation of the subject:

EXAMPLE: Āctrix in theātrō labōrat. **theātrum** *n* _____theater_____

1. Āthlēta in stadiō labōrat. _____ _____

2. Coqua in culīnā labōrat. _____ _____

3. Pīstor in pīstrīnā labōrat. _____ _____

4. Vēnditor in forō labōrat. _____ _____

5. Lanius in laniēnā labōrat. _____ _____

6. Advocātus in jūdiciō labōrat. _____ _____

7. Āctor in theātrō labōrat. _____ _____

8. Tōnsor in tōnstrīnā labōrat. _____ _____

2 Read the following story and see whether you can answer the questions that follow:

Antōnius **est** tōnsor. Ejus tōnstrīna **est** in Subūrā. Appius et Sextus ē forō vādunt et tōnstrīnam intrant. Appius quattuordecim annōs nātus **est** et Sextus trēdecim annōs nātus **est**. Appius et Sextus **sunt** amīcī bonī.

Subūra *f a noisy, busy section of Rome near the forum*

"Salvēte, puerī," dīcit Antōnius. "Vōs **estis** ad tempus. Ego **sum** ōtiōsus. Quis **est** prīmus?"

ad tempus *just in time*
ōtiōsus -a -um *not busy*

"Ego et Sextus **sumus** cupidī tōnsūrae," respondet Appius. "Coma nostra **est** longa. Sexte, tū **es** prīmus."

cupidus -a -um *eager for*
tōnsūra *f haircut*
coma -ae *f hair*
noster -ra -rum *our*

Sextus in sellā tōnsōriā cōnsīdit. Antōnius tondet et tondet et tondet.

sella tōnsōria *barber chair*
cōnsīděre *to sit down*
tondēre *to cut*

"Ō, tōnsor!" exclāmat Sextus, "coma mea **est** nimis curta! Haec tōnsūra **est** rīdicula. **Es**ne tū insānus?"

nimis *too* **curtus -a -um** *short*
insānus -a -um *crazy*

Tunc exclāmat Appius: "Ego nōlō **esse** calvus" et ē tōnstrīnā in viam currit.

nōlō *I don't want*
calvus *-a -um bald*

Āctivitās

D. Respondē ad quaestiōnēs:

1. Quis est tōnsor?

_____

2. Ubi est tōnstrīna?

_____

3. Quis tōnstrīnam intrat?

_____

4. Cūr tōnsūram optant?

_____

5. Quis prīmus in sellā tōnsōriā cōnsīdit?

_____

6. Estne tōnsūra Sextī nimis longa aut nimis curta?

_____

7. Quid exclāmat Appius ut ē tōnstrīnā currit?

_____

8. Quot annōs nātus est Appius?

_____

3 In the story you have just read, there is an important new verb: **esse** (*to be*). **Esse** is a special verb, different from all the other verb families. All its forms are different. It is, therefore, called an irregular verb. Can you pick out the verb forms in the story you have just read to match the subject pronouns below? Every form that you need occurs in the story:

ego _____   nōs _____

tū _____   vōs _____

is, ea, id _____   eī, eae, ea _____

Āctivitātēs

E. Fill in the correct form of the verb **esse:**

1. Ego _____ medicus.

2. Ea _____ actrix.

3. Frāter meus _____ pictor.

4. Pugilēs _____ āthlētae.

5. Ego et Drūsilla _____ cantrīcēs.

6. Antōnius _____ tōnsor.

7. Vōs _____ coquae bonae.

8. Quis _____ sartor bonus?

9. Īnfāns _____ amābilis.

10. Āctrix _____ ēlegāns.

11. Sculptōrēs _____ excellentēs.

12. Nōs omnēs _____ impatientēs.

F. Supply a correct subject noun or pronoun for each sentence:

1. _____ est incrēdibilis.

2. _____ sum tristis.

3. _____ sunt rōbustī.

4. _____ sumus fēlīcēs.

5. _____ est ferōx.

6. _____ estis prūdentēs.

7. _____ sunt mūsicī bonī.

8. _____ es fortūnātus.

4 Now let's look at another important verb based on **esse**. The verb is **posse** (*to be able, can*). **Posse** is a combination of the root **pot-** (*able*) and **esse** (*to be*). Let's see how the verb is formed:

ego	**poss***um*	*I can, am able*
tū	**pot***es*	*you can, are able*
is, ea, id	**pot***est*	*he, she, it can, is able*
nōs	**poss***umus*	*we can, are able*
vōs	**pot***estis*	*you can, are able*
eī, eae, ea	**poss***unt*	*they can, are able*

Look at the forms carefully. There are three forms in which the first part of the verb, (the root) **pot-**, changes to **pos-**. Which are they? _____;

_____; _____. Did you notice that in each of these three forms the Latin verb for *to be* (the second part of the verb) begins with an **s?** The Romans did not like the sound of **potsum,** and so they changed it to **possum.** For the same reason, **potsumus** became **possumus,** and **potsunt** became **possunt.**

Āctivitātēs

G. Complete the sentences with the correct forms of **posse:**

1. Ego natāre _____ .

2. Īnfāns ambulāre nōn _____ .

3. Canēs mordēre _____ .

4. Nōs amīcōs in oppidō vīsitāre _____ .

5. Tū ad mēnsam cōnsīdere _____ .

6. Quis ad quaestiōnem respondēre _____ ?

7. Ego et Claudia ad theātrum vādere nōn _____ .

8. Pīstor crūstula suāvia torrēre _____ .

9. Quōmodō tū cum laniō in laniēnā labōrāre _____ ?

10. Quōmodō nōs sine pecūniā stadium intrāre _____ ?

11. Pictor et sculptor amīcī esse _____ .

12. Nōnne senātor et advocātus multam pecūniam merēre

_____ ?

H. Here are some sentences in which a form of **esse** or **posse** is used. Match these sentences with the pictures they describe:

Āctrix est populāris.
Fabrī tignāriī sunt ūtilēs.
Ego sum mīles.
Lanius est familiāris.
Nōs discipulī sumus cōnfīdentēs.

Canis ferōx esse potest.
Tū es cantrix bona.
Gladiātōrēs sunt fortēs.
Nōs cantāre possumus.
Pugilēs sunt rōbustī.

1. _____

6. _____

2. _____

7. _____

3. _____

8. _____

4. _____

9. _____

5. _____

10. _____

CONVERSĀTIŌ

VOCĀBULA

sperāre	*to hope*	**fortasse**	*maybe*
mē paenitet	*I'm sorry*	**nimis valdē**	*too hard*
quid praetereā?	*what else?*	**per deōrum fidem**	*for heaven's sake*
merēre	*to earn*	**est multō melius**	*it is much better*
proelium	*n battle*	**cōnsilium**	*n advice*
pugnāre	*to fight*		

COLLOQUIUM

Complete the dialog with the correct expressions chosen from the following list:

Per deōrum fidem, est multō melius esse gladiātor aut pugil aut mīles.
Fabrī tignāriī nimis valdē labōrant.
Mīlitēs in proeliīs perīculōsīs pugnant.
Tū es nimis parvus.
Sculptōrēs et pictōrēs nōn multam pecūniam merent.

QUAESTIŌNĒS PERSŌNĀLĒS

1. Optāsne esse āctor aut āctrix?

   _____

2. Esne populāris in scholā?

   _____

3. Potesne sine parentibus in urbem vādĕre?

   _____

4. Potesne pecūniam merēre?

   _____

5. Estne māter tua coqua bona?

   _____

6. Estne frāter tuus āthlēta bonus?

   _____

7. Potestne soror tua bene cantāre?

   _____

8. Suntne parentēs tuī semper fēlīcēs?

   _____

RĒS PERSŌNĀLĒS

List in Latin the five professions that interest you most. Next to each profession write a sentence that describes the person in the profession. In addition to the professions listed in this lesson, you may want to consult the professions listed at the end of Lesson I and the adjectives in Lesson IV:

EXAMPLE: **Pugil. Pugil est rōbustus.**

1. _____

2. _____

3. _____

4. _____

5. _____

-ĪRE Verbs; the Verb īre

1   Meet some members of the fourth family of verbs: the **-īre** family, also called the FOURTH CONJUGATION. See whether you can guess their meanings:

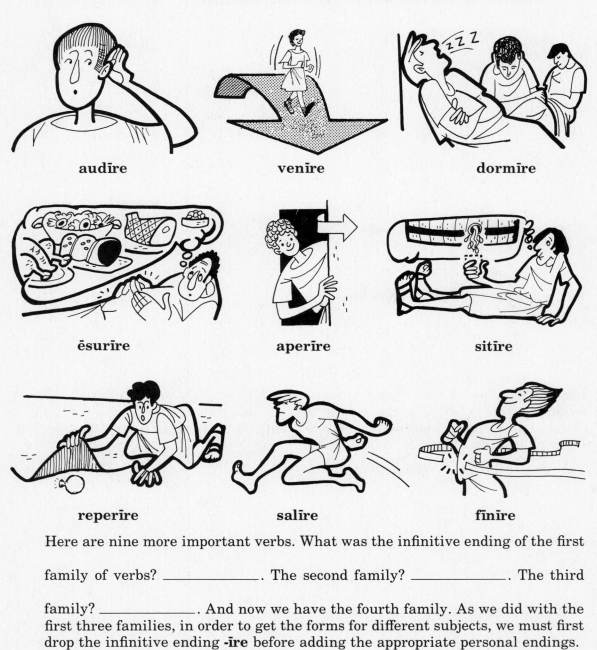

audīre

venīre

dormīre

ēsurīre

aperīre

sitīre

reperīre

salīre

fīnīre

Here are nine more important verbs. What was the infinitive ending of the first

family of verbs? _____. The second family? _____. The third

family? _____. And now we have the fourth family. As we did with the first three families, in order to get the forms for different subjects, we must first drop the infinitive ending **-īre** before adding the appropriate personal endings.

158

2 As you read the following story, look for the verbs of the **-īre** family and see whether you can spot the endings. Although the endings are similar to those of the **-ĕre** family, the stress falls usually on the next-to-last syllable because it is long:

Hodiē est diēs terribilis. Caelum est obscūrum. Discipulī in scholā fēlīcēs nōn sunt. Magister classem spectat. Ūnus discipulus **dorm*it***.

obscūr*us* -*a* -*um* *dark*

"Marcelle," dīcit magister, "Marcelle! tū **dorm*īs*.** Nōs nōn **dorm*īmus*** in scholā. Nōs domī in lectō **dorm*īmus*.**"

domī *at home*

Omnēs discipulī nunc Marcellum spectant. Marcellus oculōs lentē **aper*it*.** "Ego nōn **dorm*iō*,** magister," Marcellus tandem murmurat.

oculus *m eye*   **lentē** *slowly*
tandem *at last*
murmurāre *to murmur*

"Tū sōlus in scholā **dorm*īs*,** Marcelle," dīcit magister. "Alterī discipulī nōn **dorm*iunt*.**" Deinde ad classem sē vertēns, magister dīcit: "Nōnne vērum est? Vōs nōn in classe meā **dorm*ītis*.**"

sōl*us* -*a* -*um* *alone*
alter, alter*a*, alter*um* *the other*
deinde *then*
   sē vertēns *turning*

Discipulī ūnā voce clāmant: "Vērum est, magister; nōs nōn **dorm*īmus*;** nōs semper dīligenter studēmus."

ūnā voce *with one voice*

dīligenter *diligently*
   studēre *to study*

"Ō," clāmat Marcellus, "ego nōn **dorm*iō*,** sed tantummodo faciō ut oculī quiēscant." Alterī discipulī Marcellum inrīdent.

tantummodo *only*
faciō ut oculī quiēscant *I am resting my eyes*
inrīdēre *to laugh at*

Āctivitās

A. Vērum aut Falsum. If the sentence is true, write **Vērum** in the space provided. If the sentence is false, write **Falsum** and correct the sentence:

1. Hodiē est diēs magnificus.

_____

2. Discipulī fēlīcēs sunt.

_____

3. Marcellus sōlus dormit.

_____

4. Marcellus dīcit "Ego dormiō."

_____

5. Alterī discipulī quoque dormiunt.

_____

6. Discipulī Marcellum inrīdent.

_____

3   Now see whether you can apply the correct endings to the verb **dormīre.** Look carefully through the story and find an example of every ending you need. To

form the present tense of **-īre** verbs, drop _____ and add the endings:

ego   _____

tū   _____

is, ea, id _____

nōs   _____

vōs   _____

eī, eae, ea_____

Let's put an example of the **-ĕre** family of verbs next to an example of the **-īre** family to compare both the similiarities and the differences. Note the length of the vowels within the endings. Then, in the following columns write out those forms whose endings are spelled the same way:

dīc*ō*	ven*iō*	_____	_____
dīc*is*	ven*īs*	_____	_____
dīc*it*	ven*it*	_____	_____
dīc*imus*	ven*īmus*	_____	_____
dīc*itis*	ven*ītis*	_____	_____
dīc*unt*	ven*iunt*	_____	_____

Did you notice that, although the endings of the two families are very similar in *spelling,* there is quite a difference in the *length of the vowels* in the endings?

Āctivitātēs

B. Let's practice with other important -īre verbs. Fill in all the forms:

	audīre	ēsurīre	reperīre	sitīre
ego	_____	_____	_____	_____
tū	_____	_____	_____	_____
is, ea, id	_____	_____	_____	_____
nōs	_____	_____	_____	_____
vōs	_____	_____	_____	_____
eī, eae, ea	_____	_____	_____	_____

C. Complete with the correct forms of the verbs:

1. (dormīre) Īnfāns in lectō _____.

2. (aperīre) Puellae fenestrās et jānuās _____.

3. (ēsurīre) Nōs post scholam semper _____.

4. (audīre) Ego avēs in arbore _____.

5. (sitīre) Equī post cursum in Circō _____.

6. (venīre) Marcelle, tū ad tempus _____.

7. (fīnīre) Ego et amīcī fēlīcēs sumus ubi schola _____.

8. (salīre) Canis parvus meus trāns subsellium _____.

9. (reperīre) Quid vōs in tabernā crūstulāriā _____?

10. (venīre) Quis ad casam meam hodiē _____?

D. Circle the phrase that best completes each of the following sentences:
1. Vēnditōrēs in plaustrīs veniunt (in forum / in gallīnā).
2. Gladiātor audit (spectātōrēs / stadium).
3. Nōs ēsurīmus (ubi aquam nōn habēmus / ubi cibum nōn habēmus).
4. Servus aperit (fenestrās / canēs et fēlēs).
5. Ego nōn possum reperīre (sandalia mea / tōnsūram meam).
6. Medicus ad casam venit (ubi aegrōtī [*sick*] sumus / ubi fēlīcēs sumus).

7. In theātrō vidēmus et audīmus (cantōrēs et āctōrēs / sartōrēs et laniōs).

8. Nōs sitīmus (ubi in flūmine natāmus / ubi in agrīs labōrāmus).

9. Nōs omnēs dormīmus (in lectō / in tectō).

10. Līberī in hortō saliunt (trāns rosārium / trāns arborem).

4 A very important action verb is the Latin verb **īre** (*to go*). Its complete forms in the present tense look very much like the endings of the **-īre** verbs. Compare these two columns:

eō	*I go, am going*	**veni***o*	*I come, am coming*
īs	*you go, are going*	**ven***īs*	*you come, are coming*
it	*he, she, it goes, is going*	**ven***it*	*he, she, it comes, is coming*
īmus	*we go, are going*	**ven***īmus*	*we come, are coming*
ītis	*you go, are going*	**ven***ītis*	*you come, are coming*
eunt	*they go, are going*	**ven***iunt*	*they come, are coming*

Which two forms of **īre** are different from the endings of **venīre?**

_____   _____

Āctivitās

E. In Chapter IX, you learned that Latin verbs often have prefixes. By consulting that list of prefixes, you should be able to give the meanings of the following verbs:

1. abīre _____

2. adīre _____

3. circumīre _____

4. co(n)īre _____

5. exīre _____

6. inīre _____

7. interīre _____

8. intrōīre _____

9. perīre _____

10. praeīre _____

11. prō(d)īre _____

12. re(d)īre _____

13. subīre _____

14. trānsīre _____

5 The fourth verb in Activitās E (**coīre**) drops the **n** of the prefix **con-** (which comes from the preposition **cum**), just as in English the prefix takes different forms, depending on the first letter of the root: *con*fer, *com*plete, *co*pilot, *col*lect, *cor*rect. Look at the eleventh and twelfth verbs in Activitās E. The Romans did not like to have two vowels clash, and so they often inserted a **d** between the vowels, as in the verbs **prōdīre** and **redīre.** Many of these verbs have more than one English equivalent.

For example, **adīre** may mean *to go toward* or *to approach;* **inīre** may mean *to go into* or *to enter;* **redīre** may mean *to go back* or *to return;* **trānsīre** may mean *to go across* or *to cross;* **perīre** may mean *to perish* or *to die.* Some verbs have special meanings: **interīre** means *to perish* or *to die.*

Activitātēs

F. Match the sentences with the pictures they describe:

Avus in sellā dormit.   Medicus lectum adit.
Ego cantrīcem audiō.   Nōs ex aquā exīmus.
Coqua ē culīnā exit.   Māter cum īnfante venit.
Āthlētae sitiunt.   Equus cursum prīmus fīnit.
Ego in aquam saliō.   Nōs pecūniam reperīmus.

1. _____   4. _____

2. _____   5. _____

3. _____   6. _____

7. _____

9. _____

8. _____

10. _____

G. Complete the sentences with the correct forms of **īre** or its compounds. Be sure that if the subject is singular the verb is also singular; if the subject is plural, be sure to make the verb also plural:

1. (exīre)   Vacca ē stabulō _____.

2. (īre)   Discipula ad scholam _____.

3. (coīre)   Nōs cum amīcīs saepe _____.

4. (inīre)   Āthlētae stadium _____.

5. (circumīre) Senatōrēs oppidum _____.

6. (trānsīre)   Puerī flūmen _____.

7. (abīre)   Cūr pater _____?

8. (intrōīre)   Pugilēs in stadium nunc _____.

9. (adīre)   Nautae īnsulam parvam _____.

10. (redīre)   Fīlia ad parentēs hodiē _____.

11. (praeīre)   Servus dominō _____.

12. (interīre) Ubi rosae aquam nōn habent, _____.

VOCĀBULA

sīc *so*

cotīdiē *daily*

māne et vespere *in the morning and evening*

carō *f meat*

recēns *fresh*

igitur *then, in that case*

COLLOQUIUM

Complete the dialog with the expressions chosen from the following list:

Estne etiam lanius in forō?
Bene. Canis igitur nōbīscum in forum īre potest.
    Canis meus ēsurit et carnem amat.
Vēnditatne cerasa?
Sīc audiō. Estne pōmārius in forō?
Possum, Marce, sed ego ēsuriō.

QUAESTIŌNĒS PERSŌNĀLĒS

The school computer is assembling a personality profile for every student. You are asked to answer the following questions:

1. Quot annōs nātus (nāta) es?

   _____

2. Esne fēlix aut tristis ubi in lūdō es?

   _____

3. Studēsne cotīdiē dīligenter?

   _____

4. Dīligisne magistrum (magistram)?

   _____

5. Timēsne magistrum (magistram)?

   _____

6. Dormīsne in scholā?

   _____

7. Reperīsne multōs amīcōs et amīcās in āreā?

   _____

8. Venīsne in scholam ad tempus cotīdiē?

   _____

9. Dīligisne linguam (*language*) Latīnam?

   _____

10. Optāsne vīsitāre Rōmam?

    _____

11. Estne lingua Latīna difficilis?

    _____

12. Optāsne esse magister (magistra)?

    _____

13. Ēsurīsne ubi domum post scholam redīs?

_____

14. Dīligisne in lectō tuō manē manēre et dormīre?

_____

15. Suntne parentēs tuī sevērī?

_____

Genitive Case

1 MŌNSTRUM

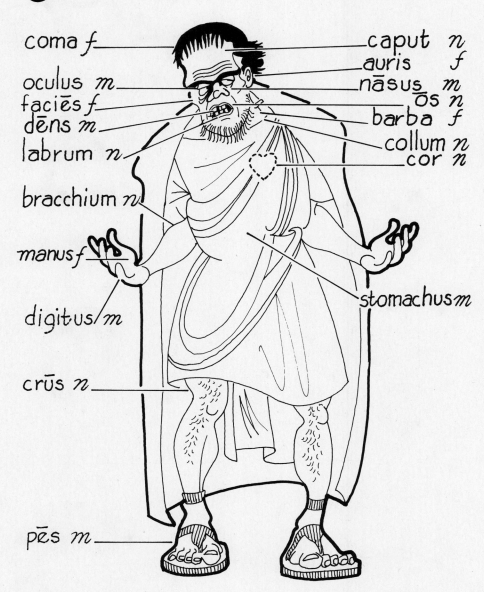

coma *f*

oculus *m*

faciēs *f*

dēns *m*

labrum *n*

bracchium *n*

manus *f*

digitus *m*

crūs *n*

pēs *m*

caput *n*

auris *f*

nāsus *m*

ōs *n*

barba *f*

collum *n*

cor *n*

stomachus *m*

This monster may look weird, but the parts of his body are the same as yours and mine. Study the Latin names for them. Here are two more parts that are not shown: **faucēs** *fpl throat;* **lingua** *f tongue.*

169

Āctivitātēs

A. Match the words with the pictures:

caput	**labra**	**auris**	**collum**
nāsus	**dentēs**	**faciēs**	**coma**
lingua	**oculī**		

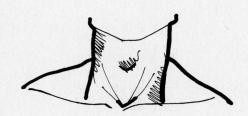

1. _____

2. _____

3. _____

4. _____

5. _____

6. _____

7. _____

8. _____

9. _____

10. _____

B. Label these parts of the face:

1. _____

5. _____

2. _____

6. _____

3. _____

7. _____

4. _____

8. _____

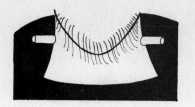

9. _____

10. _____

C. Now label these parts of the body:

1. _____

2. _____

3. _____

4. _____

5. _____

6. _____

7. _____

8. _____

D. Every part of the body can do something. Match the part of the body with the action it can perform. Sometimes more than one part of the body will share in the same action. Write the matching letter in the space provided:

1. pedēs _____
2. dentēs _____
3. manus _____
4. ōs _____
5. aurēs _____
6. faucēs _____
7. crūra _____
8. lingua _____
9. oculī _____
10. cor _____

a. audīre
b. pōtāre
c. ambulāre
d. tenēre
e. mordēre
f. currĕre
g. stāre
h. dīcĕre
i. edĕre
j. cantāre
k. vidēre
l. amāre
m. spectāre
n. respondēre
o. lavāre
p. gustare

2 Now that you know the Latin names for various parts of the body, we're ready to read the amazing story of the Roman scientist, Dr. Franciscus Frankenpetrus, and the horrible monster he created.

But first we must learn the GENITIVE (or possessive) case of nouns. In English, we express possession by using an apostrophe and s ('s): *boy's, children's.* We can express the same idea with the preposition *of:* the home *of the boy* or the *boy's* home. In Latin, there is a special genitive ending to indicate possession; for example, **puerī** means *the boy's* or *of the boy.* You can see that Latin does not use an apostrophe and s or a preposition to express possession:

Examine the following groups. Repeat each set of Latin nouns after your teacher:

AS SUBJECT	AS GENITIVE	
barba	**barb**ae	*the beard's, of the beard*
lingua	**lingu**ae	*the tongue's, of the tongue*
coma	**com**ae	*the hair's, of the hair*
stomachus	**stomach**ī	*the stomach's, of the stomach*
oculus	**ocul**ī	*the eye's, of the eye*
bracchium	**bracchi**ī	*the arm's, of the arm*
labrum	**labr**ī	*the lip's, of the lip*
dēns	**dent**is	*the tooth's, of the tooth*
caput	**capit**is	*the head's, of the head*
corpus	**corpor**is	*the body's, of the body*
crūs	**crūr**is	*the leg's, of the leg*
ōs	**ōr**is	*the mouth's, of the mouth*
auris	**aur**is	*the ear's, of the ear*
pēs	**ped**is	*the foot's, of the foot*

What is the genitive ending of a feminine noun ending in **-a?** _____. What is the genitive ending of a masculine noun ending in **-us?** _____. Of a neuter noun ending in **-um?** _____. What is the genitive ending of all the other nouns in the list? _____. These are nouns of the third declension.

In the genitive case, we see the complete stem of a noun, namely, the part of a noun that remains the same and to which the case endings are added. From now on, nouns appearing for the first time will show the nominative case, the genitive case, and the gender:

com*a* **-***ae* f *hair*	**aur***is* **-***īs* f *ear*
digit*us* **-***ī* m *finger*	**dēns -***tis* m *tooth*
labr*um* **-***ī* n *lip*	**corp***us* **-***oris* n *body*

3 We will see more of the genitive case later on. Now, on with the story:

LOCUS: Labōrātōrium physicī insānī, nōmine Doctor Frankenpetrus.

labōrātōri*um* **-***ī* n *laboratory*
  physic*us* **-***ī* m *scientist*
  insān*us* **-***a* **-***um* *mad*

PERSŌNAE: Dr. Franciscus Frankenpetrus
  Marcellus, ejus socius
  Mōnstrum, combinātiō ē variīs
  partibus corporis

soci*us* **-***ī* m *associate, assistant*
combinātiō -*nis* f *combination*
  vari*us* **-***a* **-***um* *various, different*
par*s* **-***tis* f *part*

DR. FRANKENPETRUS: Hāc nocte optō fabricāre mōnstrum horribile.
MARCELLUS: Bene, magister Frankenpetre.

hāc nocte *tonight*
  fabricāre *to make*

DR. F: Prīmum, habēsne cadāver, Marcelle?
M: Ecce! Hīc est cadāver; corpus est vetus et dēfōrme.

magis*ter* **-***trī* m *master, Mr.*
cadāver -*is* n *cadaver, corpse*
vetus, veteris *old*
dēfōrm*is* **-***is* **-***e* *ugly*

DR. F: Habēsne oculōs?
M: Habeō. Sed oculī nōn sunt similēs.

simil*is* **-***is* **-***e* *alike, similar*

DR. F: Bene! Et nunc, duo bracchia, Marcelle.
M: Hīc sunt duo bracchia. Bracchia sunt pilōsa. Ūnum est ab homine, alterum ā simiō.

pilōs*us* **-***a* **-***um* *hairy*
  homo -*inis* m *man*
  alter -*a* **-***um* *the other*
simi*us* **-***ī* m *ape*

DR. F: Perfectum! Et manūs? Habēsne manūs?
M: Hīc sunt duae manūs, magister.
DR. F: Quot digitōs habent manūs?
M: Decem, magister.
DR. M: Excellēns!
M: Sunt septem digitī in ūnā manū et tantum trēs in alterā mānū.

tantum *only*

DR. F: Bene! Et crūra? Habēmusne crūra?
M: Certē, magister. Ūnum est longum et alterum est curtum.

certē *certainly*

DR. F: Optimē! Sed ubi est caput, Marcelle?

M: Ecce, magister. Caput est magnum, cum vultū ferōcī.

DR. F: Magnificē! Vīs electrica vītam mōnstrō dabit.

    Bzzzzzzzzzzzzzzzzzzzzzz

M: Ecce mōnstrum! Id aliquid dīcere optat.

DR. F: Vītam habēs. Loquere, loquere!

MONSTRUM: Amō, amās, amat . . .

DR. F: Quāle mōnstrum! Est professor Latīnae. Est (*Fill in someone's name, someone who won't get too angry with you.*)

optimē! *very well!*

vult*us* -*ūs* *m expression*

vīs, vīs *f charge* **vīt*a* -*ae*** *f life*

mōnstrō *to the monster*
 dabit *will give*

aliquid *something*

loquere! *speak!*

quāl*is* -*is* -*e* *what a*

Āctivitātēs

E. **Vērum aut Falsum?** If the statement is true, write **Vērum** in the space. If it is false, write **Falsum** and correct the statement.

1. Doctor Frankenpetrus est physicus īnsānus.

  _____

2. Corpus mōnstrī est pulchrum.

  _____

3. Mōnstrum vultum intellegentem habet.

  _____

4. Ūnum bracchium est ā cane.

  _____

5. Mōnstrum cor nōn habet.

  _____

6. Vīs electrica vītam mōnstrō dat.

  _____

7. Mōnstrum decem digitōs habet.

  _____

8. Mōnstrum est stupidum.

  _____

F. Fill in the Latin names for the labeled parts of the body:

4 Let's learn some more about the genitive case. First, read the following story and pay particular attention to all nouns in the genitive case. Notice that the noun in the genitive case may come *before* or *after* the noun with which it goes:

Cornēliī casa procul āb oppidō est. Nōmen **oppidī** est Ardea. Cornēlius ūnum frātrem et ūnam sorōrem habet. Nōmen **frātr*is*** est

Clēmēns. Nōmen **sorōr***is* est Līvia. **Cornēliī** pater agricola est. Dum pater in agrīs labōrat, līberī in hortō lūdunt. Cornēlius **pat***ris* tunicam gerit. Līvia **mātr***is* stolam caeruleam gerit. Clēmēns **pat***ris* togam et calceōs gerit.

Tum **vicīnī** canis lūdibundus hortum intrat. Prīmum is stolam **Līvi***ae* vellit. Deinde **Cornēliī** tunicam vellit. Dēnique togam **Clēment***is* vellit. Paulō post canis lūdibundus manum **Clēment***is* et faciem **Līvi***ae* lambit. Deinde **Cornēliī** bracchium lambit. Līberī cum gaudiō clāmant et currunt. Māter clāmōrēs audit, hortum intrat et canem permulcet.

dum *while*

caerule*us* **-***a* **-***um* *blue*
calce*us* **-***ī* *m shoe*

vicīn*us* **-***ī* *m neighbor*
  lūdibund*us* **-***a* **-***um* *playful*
vellĕre *to tug at*
  deinde *then, next*
dēnique *finally*
paulō post *a little later*
lambĕre *to lick*

permulcēre *to pet*

NOTE: The genitive usually indicates possession, but not always:

Plaustrum est plēnum lignī. *The wagon is full of wood.*

Āctivitās

G. Supply the genitive endings:

1. Cornēli____ casa procul ab oppidō est.

2. Nōmen oppid____ est Ardea.

3. Frātr____ nōmen est Clēmēns.

4. Nōmen sorōr____ est Līvia.

5. Cornēli____ pater est agricola.

6. Līvia stolam caeruleam mātr____ gerit.

7. Cornēlius patr____ tunicam gerit.

8. Canis vicīn____ in hortum currit.

9. Canis lūdibundus bracchium Clēment____ lambit.

10. Cornēli____ māter canem permulcet.

5 The genitive singular of a noun like **fīlia** or **oculus** has the same form as the nominative plural. Compare the following sentences:

Coma fīli*ae* **est pulchra.**
The daughter's hair is beautiful.

Fīli*ae* **comam pulchram habent.**
The daughters have beautiful hair.

Color oculī est caeruleus.
The color of the eye is blue.

Puellae oculī sunt caeruleī.
The girl's eyes are blue.

How can you tell whether the form is the genitive singular or the nominative plural? The rest of the sentence provides the clues. Look carefully for these clues in the following sentence:

Puerī pater senātor Rōmānus est.

The word **puerī** by itself could be either the genitive singular or the nominative plural subject of the sentence. But the next word, **pater,** can be only the subject of the sentence. This function is confirmed by the singular verb **est.** Therefore, **puerī** in this sentence must be in the genitive case. Besides, the sense of the sentence as a whole gives us another clue. After all, boys were not senators in ancient Rome. Furthermore, the words **puerī pater** form a phrase and should be read together as a phrase. (A phrase is a group of two or more words that belong together as a unit.) To understand Latin, it is very important for you to read sentences in word groups.

Activitās

H. Read the following sentences aloud with proper pauses between phrases:

1. Līviae māter   in culīnā   semper valdē labōrat.
2. Canis vicīnī   puellās et puerōs   terret.
3. Līvia   caeruleam stolam mātris   gerĕre amat.
4. Canis lūdibundus   Clēmentis tunicam   vellit.
5. Mōnstrī caput   magnum et dēfōrme   est.
6. Faciēs mōnstrī   vultum ferōcem   semper habet.

6 Now that you have learned to recognize the genitive case in the singular, examine the following groups in the plural. Repeat each set of nouns after your teacher:

AS SUBJECT		AS GENITIVE	
lingu*ae*	FIRST DECLENSION	**lingu***ārum*	*of the tongues*
stol*ae*		**stol***ārum*	*of the gowns*
digit*ī*		**digit***ōrum*	*of the fingers*
nās*ī*	SECOND DECLENSION	**nās***ōrum*	*of the noses*
labr*a*		**labr***ōrum*	*of the lips*
dent*ēs*		**dent***ium*	*of the teeth*
ped*ēs*	THIRD DECLENSION	**ped***um*	*of the feet*
corpor*a*		**corpor***um*	*of the bodies*
cord*a*		**cord***um*	*of the hearts*

What is the genitive plural ending of nouns of the first declension? _____.

What is the genitive plural ending of nouns of the second declension? _____.

If you look carefully at the nouns of the third declension, notice that the genitive plural ending is sometimes **-ium** and sometimes **-um.**

Āctivitātēs

I. Match the following sentences with the pictures they describe:

Oculī feminae sunt tristēs.
Musculī āthlētae sunt magnī.
Bracchia mōnstrī sunt pilōsa.
Vir vetus comam nōn habet.
Magnum nāsum habēs.

Avī faciēs vultum fēlīcem habet.
Vultus discipulī est intellegēns.
Crūra elephantī sunt ēnorma.
Decem digitōs habeō.
Stomachus senātōris est magnus.

1. _____

2. _____

3. _____

4. _____

5. _____

6. _____

7. _____   9. _____

8. _____   10. _____

J. Supply the genitive plural endings:

1. Dentēs puer_____ sunt albī.

2. Pedēs īnfant_____ sunt parvī.

3. Ego in casā amīc_____ saepe dormiō.

4. Līberī tunicās parent_____ gerĕre dīligunt.

5. Fīliī senātor_____ cotīdiē in scholā sunt.

6. Avēs in tectīs cas_____ sedent.

7. Pōma arbor_____ sunt magna.

8. Pretium ros_____ est altum.

9. Medicus ōra līber_____ inspectat.

10. Stolae fēmin_____ sunt ēlegantēs.

VOCĀBULA

quid est? *what's wrong?*
aegrōtus -a -um *sick*
dolor -ōris m *ache*
dolēre *to ache, hurt*

appetentia -ae f *appetite*
jam *already*
mē melius habeō *I feel better*

COLLOQUIUM

Complete the dialog with expressions chosen from the following list:

aegrōta	multās grātiās	dolent
ēsuriō	scholam	medicīnam
in lectō	dolet	quid
tristis	appetentiam	stomachī

QUAESTIŌNĒS PERSŌNĀLĒS

Answer the questions in complete Latin sentences:

1. Habēsne comam longam aut curtam?

   _____

2. Habēsne pedēs magnōs aut parvōs?

   _____

3. Habēsne cor bonum aut malum?

   _____

4. Habēsne dentēs albōs?

   _____

5. Lavāsne manūs et faciem cotīdiē?

   _____

6. Habēsne oculōs bonōs aut infirmōs?

   _____

7. Habēsne appetentiam bonam aut malam?

   _____

8. Vīsitāsne medicum saepe?

   _____

Recōgnitiō III (Lectiōnēs IX-XII)

Lectiō IX

a. To conjugate an **-ĕre** verb, drop **-ĕre** from the infinitive and add the proper endings:

> EXAMPLE: **scrībĕre**

If the subject is **ego**   add **ō**   to the remaining stem: **ego scrībō**

tū	is	**tū scrīb***is*
is, ea, id	it	**is, ea, id scrīb***it*
nōs	imus	**nōs scrīb***imus*
vōs	itis	**vōs scrīb***itis*
eī, eae, ea	unt	**eī, eae, ea scrīb***unt*

b. Verbs of the **-ĕre** family:

cadĕre	*to fall*	**legĕre**	*to read*
currĕre	*to run*	**lūdĕre**	*to play*
dīcĕre	*to say*	**quaerĕre**	*to ask; to acquire*
dūcĕre	*to lead*	**scrībĕre**	*to write*
edĕre	*to eat*	**vādĕre**	*to go*
emĕre	*to buy*	**vēndĕre**	*to sell*
frangĕre	*to break*	**vincĕre**	*to win; to defeat*
gerĕre	*to wear*		

c. By adding prefixes to a verb, new words are formed. Some of the common Latin prefixes are:

ā- or **ab-**	*from, away*
ad-	*to, toward*
circum-	*around*
con- or **com-**	*with, together; completely, up* (**comedere** *to eat up*)
contrā-	against
dē-	down, away from
ē- or **ex-**	out of, from
in-	in, into
inter-	between
intrō-	in, inward
per-	completely; through
post-	after, behind
pre- or **prae-**	before, ahead
prō-	forward, forth
re-	back; again
trāns	across
sub- or **suc-**	under, beneath; from beneath, up

Lectiō X

a. The verb **esse** (*to be*) is an irregular verb. Memorize all its forms:

ego sum	nōs sumus
tū es	vōs estis
is, ea, id est	eī, eae, ea sunt

b. The verb **posse** (*to be able, can*) is a combination of the root **pot-** (*able*) and **esse**. The **t** of **pot-** changes to **s** whenever the form of the verb **esse** begins with an **s**:

ego possum	nōs possumus
tū potes	vōs potestis
is, ea, id potest	eī, eae, ea possunt

Lectiō XI

a. To conjugate an **-īre** verb, drop **-īre** from the infinitive and add the proper endings:

EXAMPLE: **fīnīre**

If the subject is		add		to the remaining stem:
ego	tū	iō	īs	ego fīn*iō*
	is, ea, id		it	tū fīn*īs*
	nōs		īmus	is, ea, id fīn*it*
	vōs		ītis	nōs fīn*īmus*
	eī, eae, ea		iunt	vōs fīn*ītis*
				eī, eae, ea fīn*iunt*

b. Verbs of the **-īre** family:

aperīre	*to open*	**reperīre**	*to find*
audīre	*to hear*	**salīre**	*to jump*
dormīre	*to sleep*	**sitīre**	*to be thirsty*
ēsurīre	*to be hungry*	**venīre**	*to come*
fīnīre	*to end, finish*		

c. Forms of the verb **īre** (*to go*) look very much like the endings of verbs of the **-īre** family:

ego eō	nōs īmus
tū īs	vōs ītis
is, ea, id it	eī, eae, ea eunt

Lectiō XII

a. Parts of the body:

aur*is* -*is* *f*	ear	**crūs -*ris*** *n*	leg
barb*a* -*ae* *f*	beard	**dēns -*tis*** *m*	tooth
bracchi*um* -*ī* *n*	arm	**digit*us* -*ī*** *m*	finger
cap*ut* -*itis* *n*	head	**faciēs -*ēī*** *f*	face
coll*um* -*ī* *n*	neck	**faucēs -*ium*** *fpl*	throat
com*a* -*ae* *f*	hair	**labr*um* -*ī*** *n*	lip
cor -*dis* *n*	heart	**lingu*a* -*ae*** *f*	tongue

manus -ūs f	hand	pēs pedis m	foot
nāsus -ī m	nose	stomachus -ī m	stomach
oculus -ī m	eye	vultus -ūs m	expression
ōs ōris n	mouth		

b. The GENITIVE case sometimes shows possession, but it also has other uses. We can see the full stem of the noun in the GENITIVE case. All four cases that we have learned so far, including the GENITIVE case, are shown below:

	SINGULAR					
	FIRST DECLENSION	SECOND DECLENSION		THIRD DECLENSION		
NOMINATIVE	com*a*	nās*us*	bracchi*um*	dēns	aur*is*	cap*ut*
ACCUSATIVE	com*am*	nās*um*	bracchi*um*	dent*em*	aur*em*	cap*ut*
ABLATIVE	com*ā*	nās*ō*	bracchi*ō*	dent*e*	aur*e*	capit*e*
GENITIVE	com*ae*	nās*ī*	bracchi*ī*	dent*is*	aur*is*	capit*is*

	PLURAL					
	FIRST DECLENSION	SECOND DECLENSION		THIRD DECLENSION		
NOMINATIVE	com*ae*	nās*ī*	bracchi*a*	dent*ēs*	aur*ēs*	capit*a*
ACCUSATIVE	com*ās*	nās*ōs*	bracchi*a*	dent*ēs*	aur*ēs*	capit*a*
ABLATIVE	com*īs*	nās*īs*	bracchi*īs*	dent*ibus*	aur*ibus*	capit*ibus*
GENITIVE	com*ārum*	nās*ōrum*	bracchi*ōrum*	dent*ium*	aur*ium*	capit*um*

Āctivitātēs

A. Search for the Latin equivalents of the English words listed below. You will find them all in the puzzle on page 187. Circle each word as you find it and write it next to the English word:

1. vendor _____

2. friends _____

3. doctor _____

4. maid _____

5. barber _____

6. seamstress _____

7. musician _____

8. butcher _____

9. singer _____

10. boxer _____

11. lawyer _____

12. soldier _____

13. baker _____

14. senators _____

15. painter _____

16. cook _____

17. eyes	_____	**24.** leg	_____
18. nose	_____	**25.** foot	_____
19. expression	_____	**26.** to go	_____
20. teeth	_____	**27.** to lead	_____
21. throat	_____	**28.** to buy	_____
22. mouth	_____	**29.** to wear	_____
23. heart	_____	**30.** to go out	

```
O  S  Q  S  E  N  A  T  O  R  E  S
C  O  R  X  Z  P  I  S  T  O  R  A
U  F  A  U  C  E  S  E  R  V  A  R
L  A  N  I  U  S  A  M  I  C  I  T
I  Q  Y  Z  V  E  N  D  I  T  O  R
M  E  D  I  C  U  S  L  Y  W  Q  I
C  O  Q  U  A  B  P  U  G  I  L  X
A  D  V  O  C  A  T  U  S  I  R  E
N  A  S  U  S  Z  B  D  G  E  M  A
T  O  N  S  O  R  V  U  E  Q  U  P
R  C  T  R  I  X  U  C  R  H  S  I
I  M  I  L  E  S  L  E  E  C  I  C
X  E  M  E  R  E  T  R  R  R  C  T
I  E  X  I  R  E  U  E  E  U  U  O
X  D  E  N  T  E  S  H  Q  S  S  R
```

B. Jumble: Unscramble the words. The unscrambled words will form a sentence:

P R M S U I □ □ □ □ □ □

U Q S E U □ □ □ □ □

P S E M R E □ □ □ □ □ □

T I C N I V □ □ □ □ □ □

C. Acrostic. After filling in all the horizontal slots, look at the vertical box to find the mystery word.

1. second   __ __ __ __ __ __ __

2. to break   __ __ __ __ __ __ __

3. city   __ __ __ __

4. baker   __ __ __ __ __ __

5. shop, booth   __ __ __ __ __ __

6. I can   __ __ __ __ __

7. neck   __ __ __ __ __ __

8. to lead   __ __ __ __ __ __

9. to sleep   __ __ __ __ __ __

D. Place the Latin words describing the pictures in their proper places in the puzzle:

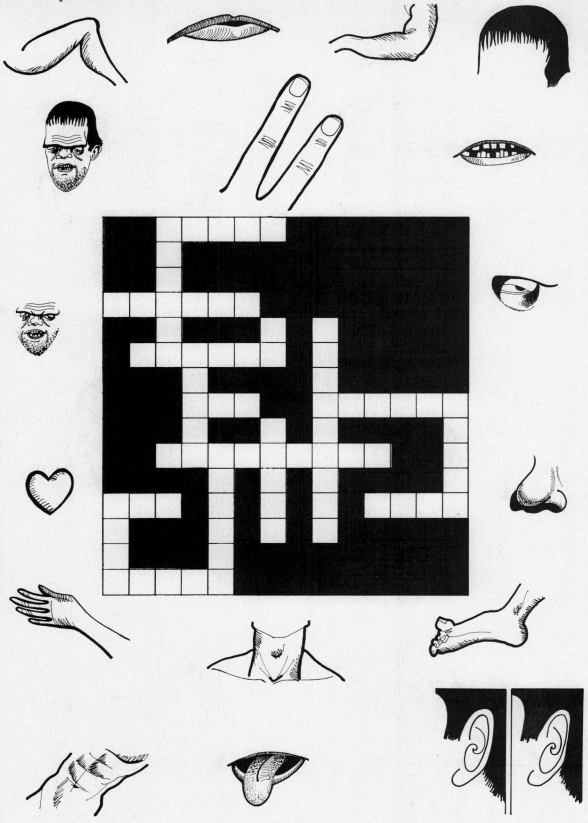

E. Identify with the person in each picture as you express the problem illustrated. Use the first person of the Latin verb. Some problems can be described by the verb alone, others by an adjective and verb:

1. _____

2. _____

3. _____

4. _____

5. _____

6. _____

F. Picture Stories. Can you read these stories? Much of them is in picture form. Whenever you come to a picture, read it as if it were a Latin word. Be sure to use the correct endings:

Salvē. Ego sum Cornēlius. Trēdecim annōs nātus sum.

Ego sum  intellegēns et studiōsus. Ego in

parvō habitō et parvam frequentō, ubi in classe

octāvā sum. Meus est et in

labōrat. Ego spērō esse . Cotīdiē post scholam ego circum

cursum in currō et etiam per oppidī

currō, quia optō habēre robusta. Ego spērō in

lūdīs Olympicīs currere.

Salvē. Ego sum Silvia. Duodecim annōs nāta sum. Ego sum

intellegēns et studiōsa. Mea est atra et meī sunt caeruleī.

Ego nōn frequentō. Ego cum mēa in

labōrō, praecipuē in . Meus est et in

 docet. In familiā mēa sunt trēs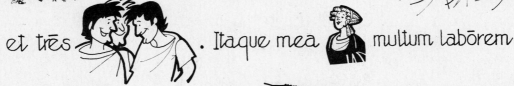

et trēs . Itaque mea multum labōrem

semper habet. Ego saepe frequentō, ubi ego

actōrēs et actrīcēs vidēre possum. Ego spērō esse

in Rōmānō.

Achievement Test I (Lessons I-XII)

1 Vocabulary [15 points]

    A. Label the following pictures in Latin:

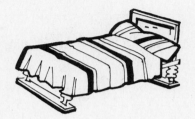

1. _____

2. _____

3. _____

4. _____

5. _____

6. _____

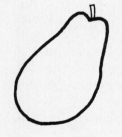

7. _____

8. _____

 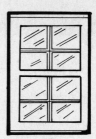

9. _____ 10. _____

B. Name the parts of the body that are used for the following human activities. Give your answer first in Latin and then in English:

1. vidēre   _____ _____

2. ambulāre   _____ _____

3. amāre   _____ _____

4. dīcĕre   _____ _____

5. audīre   _____ _____

2 **Vērum aut Falsum?** Tell whether the following statements are true or false. If they are false, correct them: [5 points]

1. Pōmārius in tōnstrīnā labōrat. _____

2. Magister in lūdō docet. _____

3. Āthlētae in stadiō sē exercent. _____

4. Quattuor et octō sunt trēdecim. _____

5. Tōnsor comām tondet. _____

3 Verbs (**-āre, -ēre, -ĕre, -īre**) [20 points]

Supply the verb with the correct ending:

1. (cantāre) Nōs in classe _____

2. (natāre) Puellae in flūmine _____

3. (vīsitāre) Avus et avia familiam meam _____

4. (currĕre et salīre) Āthlētae in stadiō _____

5. (gerĕre) Āctrix stolam pulchram _____

6. (vēndĕre) Crūstulārius crūstula _____

7. (legĕre et scrībĕre) Vōs in scholā _____

8. (cadĕre) Pōma dē arboribus _____

9. (posse) Equus crūs in Circō frangĕre _____

10. (edĕre) Ubi post scholam ēsuriō, crūstulum _____

11. (dormīre) Avus in subselliō in hortō _____

12. (dīcĕre) Quid magistra dē theātrō _____

13. (labōrāre) Servī et servae in culīnā _____

14. (audīre) Ego mūsicam pulchram _____

15. (aperīre) Ante scholam magistra fenestrās _____

16. (lūdĕre) Discipulae in āreā nunc _____

17. (emĕre) Pater vīllam novam _____

18. (dīligĕre) Līberī fēlēs et canēs _____

19. (excēdĕre) Senātōrēs ē forō _____

20. (abīre) Ego "Valē" dīcō, ubi tū _____

4   Prepositions [10 points]

From the forms in parentheses, select the appropriate object or objects and write them in the space provided. In some sentences, two objects are possible:

1. Oppidum est prope (urbe, flūmen, urbs). _____

2. Magister fābulam nārrat dē (equīs, vaccam, fēlēs). _____

3. Quō vādis cum (amīcō, fratrem, amīca)? _____

4. Pater valdē labōrat prō (māter, familiā, īnfāns). _____

5. Āthlēta salit in (aqua, aquam, aquae). _____

6. Magister et discipulī ambulant per (agrōs, oppidō, viās). _____

7. Ego in forum ineō sine (pecūniam, pecūniā, nummōs). _____

8. Avēs volant super (arborēs, casīs, vīllae). _____

9. Via angusta currit inter (tabernae, oppidō, tabernās). _____

10. Gladiātōrēs prōcēdunt ad (arēnā, arēnam, stadium). _____

5 The verb esse [5 points]

Supply the correct form of the verb **esse:**

1. Vaccae in stabulō _____

2. Ego et amīca mea in hortō _____

3. Vōs ad tempus in theātrō _____

4. Parentēs meī sevērī _____

5. Fēlēs mea sub mēnsā in culīnā _____

6 The verb posse [5 points]

Supply the correct form of the verb **posse:**

1. Avēs volāre _____

2. Nōs urbem ā vīllā vidēre _____

3. Canis meus super rosārium salīre _____

4. Actrīcēs cantāre _____

5. Tū post scholam cum amīcīs lūdĕre _____

7 Numbers [10 points]

Write out the numbers in answer to the following problems:

1. Quot sunt duo et quattuor? _____

2. Quīnque et duodecim sunt _____

3. Quot sunt ūndēvīgintī et novem? _____

4. Quot sunt decem et octō? _____

5. Quot sunt trēdecim dē vīgintī? _____

6. Quot sunt septem dē octō? _____

7. Decem dē vīgintī sunt _____

8. Quīndecim et quīndecim sunt _____

9. Quot sunt sex dē duodētrīgintā? _____

10. Quot sunt sex et sex et decem? _____

8 Adjectives [10 points]

Supply the correct forms of the Latin adjectives:

1. (good)   Cornēlius est puer _____

2. (happy)   Parentēs meī sunt _____

3. (big)   Āthlēta in stadiō est _____

4. (beautiful)   Āctrix est _____

5. (intelligent) Magistrae sunt _____

6. (dangerous)   Animal est _____

7. (cold)   Aqua in flūmine est _____

8. (small)   Ego habeō canem _____

9. (black)   Claudia habet comām _____

10. (ferocious) Frāterculus meus timet mōnstra _____

9 Problem solving [10 points]

Each of the following problems includes a knowledge of Roman numbers. Write the correct answer in the space provided. Be sure to write out the numbers in Latin and then in Roman numerals:

1. Sunt multae persōnae hodiē in theātrō. Sunt trēs āctrīcēs, septem actōrēs, trēs mūsicī et trēs mūsicae. Quot persōnae in theātrō sunt?

_____

2. Līberī in flūmine prope vīllam natant. Ūnus puer est in aquā, quīndecim puellae stant prope aquam, duo frāterculī in aquam saliunt et ūna puella ex aquā excēdit. Quot līberī ad flūmen sunt?

_____

3. Sunt multī vēnditōrēs in forō. Sunt trēs pīstōrēs, quattuor pōmāriī, duo crūstulāriī. Quot vēnditōrēs in forō sunt?

_____

4. Māter mea ad forum it. Ea trīgintā nummōs habet. Emit ūvās tribus nummīs, pōma emit decem nummīs, crūstula emit quīnque nummīs. Quot nummōs nunc māter habet?

_____

5. Sunt multa animālia in hortō meō. Ūna fēlēs sub arbore sedet. Trēs fēlēs inter rosās latent. Quīnque canēs ad portam jacent, et ūnus canis sub mēnsā jacet. Quot animālia in hortō sunt?

_____

10 Genitive case [5 points]

Supply the Latin noun in the genitive:

1. (grandfather's) _____ vīlla procul ab oppidō est.

2. (the teacher's) _____ liber in subselliō jacet.

3. (Claudia's) _____ oculī sunt caeruleī.

4. (the senator's) _____ stomachus est magnus.

5. (sister's) _____ amīcus est cantor.

11 Reading Comprehension [5 points]

Read the following passage and then circle the expression that best completes each statement:

Terentius prope Rōmam in suburbiō habitat. Māter Terentiī est coqua excellēns et in culīnā dīligenter labōrat. Terentiī pater est tōnsor et in tōnstrīnā comam tondet. Terentius in scholā dīligenter studet, sed post scholam patrem in tōnstrīnā interdum (_sometimes_) vīsitat.

1. Terentius habitat
   (a) in scholā; (b) in suburbiō; (c) in tōnstrīnā; (d) in culīnā.
2. Māter Terentiī labōrat
   (a) in pīstrīnā; (b) in scholā; (c) in tōnstrinā; (d) in culīnā.
3. Pater Terentiī tondet
   (a) mātrem; (b) tōnstrīnam; (c) comam; (d) coquam.
4. Terentius est
   (a) āthlēta; (b) vēnditor; (c) tōnsor; (d) discipulus.
5. Post scholam Terentius vīsitat
   (a) tōnstrīnam; (b) culīnam; (c) mātrem; (d) scholam.

12 Slot Completion [5 points]

Underline the expression that best completes the sentence:

Rūfus est gladiātor __(1)__ . Musculōs __(2)__ habet. Rūfus in stadiō saepe __(3)__ . Omnēs puerī et puellae Rūfum amant, quia Rūfus semper __(4)__ . Omnēs dīcunt: "Rūfus est __(5)__ magnificus!"

1. (a) calidus
   (b) fragilis
   (c) rōbustus
   (d) lātus
2. (a) parvōs
   (b) justōs
   (c) magnōs
   (d) vacuōs
3. (a) cantat
   (b) pugnat
   (c) dormit
   (d) studet
4. (a) scrībit
   (b) legit
   (c) vincit
   (d) volat
5. (a) medicus
   (b) tōnsor
   (c) discipulus
   (d) āthlēta

Pars Quārta

Cibus et colōrēs

-IŌ Verbs

1   You should enjoy learning this vocabulary:

carō *-nis f*

jūs, jūr*is n*

carōta *-ae f*

acētāria *-ōrum npl*

olīv*a -ae f*

pān*is -is m*

lactūc*a -ae f*

lac lact*is n*

tomāc*lum n*

ariēn*a -ae f*

cāse*us -ī m*

pisc*is -is m*

203

perna -ae *f*　　　　**cucumis -eris** *m*　　　　**placenta -ae** *f*

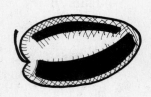

asparagus -ī *m*　　　　**pīsa -ōrum** *npl*　　　　**prūnum -ī** *n*

Āctivitātēs

A. Identify in Latin:

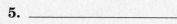

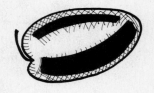

1. _____　　4. _____　　7. _____

2. _____　　5. _____　　8. _____

3. _____　　6. _____　　9. _____

10. _____   **11.** _____   **12.** _____

B. Write out the genitive form and give the gender of the following nouns:

1. carō _____ _____

2. jūs _____ _____

3. acētāria _____ _____

4. cucumis _____ _____

5. lac _____ _____

6. pīsa _____ _____

7. prūnum _____ _____

C. The Romans did not have some of the vegetables and fruits that we enjoy today. Tomatoes, potatoes, and corn came from the New World when America was discovered, and coffee was unknown for over a thousand years after the Romans. From the list below, pick out the vegetables (**holer***a* **-***um npl*) and write them in the first column. Then write the plural form after each one. Write the various types of fruit (**fruct***us* **-***ūs m*) in the column under **fructus** and give the plural forms:

ūva	cucumis	cerasum
lactūca	pīsum	mālum
ariēna	pirum	olīva
carōta	asparagus	persicum

holera	PLURAL	**fructus**	PLURAL
_____	_____	_____	_____
_____	_____	_____	_____
_____	_____	_____	_____
_____	_____	_____	_____
_____	_____	_____	_____

2 Now see whether you can understand this story about a busy day in the kitchen:

Hodiē est diēs festus. Tōta familia in culīnā cēnam splendidam parat. Māter acētāria facit. Lactūcam et olīvās et carōtās et asparagōs et cucumerēs immiscet cum acētō et oleō.

Pater tomāclum et pernam in culīnam portat. Carnem et piscēs in furnō coquit. Deinde jūs cum pīsīs coquit.

Claudia et Septimius parentēs adjuvant. Mēnsam secundam parant. Claudia persica et māla et ūvās et ariēnās et prūna ab hortō portat.

Septimius pānem et cāseum et placentam et vīnum in culīnam portat.

Ut pater tomācla ā mēnsā ad furnum portat, ūnum tomāclum ad pavīmentum cadit. Canis tomāculum cito rapit et cum tomāclō ē culīnā fugit. "Aha!" inquit pater, "nunc canis quoque cēnam bonam habet." Tōta familia rīdet.

tōtus -a -um whole
cēna -ae f *dinner*
  parāre to prepare
facěre to make
immiscēre to mix in
  acētum -ī n *vinegar*
oleum -ī n *oil*

furnus -ī m *oven*
  coquěre to cook

adjuvāre to help
mēnsa secunda f *dessert*

ut as
pavīmentum -ī n *floor*
cito quickly
  rapěre to grab, seize
fugěre to run away, flee
  inquit (he says)

Activitās

D. Respondē ad quaestiōnēs:

1. Quis acētāria facit? _____

2. Quid pater in culīnam portat? _____

3. Quid pater in furnō coquit? _____

4. Quis mēnsam secundam parat? _____

5. Quid Claudia ab hortō portat? _____

6. Quid Septimius in culīnam portat? _____

7. Quid ad pavīmentum cadit? _____

8. Quis tomāclum cito rapit? _____

3 In the story you have just read, there are three verbs that don't exactly fit into any of the four families of verbs you have learned. These verbs are **facěre** (*to make, do*), **rapěre** (*to grab, seize*), and **fugěre** (*to run away, flee*). They are formed somewhat like the **-ěre** family of verbs and somewhat like the **-īre** family. We will call this the **-iō** family.

Let's put the forms of **facĕre** between the **-ĕre** and **-īre** families to see the difference:

-ĕre FAMILY		NEW **-iō** FAMILY		**-īre** FAMILY	
dīcō	(*I say*)	**faciō**	(*I make, do*)	**veniō**	(*I come*)
dīcis		**fac**is		**ven**īs	
dīcit		**fac**it		**ven**it	
dīcimus		**fac**imus		**ven**īmus	
dīcitis		**fac**itis		**ven**ītis	
dīcunt		**fac**iunt		**ven**iunt	

All endings of **facĕre** are exactly the same as the endings of **dīcĕre** except two.

Which are they? _____ _____ There are three endings of **dīcĕre** in which the length of the **i** is different from the **i** of **venīre**. Which are they?

_____ _____ _____

Āctivitātēs

E.   Let's practice with some other verbs like **facĕre**. Fill in all the forms:

rapĕre (*to grab, seize*)   **capĕre** (*to take*)   **fugĕre** (*to run away, flee*)

_____   _____   _____

_____   _____   _____

_____   _____   _____

_____   _____   _____

_____   _____   _____

_____   _____   _____

F.   Supply the correct forms of the verbs:

1. (rapĕre)   Canis tomāclum _____ .

2. (facĕre)   Coquī acētāria _____ .

3. (capĕre)   Claudia et Septimius placentam _____ .

4. (facĕre)   Māter, nonne jūs cum pīsīs _____ ?

5. (facĕre)   Coquae cēnam bonam prō familiā _____ .

6. (capĕre) Puerī pānem et cāseum _____.

7. (facĕre) Ego et māter pānem _____.

8. (fugĕre) Canis ē culīnā _____.

4 In Lesson 9, you learned how to increase your Latin word power by combining prefixes with verbs. When a prefix is added to a verb with an **a** in the stem, that **a** changes to **i**:

> **re** + **capĕre** = **recipĕre** (*to get back, receive*)
> **re** + **facĕre** = **reficĕre** (*to redo, repair*)

Note that the prefix often changes according to the first letter of the verb:

> **ad** + **capĕre** = **accipĕre** (*to accept, receive*)
> **ex** + **fugĕre** = **effugĕre** (*to flee out of, escape*)

Āctivitās

G. Now let's try a few combinations. First review the prefixes in Lesson 9:

1. con + capĕre = _____ (*to conceive*)

2. dē + capĕre = _____ (*to deceive*)

3. in + capĕre = _____ (*to begin*)

4. per + capĕre = _____ (*to perceive, notice, understand*)

5. con + facĕre = _____ (*to do completely, complete*)

6. dē + facĕre = _____ (*to run low, be deficient*)

7. per + facĕre = _____ (*to do completely, to perfect*)

5 Now you will learn the Latin names of some colors. You should have no trouble identifying them:

Lac est *album.*

Mālum est *rubrum.*

Lactūca est *prasina.*

Ariēna est *flāva*. **Carō est *rubra*.** **Ōvum est *album*.**

Pīsa sunt *prasina*. **Rosa est *rubra*.** **Ūvae sunt *purpureae*.**

  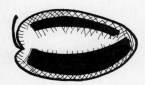

Cucumis est *prasinus*. **Perna est *rubra*.** **Prūnum est *purpureum*.**

Arbor est *prasina*. **Caelum est *caeruleum*.** **Fēlēs est *ātra*.**

Āctivitātēs

H. See whether you can figure out this familiar poem, which names certain colors:

> Rosae sunt rubrae,
> Violae sunt caeruleae,
> Saccarum est dulce
> Et sīc es tū.

I. Here are a few other objects whose colors you should recognize:

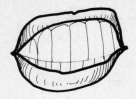 

1. Dentēs sunt albī. **2.** Labra sunt rubra. **3.** Ātrāmentum est ātrum.

4. Vexillum est rubrum, album et caeruleum.

6 Other common colors:

candidus **-a -um** (*glistening*) white	**ros**eus **-a -um** *pink*
cānus **-a -um** grey	**virid**is **-is -e** (*light*) *green*
fuscus **-a -um** brown	

Activitās

J. Complete the sentences with the correct forms of the Latin colors:

1. Ūvae sunt _____.

2. Pīsa sunt _____.

3. Mālum est _____.

4. Ōvum est _____.

5. Ariēnae sunt _____.

6. Toga est _____.

7. Coma avī meī est _____.

8. Cucumerēs sunt _____.

9. Lac est _____.

10. Carō est _____.

CONVERSĀTIŌ

VOCĀBULA

haec *this*
popīna *-ae* f *restaurant*

appetentia *-ae* f *appetite*

COLLOQUIUM

Imagine yourself in a Roman restaurant. The restaurant owner asks you some questions. Write an original response to each question.

VOCĀBULA

prandium -ī *n lunch*   **quaesō** *please*
an *or*   **quae holera** *which vegetables*

THE LATIN CONNECTION

Look over the list of Latin words and the list of English words (called derivatives) that come from the Latin words. Write the English word in the space next to the Latin word that is connected with it in meaning:

1. lactūca _____

2. carōta _____

3. olīva _____

4. cucumerēs _____

5. pīsa _____

6. prūnum _____

7. asparagus _____

8. furnus _____

9. pavīmentum _____

10. candidus _____

prune
pavement
furnace
asparagus
lettuce
candid
peas
olive
carrot
cucumbers

RĒS PERSŌNĀLĒS

You are having guests at your home. Prepare a menu for lunch and dinner:

Prandium

_____ _____

_____ _____

_____ _____

Cēna

_____ _____

_____ _____

_____ _____

_____ _____

 Nātūra

Fourth-Declension Nouns; Dative Case

1 Look at the pictures and try to guess the meanings of the new words:

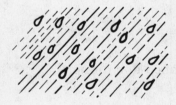

sōl *-is* m

lūna *-ae* f

nūbēs *-is* f

pluvia *-ae* f

nix nivis f

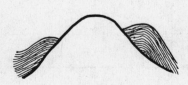

ventus *-ī* m

collis *-is* m

vallēs *-is* f

mōns *-tis* m

herba -ae *f*

stāgnum -ī *n*

fōns -tis *m*

astrum -ī *n*

saxum -ī *n*

campus -ī *m*

ager agrī *m*

silva -ae *f*

rīvus -ī *m*

flōs flōris *m*

lacus -ūs *m*

Āctivitātēs

A. Match the words with the pictures:

astrum   stāgnum   lūna
mōns   campus   vallēs
fontēs   sōl   flōrēs
silva   pluvia   herba

1. _____

5. _____

2. _____

6. _____

3. _____

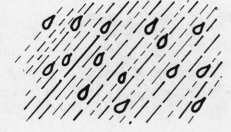

7. _____

4. _____

8. _____

9. _____

11. _____

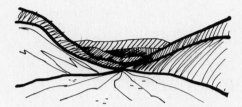

10. _____

12. _____

B. Write out the complete form of the genitive and give the gender of each of the following nouns:

1. ager _____ _____   **5.** mōns _____ _____

2. nix _____ _____   **6.** flōs _____ _____

3. collis _____ _____   **7.** vallēs _____ _____

4. nūbēs _____ _____   **8.** saxum _____ _____

C. Complete the sentences with the correct form of the noun:

1. Equī _____ in campō edunt. (herba, herbam, herbae)

2. Multa saxa in _____ sunt. (vallem, valle, vallēs)

3. Nix in _____ jacet. (montēs, mōns, montibus)

4. Multa animālia in _____ habitant. (silva, silvam, silvā)

5. Sōl post _____ latet. (nūbem, nūbis, nūbe)

6. Flōrēs prope _____ sunt. (stāgnum, stāgnō, stāgnī)

7. Vallēs pulchra inter _____ est. (mōns, montēs, montibus)

8. Vaccae aquam ē _____ pōtant. (fōns, fontem, fonte)

2 One of the words you have just learned belongs to a new class of nouns: **lacus -ūs** *m* (*lake*). In Lesson 13, you learned **fructus -ūs** *m* (*fruit*). Almost all of the nouns of this fourth declension are masculine, but there are some important exceptions. The forms of fourth-declension nouns follow:

	SINGULAR			PLURAL	
NOMINATIVE	**lacus**	(*a/the lake*)		**lacūs**	(*the lakes*)
GENITIVE	**lacūs**	(*of a/the lake*)		**lacuum**	(*of the lakes*)
ACCUSATIVE	**lacum**	(*a/the lake*)		**lacūs**	(*the lakes*)
ABLATIVE	**lacū**	(*by/in/with a/the lake*)		**lacibus**	(*by/in/with the lakes*)

Note the length of the vowel in the endings. **Lacūs** occurs in three different cases. Which are they?

_____

_____

_____

Activitās

D. Give the correct forms of the fourth-declension nouns **fructus** *m*, **ūsus** *m* (*use, experience*), **manus** *f*:

SINGULAR

NOMINATIVE	_____	_____	_____
GENITIVE	_____	_____	_____
ACCUSATIVE	_____	_____	_____
ABLATIVE	_____	_____	_____

PLURAL

NOMINATIVE	_____	_____	_____
GENITIVE	_____	_____	_____
ACCUSATIVE	_____	_____	_____
ABLATIVE	_____	_____	_____

3 Now read this story about a visit to the country:

Ego sum Aulus. Familia mea in urbe magnā et prosperā habitat. Sed vēre post longam hiemem rūs īre amāmus et vīsitāmus avum et aviam, quī in fundō rūrī habitant.

vēr vēris *n spring*
hiems hiemis *f winter*
   rūs *to the country*
quī *who*
   rūrī *in the country*

Eōrum vīlla in valle inter collēs sita est. Nōn procul ā vīllā sunt silva et mōns altus. In summō monte nix inter saxa jacet.

Vēr semper est pulchrum. In collibus et vallibus sunt multī flōrēs dīversōrum colōrum. Vaccae et equī in campō ambulant et aquam frīgidam ē rīvō aut stāgnō bibunt. Modo ego flōrēs in campō prō aviā carpō; modo in rīvō pedibus nūdīs ambulō aut in stāgnō natō. Avus et pater agrōs arant, sed māter aviam in vīllā adjuvat. Antequam ad urbem redīmus, cēnam magnificam sumimus, nam sunt semper holera recentia in aviae hortō. Quam mīrābilis est nātūra!

eōrum *their*
  sita est *is located*

in summō monte *on the top of the mountain*

dīvers*us -a -um* *various, different*

modo ... modo *sometimes ... sometimes*
  carpĕre *to pick*
nūd*us -a -um* *bare, nude*
arāre *to plough*
antequam *before*

nam *for* recēns *-tis* *fresh*
quam *how*
  mīrābil*is -is -e* *wonderful*
  nātūr*a -ae* f *nature*

Activitās

E. Respondē ad quaestiōnēs:

1. Ubi Aulus cum familiā habitat?

  _____

2. Quandō familia avum et aviam vīsitant?

  _____

3. Ubi avus et avia habitant?

  _____

4. Ubi vīlla sita est?

  _____

5. Quandō est rūs pulchrum?

  _____

6. Ubi jacet nix?

  _____

7. Ubi sunt multī flōrēs?

  _____

8. Quid vaccae et equī in campō faciunt?

  _____

9. Ubi vaccae et equī aquam bibunt?

_____

10. Ubi ambulat Aulus pedibus nūdīs?

_____

11. Quid faciunt avus et pater?

_____

12. Quid māter in vīllā facit?

_____

13. Quid familia facit antequam ad urbem redeunt?

_____

14. Cūr est cēna bona?

_____

4 There is one more case of the noun that you need to know: the case of the indirect object, or the DATIVE CASE. "Dative" means "connected with giving" and so the meaning of "dative case" is "the form of a noun or pronoun after a verb of giving." As you will see, however, it developed other uses. In English, we can say: "I gave _my friend_ a book" or "I gave a book _to my friend_." In the first example, _my friend_ is the indirect object; in the second example, _my friend_ is the object of the preposition _to_. Latin never uses a preposition to express this idea; it simply uses the DATIVE CASE. Look carefully at the following two sentences:

Magister librum discipulō dat.   **Magister ad scholam it.**
The teacher gives a book to the boy.   _The teacher is going to the school._

In the first sentence, **discipulō** is in the dative case; in the second sentence, _to the school_ indicates movement over space. Even though we use the preposition _to_ in both situations, in Latin there is always a clear distinction. Look at these two sentences:

Epistulam mātrī scrībō.   **Epistulam ad mātrem mittō.**
I am writing my mother a letter.   _I am sending my mother a letter._
I am writing a letter to my mother.   _I am sending a letter to my mother._

In the first sentence, the dative (or indirect object) is used. The second sentence suggests that the letter will move over space; the Romans, therefore, used the preposition **ad**, followed by the accusative case.

The following table shows the nominative, dative, and ablative cases of the four noun declensions that you have learned thus far:

	SINGULAR				
	FIRST DECLENSION	SECOND DECLENSION		THIRD DECLENSION	FOURTH DECLENSION
NOMINATIVE	silv*a*	camp*us*	stāgn*um*	fons	lac*us*
DATIVE	silv*ae*	camp*ō*	stāgn*ō*	font*ī*	lac*uī*
ABLATIVE	silv*ā*	camp*ō*	stāgn*ō*	font*e*	lac*ū*

	PLURAL				
	FIRST DECLENSION	SECOND DECLENSION		THIRD DECLENSION	FOURTH DECLENSION
NOMINATIVE	silv*ae*	camp*ī*	stāgn*a*	font*ēs*	lac*ūs*
DATIVE	silv*īs*	camp*īs*	stagn*īs*	font*ibus*	lac*ibus*
ABLATIVE	silv*īs*	camp*īs*	stagn*īs*	font*ibus*	lac*ibus*

Look at the singular forms. In which declension is the DATIVE form the same as the ABLATIVE form? _____ .

Now look at the plural forms. In which declensions is the DATIVE form the same as the ABLATIVE form? _____

Āctivitātēs

F. Complete each sentence with the dative form of the noun in parentheses:

1. (māter)   Ego epistulam _____ scrībō.

2. (fēminae [*pl*])   Pōmārius ariēnās _____ vēndit.

3. (Claudia)   Avus fābulam _____ nārrat.

4. (līberī)   Avia crūstula _____ dat.

5. (magister)   Discipulus poēmata _____ legit.

6. (canis)   Lānius carnem _____ dat.

7. (īnfantēs)   Māter lac _____ dat.

8. (fīliī)   Pater fābulam _____ nārrat.

G. Read the following sentences and then rewrite them, changing the nouns in the dative from singular to plural:

1. Senātor Rōmānus epistulam amīcō scrībit.

2. Māter lac īnfantī dat.

_____

3. Pōmārius prūna et cerasa fēminae vēndit.

_____

4. Lanius carnem canī dat.

_____

5. Coquus cēnam bonam amīcō parat.

_____

6. Coquae jūs virō coquunt.

_____

Note in the last two sentences that the noun in the dative is not equivalent to an English noun with the preposition _to_. Which English preposition would you

use in these two situations? _____.

5 Certain verbs take the dative case instead of the accusative case:

> **Fundus famili_ae_ me_ae_ placet.**
> _The farm pleases my family._ (My family likes the farm.)

> **Pluvia agricol_ae_ placet.**
> _Rain pleases the farmer._ (The farmer likes rain.)

> **Patrī et mātrī semper pareō.**
> _I always obey my father and mother._

Some other verbs that take the dative case instead of the accusative case are:

confīdĕre _to trust_	**ignōscĕre** _to pardon_
crēdĕre _to believe_	**nocēre** _to hurt, injure_
invidēre _to envy_	**servīre** _to serve_

Activitātēs

H. Complete the sentences with the dative forms of the expressions in parentheses:

1. (puella pulchra) Quis _____ nōn invidet?

2. (vēnditor) Cūr _____ nōn confīdis?

3. (flōrēs) Nix et ventus frīgidus _____ nocent.

4. (senātor novus) Populus Rōmānus _____ crēdit.

5. (dominus bonus) Multī servī _____ libenter serviunt.

6. (fīlius malus) Pater bonus _____ ignōscit.

I. Read the following sentences and then rewrite them, changing the dative noun to the plural form:

1. Aqua frīgida animālī placet. _____

2. Magister discipulō ignōscit. _____

3. Servus equō nōn nocet. _____

4. Gladiātor āthlētae invidet. _____

5. Ego amīcō meō confīdō. _____

6. Quis medicō nōn crēdit? _____

J. Using the verb **placēre,** express the following sentences in Latin:

EXAMPLE: My family likes the farm. **Fundus familiae meae placet.**

1. The farmer likes the sun.

_____

2. Cows like grass.

_____

3. Flowers like rain.

_____

4. Claudia likes the mountains.

_____

6 The dative is sometimes used to express ownership. As we may say in English, "There is no lid _to the bottle_" or "There is no truth _to the story_," so the Romans could say, "There is no money _to the boy_" instead of "The boy has no money":

> **Liber discipulō nōn est.**   **Vaccae agricolae nōn sunt.**
> _The pupil has no book._   _The farmer has no cows._

Activitātēs

K. Change the following sentences to express the dative of possession:

EXAMPLE: Familia canem habet.   **Canis familiae est.**

1. Avus fundum habet. _____

2. Puella flōrēs habet. _____

3. Vīlla tectum habet. _____

4. Lānius tomācla habet. _____

5. Fundus fontem et stāgnum habet. _____

6. Pōmāriī prūna habent. _____

7. Caelum nūbēs habet. _____

8. Īnfantēs lac nōn habent. _____

9. Coquī holera viridia habent. _____

10. Montēs saxa magna habent. _____

L. Look at the following pictures. Then express possession first with the verb **habēre** and then with the dative:

1. _____

2. _____

3. _____

4. _____

7 The dative case is also used after certain adjectives whose English equivalents are followed by *to*:

amīc*us -a -um*	*friendly*	ūtil*is -is -e*	*useful*
simil*is -is -e*	*similar, like*	grāt*us -a -um*	*pleasing, welcome*
benign*us -a -um*	*kind*	propinqu*us -a -um*	*close, near*
nōt*us -a -um*	*known, familiar*	molest*us -a -um*	*annoying*

EXAMPLES:

Senātōrēs avō meō amīcī sunt.
The senators are friendly to my grandfather.

Pluvia agricolīs ūtilis est.
Rain is useful to farmers.

Āctivitās

M. Complete the sentences with the dative case of the nouns in parentheses:

1. (Sicilia) Ītalia est propinqua _____.

2. (māter) Fīlia est similis _____.

3. (vēnditōrēs) Oppidum est nōtum _____.

4. (agricolae) Sōl et pluvia sunt ūtilēs _____.

5. (līberī) Ventī frīgidī nōn sunt grātī _____.

6. (lacus) Arborēs sunt propinquae _____.

7. (vaccae) Puerī sunt benignī _____.

8. (discipulī) Schola est molesta _____.

9. (nūbēs [*pl*]) Astra et lūna sunt propinqua _____.

10. (rosae) Līlia nōn sunt similia _____.

8 So far we have seen the pronouns **ego, tū,** etc., used as subjects of sentences. Now learn their dative forms:

NOMINATIVE	DATIVE	NOMINATIVE	DATIVE
ego	**mihi**	**nōs**	**nōbīs**
tū	**tibi**	**vōs**	**vōbīs**
is	**eī**	**eī**	**eīs**
ea	**eī**	**eae**	**eīs**
id	**eī**	**ea**	**eīs**

Look at the first dative column. What are the three possible meanings of **eī**?

_____ _____ _____. Look at the second dative column.

What three genders can **eīs** be? _____ _____ _____

Āctivitātēs

N. Change the following sentences to express the dative of possession:

EXAMPLE: Ego pecūniam habeō.   **Pecūnia mihi est.**

1. Ea pānem et cāseum habet.   _____

2. Nōs vīllam habēmus.   _____

3. Eī fructūs et holera habent.   _____

4. Ego fundum inter montēs habeō.   _____

5. Eae carōtās et lactūcam habent.   _____

6. Vōs acētāria et carnem habētis.   _____

7. Is tomāclum et pānem habet.   _____

8. Tū tunicam longam habēs.   _____

O. Change the following sentences to new sentences with the dative of possession, but substitute the proper pronoun for the noun:

EXAMPLE: Agricola vaccās habet.   **Vaccae eī sunt.**

1. Equī herbam habent.   _____

2. Claudia et soror fēlem habent.   _____

3. Medicus medicīnam habet.   _____

4. Fundus rīvum et stāgnum habet.   _____

5. Mātrēs īnfantēs habent.   _____

P. Reverse the subject and the noun in the dative case in the following sentences:

EXAMPLE: Ego sum similis sorōrī.   **Soror est similis mihi.**

1. Tū es nōtus senātōrī.   _____

2. Nōs parentibus ūtilēs sumus.   _____

3. Ego sorōrī molestus sum.   _____

4. Is propinquus jānuae est.   _____

5. Vōs grātī magistrō estis.   _____

6. Eae sunt propinquae urbī.   _____

CONVERSĀTIŌ

VOCĀBULA

fertil*is* **-is -e** *fertile*
prāt*um* **-ī** n *meadow*
minim*us* **-a -um** *very little*

commod*us* **-a -um** *comfortable, cosy*
trāns*īre* *to move*
vērō *really*

COLLOQUIUM

Complete this conversation by using expressions chosen from the following list:

Ita, vērō. Sed rīvus nōn est propinquus prātō.
Habeō. Sed aqua nōn satis alta est. Est minima pluvia aestāte.
Salvē, Claudī! Fundus in valle inter collēs nunc mihi est.
Numquam, numquam! Crēdē mihi, ego fundum et vīllam vērō amō.
Sānē. Sed sunt nimis multa saxa in agrīs.
Sānē. Sed vīlla nimis parva est.

THE LATIN CONNECTION

Look over the list of Latin words and the list of English words (derivatives) that come from the Latin words. Then write the English word in the space next to the Latin word that is connected with it in meaning:

1. lacus -ūs   _____

2. mōns montis   _____

3. vallēs -is   _____

4. herba -ae   _____

5. flōs flōris   _____

6. fōns fontis   _____

7. similis   _____

8. benignus   _____

9. nōtus   _____

10. rīvus   _____

11. manus -ūs   _____

12. astrum -ī   _____

13. arāre   _____

14. prōsperus   _____

15. nātūra   _____

16. mīrābilis   _____

astronaut
valley
noted
similar
mountain
lake
manual
herb
river
floral
benign
fountain
admirable
nature
arable
prosperous

RĒS PERSŌNĀLĒS

1. Habitāsne in urbe an rūrī?

   _____

2. Estne domus tua propinqua collibus an montibus?

   _____

3. Placetne tibi nix hieme?

   _____

4. Flōrēsne prō mātre an aviā carpis?

_____

5. Placetne tibi rūs?

_____

6. Spectāsne nocte astra et lūnam?

_____

Possessive Adjectives

1   A Roman house looked quite different from a modern American house. Only the richer people in Rome lived in single-family homes. All the others lived in apartment buildings (**īnsulae**). The Roman house did not have a front yard or backyard, and the walls of the house had no windows looking to the outside.

Stepping up from a very narrow sidewalk, one passed through the entrance way (**vēstibulum**) to a large room (**ātrium**) with a large skylight (**compluvium**) in the center of the roof that let in light and rain. In the center of the floor was a collecting pool (**impluvium**) to catch the rain water, which was stored in cisterns below the floor of the **ātrium** to supply the family with water. On either side of the **ātrium** were bedrooms.

Passing beyond the **ātrium,** one reached the combination living room and study (**tablīnum**) and dining room (**trīclīnium**), where members of the family reclined on couches around the table. A corridor led to a garden with a covered colonnade or walk (**peristȳlium**) around the garden. The rooms leading off from the garden were the kitchen (**culīna**), bath (**balneum**), workshop (**officīna**), storerooms, servants' quarters, and stables. The exact arrangement of rooms varied from house to house. The rooms along the street in front of the house were often used as stores (**tabernae**) or workshops.

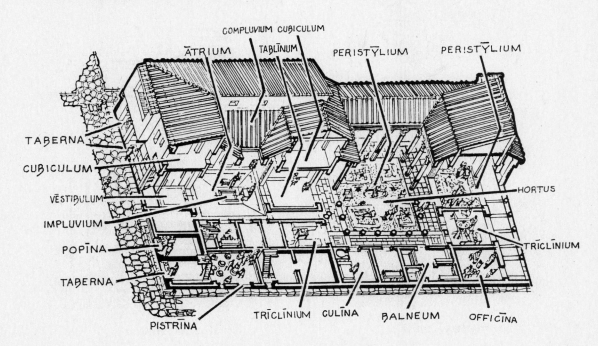

231

2   Look at the new words and try to guess their meanings:

īnsul*a* -*ae* *f*

culīn*a* -*ae* *f*

ātri*um* -*ī* *n*

vēstibul*um* -*ī* *n*

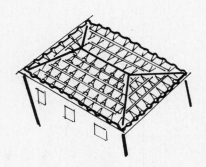

tect*um* -*ī* *n*

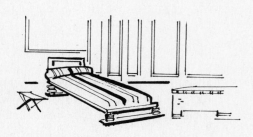

cubicul*um* -*ī* *n*

compluvi*um* -*ī* *n*

impluvi*um* -*ī* *n*

balne*um* -ī *n*

trīclīni*um* -ī *n*

tablīn*um* -ī *n*

peristȳli*um* -ī *n*

hort*us* -ī *m*

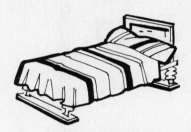

lect*us* -ī *m*

mēns*a* -*ae f*

candēl*a* -*ae f*

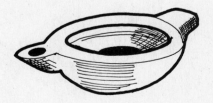

lucern*a* -*ae f*

sell*a* -*ae f*

Āctivitātēs

A. **Quid id est?** Name the objects. Give the gender of each word:

1. _____

5. _____

2. _____

6. _____

3. _____

7. _____

4. _____

8. _____

9. _____

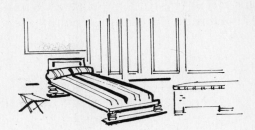

11. _____

10. _____

12. _____

B. Different parts of the Roman house were used for different purposes. See whether you can find your way around the house by completing the following statements in Latin:

1. Dormiō in _____ .

2. Cibum coquō in _____ .

3. Cibum edō in _____ .

4. Sedeō in _____ .

5. Corpus meum lavō in _____ .

6. Domum intrō per _____ .

7. Impluvium est in _____ .

8. Compluvium est in _____ .

9. Lectus est in _____ .

10. Arborēs et flōrēs sunt in _____ .

3 The Latin noun **domus,** a very important word, has some unusual forms. In some cases, it has the forms of the second declension (like **lectus**), and in some cases the Romans preferred the endings of the fourth declension (like **manus**). **Domus** is a feminine noun. The forms in parentheses are the less frequent forms:

	SINGULAR	PLURAL
NOMINATIVE	dom*us*	dom*ūs*
GENITIVE	dom*ī* (-*ūs*)	dom*ōrum* (-*uum*)
ACCUSATIVE	dom*um*	dom*ōs* (-*ūs*)
DATIVE	dom*ō* (-*uī*)	dom*ibus*
ABLATIVE	dom*ō* (-*ū*)	dom*ibus*

Domī means *at home,* rarely *of home* or *of the house;* **domum** means *home* in a sentence like *I am going home.* **Domō** means *from home,* but **ā domō** means *from the house* and **ē domō** means *out of the house.* **Domī tuae** means *at your home.*

Āctivitās

C. Fill in the correct forms of **domus.** Use the more frequent forms:

1. Familia _____ it.

2. Tecta Rōmānārum _____ sunt rubra.

3. Quis _____ suam nōn amat?

4. Māter ē _____ venit.

5. Sunt multae _____ in oppidō.

6. Estne pater _____ ?

7. _____ mea est pulchra et commoda.

8. Senātor duās _____ habet.

9. Domus mea est similis _____ tuae.

10. Sunt quattuor cubicula in _____ meā.

11. Frāter meus _____ nunc venit.

12. Claudia, ego _____ tuae lūdĕre optō.

4   Certain adjectives express possession. These adjectives tell us to whom someone or something belongs (*my* father, *their* farm). They are called POSSESSIVE ADJECTIVES. In the first column below, you see the subject pronouns; in the second column, you see the corresponding possessive adjectives:

	I		II	
SINGULAR:	**ego** *I*	**me*us* -*a* -*um***	*my*
	tū *you*	**tu*us* -*a* -*um***	*your*
	is *he*	**ejus**	*his*
	ea *she*	**ejus**	*her*
	id *it*	**ejus**	*its*
PLURAL:	**nōs** *we*	**nos*ter* -*tra* -*trum***	*our*
	vōs *you*	**ves*ter* -*tra* -*trum***	*your*
	eī *they* (masculine)	**eōrum**	*their*
	eae *they* (feminine)	**eārum**	*their*
	ea *they* (neuter)	**eōrum**	*their*

Which possessive adjectives in column II have masculine, feminine, and neuter endings like **bon*us* -*a* -*um?***

_____   _____

Which possessive adjectives have masculine, feminine, and neuter endings like **pulch*er* pulchr*a* pulchr*um?***

_____   _____

Which three different meanings can **ejus** have?

_____ _____ _____

In Latin, there are no possessive adjectives for *his, her, its.* Instead, the Romans said "of him," "of her," "of it," when we say simply "his," "her," "its." Note that possessive adjectives can come before or after the noun they belong to:

Hīc est puer.   *Domus ejus* est magna.
Here is the boy. His house [the house of him] is big.

Hīc est puella. Est lucerna in *ejus cubiculō*.
Here is a girl.   There is a lamp in her bedroom [the bedroom of her].

Hīc est oppidum. *Mūrī ejus* sunt altī.
Here is a town.   Its walls [the walls of it] are high.

There is also no possessive adjective for *their.* Instead, the Romans said "of them," when we say simply "their":

Hīc sunt puerī.   *Eōrum domus* est magna.
Here are the boys. Their house [the house of them] is big.

Hīc sunt puellae. *Domus eārum* est commoda.
Here are the girls. Their house [the house of them] is cozy.

Hīc sunt oppida.   *Eōrum mūrī* sunt altī.
Here are the towns. Their walls [the walls of them] are high.

Āctivitātēs

D. Fill in the correct form of **me*us* -*a* -*um*:**

1. domus _____

2. cubiculum _____

3. lucernae _____

4. candēla _____

5. lectus _____

6. vēstibulum _____

7. pater _____

8. māter _____

E. Fill in the correct form of **tu*us* -*a* -*um*:**

1. balneum _____

2. culīna _____

3. sellae _____

4. frātrēs _____

5. īnsula _____

6. sorōrēs _____

7. tablīnum _____

8. hortus _____

F. Fill in the correct form of **nost*er* -*tra* -*trum*:**

1. candēlae _____

2. domus _____

3. vēstibulum _____

4. mēnsa _____

5. fenestrae _____

6. jānua _____

7. mātrēs _____

8. impluvium _____

G. Fill in the correct form of **vest*er* -*tra* -*trum*:**

1. tectum _____

2. lucernae _____

3. peristȳlium _____

4. frātrēs _____

5. culīnae _____

6. trīclīnium _____

7. pictūrae _____

8. subsellium _____

H. Fill in the correct form of **eōrum, eārum, eōrum:**

1. Puellae in īnsulā habitant. Īnsula _____ est alta.

2. Claudius et Aulus in cubiculō dormiunt. Cubiculum _____ est obscūrum.

3. Frātrēs canem habent. _____ canis est rapidus.

4. Cubicula fenestrās habent. _____ fenestrae sunt parvae.

5. Āthlētae sunt rōbustī. Musculī _____ sunt magnī.

6. Silvia et Jūlia in urbe habitant. _____ domus est spatiōsa.

5 Note the possessives in the following sentences:

> **Claudius Licinium saepe vīsitat, quia canem *ejus* amat.**
> *Claudius often visits Licinius because he likes his [Licinius'] dog.*

But:

> **Fabius cum cane *suō* rūs it.**
> *Fabius is going to the country with his (own) dog.*

> **Puerī in lectīs *suīs* jacent.**
> *The boys are lying on their (own) beds.*

The possessive adjective **su*us -a -um*** means *his (own)*, *her (own)*, *its (own)*, or *their (own)*. There is no special form for the other persons. Thus, **me*us -a -um*** means *my* or *my own*; **tu*us -a -um*** means *your* or *your own*; **nos*ter -tra -trum*** means *our* or *our own*; **ves*ter -tra -trum*** means *your* or *your own*. The special "reflexive" adjective **su*us -a -um*** is used only for the third person singular and plural.

Activitās

I. Complete the sentences with the correct possessive:

1. Claudia manūs _____ in balneō lavat.
   (ejus / suās)

2. Gaium et Aulum saepe vīsitō. Ego in _____ trīclīniō prandium sūmō.
   (eōrum / suō)

3. Aurēlia et Claudia rūrī habitant. Vīlla _____ est remōta.
   (eārum / sua)

4. Puer ē cubiculō _____ exit.
   (ejus / suō)

5. Pater epistulās in tablīnō _____ scrībit.
   (ejus / suō)

6. Puellae in lectīs _____ dormiunt.
   (suīs / eārum)

6 Read the following story about two girls trying to impress each other. Pay particular attention to the possessives:

JŪLIA: Salvē, Silvia. Quid agis?

SILVIA: Salvē, Jūlia. Multum labōrem habeō.

labor -ōris *m work, labor*

JŪLIA: Multum labōrem? Cūr?

SILVIA: Familia nostra in īnsulā magnā habitat. Quīnque conclāvia cēnāculō sunt. Parentēs meī in cubiculō magnō dormiunt. Ego et soror mea quoque magnum cubiculum habēmus, et meus frāter cum frāterculō in magnō cubiculō dormit.

īnsula -ae *f apartment building*
conclāve -is *n room*
  cēnāculum -ī *n apartment*

JŪLIA: Habētisne balneum in domō vestrā?

SILVIA: Balneum nōn habēmus. Balneum publicum frequentāmus. Sed culīnam magnam habēmus, ubi māter et serva nostra cibum bonum parant. Et trīclīnium nostrum pictūrās pulchrās habet. Jūlia, habetne familia tua cēnāculum magnum?

publicus -a -um *public*
  frequentāre *to go regularly to; to use*

JŪLIA: Nōs nōn in īnsulā habitāmus! Familia mea magnam domum habet. Domus nostra decem conclāvia habet. Ūnus servus in vēstibulō semper stat et jānuam aperit et claudit. Parentēs meī in cubiculō ēnormī dormiunt. Ego ipsa cubiculum magnum habeō et frāter meus cubiculum suum habet, et frāterculus meus quoque cubiculum suum habet. Trēs servae mātrem meam in culīnā adjuvant. Pater meus in tablīnō semper occupātus est. In tablīnō pater epistulās scrībit et hospitēs excipit. In nostrō tablīnō sunt statuae et pictūrae pulchrae. Et nostrum balneum est tam magnum . . .

claudĕre *to close*
ipsa *myself*

hospes -itis *mf guest*
  excipĕre *to welcome*
tam *so*

Tunc maximē māter Jūliae ā fenestrā īnsulae proximae Jūliam vocat: "Jūlia! Ubi es, Jūlia? Adjuvā mē in culīnā. Pater ab officīnā mox venit."

tunc maximē *just then*
proximus -a -um *nearby, next-door*
officīna -ae *f workshop*

SILVIA: Aha! Ūnus servus in vēstibulō . . . trēs servae in culīnā . . . Quālis fābula!

quālis -is -e *what a . . . !*
  fābula -ae *f story, tale*

Activitās

J. Respondē ad quaestiōnēs:

1. Ubi familia Silviae habitat?

   _____

2. Quot conclāvia in cēnāculō Silviae sunt?

   _____

3. Ubi parentēs Silviae dormiunt?

   _____

4. Ubi frāter et frāterculus Silviae dormiunt?

   _____

5. Quid familia Silviae frequentat?

   _____

6. Quid habet trīclīnium Silviae?

   _____

7. Secundum (*according to*) Jūliam, quot conclāvia in Jūliae domō sunt?

   _____

8. Quid facit servus in vēstibulō?

   _____

9. Secundum Jūliam, quot servae mātrem Jūliae adjuvant?

   _____

10. Quid pater Jūliae in tablīnō facit?

    _____

11. Secundum Jūliam, quid est in tablīnō?

    _____

12. Dicitne Jūlia vērum an falsum?

    _____

THE LATIN CONNECTION

You have seen that **domus** is a house or home. *Domestic* products are products made "at home," in this country, as opposed to products made in foreign countries. Another word for servants in a home is *domestics*. To *domesticate* is "to make suitable for the home" or "to tame." A **dominus** is an owner of a **domus**. A **domina** is a lady of the house. A *domicile* is a home or place of residence. *Dominium* is ownership of a home. A *condominium* is an apartment in a building owned by several persons.

Look over the list of Latin words and the list of English words (derivatives) that come from the Latin words. Then write the English word in the space next to the Latin word that is connected with it in meaning:

1. culīna   _____

2. officīna   _____

3. vēstibulum _____

4. cubiculum _____

5. candēla   _____

6. fābula   _____

fable
vestibule
culinary
office
cubicle
candle

In Lesson XIII, you saw that, when a prefix is added to a verb, the vowel in the stem sometimes changes, as happens with the verb **claudĕre,** which changes to **-clūdĕre** when a prefix is added.

Try a few combinations. First review the prefixes in Lesson IX:

PREFIX	ROOT		LITERAL ENGLISH MEANING	ENGLISH DERIVATIVE
con	+ **claudĕre**	= _____	*close up*	*conclude*
ex	+ **claudĕre**	= _____	*close out*	_____
in	+ **claudĕre**	= _____	*close in*	_____
sē	+ **claudĕre**	= _____	*close off*	_____

242   *LECTIO XV*

CONVERSĀTIŌ

VOCĀBULA

Mīrum est! *That's strange.*
quālis tandem *just what kind of*

domus canīna *dog house*
Dī superī! *Ye gods!*

COLLOQUIUM

Complete the dialog with expressions chosen from the following list:

prō cane meō   Salvē!

nōn optō   Minimē, vērō!

cum magnā culīnā   Dī superī!

Quālem tandem domum   Mīrum est.

RĒS PERSŌNĀLĒS

1. Habitāsne in domō an in īnsulā?

   _____

2. Quot cubicula in domō tuā an in cēnāculō tuō sunt?

   _____

3. Quot conclāvia in domō tuā sunt?

   _____

4. Estne culīna tua magna an parva?

   _____

5. Habēsne servam in domō tuā?

   _____

6. Habetne pater tuus tablīnum?

   _____

XVI Hōrae, diēs, mēnsēs, tempora annī

Telling Time in Latin; Fifth Declension

1 The Romans were not as concerned about telling exact time as we are today. For hundreds of years after the founding of Rome, they didn't have any clocks at all. Later they used sundials and water clocks. The Roman day began at sunrise (not at midnight, as ours does) and lasted until sunset. The night began at sunset and lasted until sunrise. There were twelve hours in the day and twelve hours in the night. The hour (**hōra -ae** *f*) was divided into half hours (**sēmihōra -ae** *f*), but the Romans did not divide the hour into quarter hours, minutes, or seconds. The Romans did not say "three o'clock," "five o'clock," and so on. Instead, they said "first hour," "second hour," and so on. Review the Latin ordinal numbers in Lesson VIII.

Activitās

A. Match each ordinal number in the left column with the correct numeral in the right column. Write out the cardinal number next to the matching Roman numeral. There are two ordinal numbers you have not met before, but you should have no trouble recognizing them:

1. ūndecimus	_____	_____	I
			II
2. tertius	_____	_____	III
			IV
3. sextus	_____	_____	V
			VI
4. quīntus	_____	_____	VII
			VIII
5. decimus	_____	_____	IX
			X
6. septimus	_____	_____	XI
			XII
7. duodecimus	_____	_____	
8. prīmus	_____	_____	
9. octāvus	_____	_____	
10. quārtus	_____	_____	

246

11. secundus _____ _____

12. nōnus _____ _____

B. Now you are ready to tell time. The Romans might ask **Quota hōra est?** (*What hour is it?* or *What time is it?*), and the answer might be **Tertia hōra est** (*It is the third hour*). Or the Romans might ask **Quot hōrae sunt?** (*How many hours are there?*) and the answer might be **Trēs hōrae sunt** (*It is three o'clock*). Following the examples, tell what time each clock shows:

Septima hōra est.
Septem hōrae sunt.

Ūndecima hōra est.
Ūndecim hōrae sunt.

1. _____

_____

4. _____

_____

2. _____

_____

5. _____

_____

3. _____

_____

6. _____

_____

7. _____   8. _____

_____   _____

2 Our new day starts at midnight, but the Roman day started at 6:00 in the morning. Their first hour (**prīma hōra**) would be equivalent to our 7:00 A.M., the second hour (**secunda hōra**) would be our 8:00 A.M.

Āctivitās

C. For each Roman time of day, give the corresponding modern time of day:

EXAMPLE: hōra prīma = 7:00 A.M.

1. hōra quārta   = _____   6. hōra duodecima = _____

2. hōra sexta   = _____   7. hōra quinta   = _____

3. hōra decima   = _____   8. hōra ūndecima = _____

4. hōra tertia   = _____   9. hōra septima   = _____

5. hōra octāva   = _____   10. hōra nōna   = _____

3 Since day and night were divided into twelve hours each, the Romans had to make a clear distinction, just as we use A.M. and P.M. If the Romans wanted to give the time of day, they would say, for example, **hōra diēī secunda** (*the second hour of the day*). If they wanted to give the time of night, they would say, for example, **hōra noctis quārta** (*the fourth hour of the night*). The Latin noun **nox, noctis** *f* (*night*) is a regular noun of the third declension. But the Latin noun **diēs** is a noun of the fifth declension. Most nouns of this declension are feminine, but the Romans regarded **diēs** as sometimes masculine and sometimes feminine. They mostly regarded it as masculine, however. Here are its forms:

	SINGULAR	PLURAL
NOMINATIVE	**diēs**	**diēs**
GENITIVE	**diēī**	**diērum**
ACCUSATIVE	**diem**	**diēs**
DATIVE	**diēī**	**diēbus**
ABLATIVE	**diē**	**diēbus**

Āctivitās

D. Now see whether you can give the correct forms of other nouns of the fifth declension: **merīdiēs** *m noon*, **faciēs** *f face*, **rēs** *f thing*:

SINGULAR

NOMINATIVE _____ _____ _____

GENITIVE _____ _____ _____

ACCUSATIVE _____ _____ _____

DATIVE _____ _____ _____

ABLATIVE _____ _____ _____

PLURAL

NOMINATIVE _____ _____ _____

GENITIVE _____ _____ _____

ACCUSATIVE _____ _____ _____

DATIVE _____ _____ _____

ABLATIVE _____ _____ _____

Merīdiēs means *noon*. What does **ante merīdiem** mean? _____

What is the abbreviation we use for it? _____. What does **post merīdiem** mean? _____. What is our abbreviation for it?

_____

4 Sunt septem diēs in ūnā septimānā:

diēs Sōlis	*(sun's day)*	*Sunday*
diēs Lūnae	*(moon's day)*	*Monday*
diēs Mārtis	*(Mars' day)*	*Tuesday*
diēs Mercuriī	*(Mercury's day)*	*Wednesday*
diēs Jovis	*(Jove's day)*	*Thursday*
diēs Veneris	*(Venus' day)*	*Friday*
diēs Sāturnī	*(Saturn's day)*	*Saturday*

If you want to say *on Monday*, *on Tuesday*, use the ablative case of **diēs**: *diē* **Lūnae,** *diē* **Mārtis,** and so on.

Āctivitātēs

E.   Complete the days of the week:

1. diēs L__n____   5. diēs Me__c__r____

2. diēs S__t__rn__   6. diēs V__n_____s

3. diēs S__l__s   7. diēs J__v____

4. diēs M__rt____

F.   Fill in the days before and after the days given:

1. _____   diēs Lūnae   _____

2. _____   diēs Mercuriī   _____

3. _____   diēs Veneris   _____

4. _____   diēs Sōlis   _____

5   Now read this passage about the days of the week:

Quis est tuus diēs grātiōsissimus septi-   **grātiōsissimus** *most pleasant*
mānae? Cūr?

CAECILIUS: Diēs Sōlis, quia cum amīcīs in
āreā lūdĕre possum.

PAULUS: Diēs Sāturnī, quia ad merīdiem
dormīre possum.

CLAUDIA: Diēs Mercuriī, quia cum mātre ad
tabernās vādō.

SEPTIMIUS: Diēs Veneris, quia schola est
finīta.

ANNA: Diēs Jovis, quia vīllam avī et aviae
vīsitō.

LUCIUS: Diēs Mārtis, quia cum patre ad lūdōs
gladiātōriōs in amphitheātrum eō.

Āctivitātēs

G.   Match the person with his or her favorite day. Write the matching letter in
the space provided:

1. Anna _____   4. Caecilius _____   a. diēs Jovis
                                              b. diēs Sōlis
2. Paulus _____   5. Septimius _____   c. diēs Sāturnī
                                              d. diēs Veneris
3. Lūcius _____   6. Claudia _____   e. diēs Mercuriī
                                              f. diēs Mārtis

H. Give the reason in Latin why each person prefers his or her favorite day. (Be sure to change the verb to the third person in each answer.):

1. Claudia _____

2. Anna _____

3. Caecilius _____

4. Septimius _____

5. Lūcius _____

6. Paulus _____

6 Annus (*the year*) duodecim mēnsēs habet:

Jānuārius	**Māius**	**September**
Februārius	**Jūnius**	**Octōber**
Mārtius	**Jūlius**	**November**
Aprīlis	**Augustus**	**December**

Look over the names of the months. What number is contained in **September?**

_____. In **Octōber?** _____. In **November?**

_____. In **December?** _____. Early in Roman times, the year began with March (**mēnsis Mārtius**), sacred to Mars, the god of war, because in that month the Roman army would often go to war. In those early times, therefore, which month of the year was **September?**

_____. **Octōber?** _____ **November?** _____

December? _____.

The names of the months are adjectives and modify the masculine noun **mēnsis** (*month*). The Romans would say **mēnse Februāriō** (*in the month of February*) or simply **Februāriō.** Some of the months have endings like **bon*us* -*a* -*um*,** while some have endings like **fort*is* -*is* -*e*** (*brave, strong*) or **ācer, ācris, ācre** (*sharp*).

Āctivitātēs

I. List the months that have endings like **bon*us* -*a* -*um*:**

1. _____   5. _____

2. _____   6. _____

3. _____   7. _____

4. _____

J. Now list the months that have endings like **fort*is* -*is* -*e*** or **ācer, ācris, ācre:**

1. _____   4. _____

2. _____   5. _____

3. _____

K. Fill in the months that come before and after the months given:

1. _____   Februārius   _____

2. _____   Māius   _____

3. _____   Augustus   _____

4. _____   Jānuārius   _____

5. _____   November   _____

6. _____   Aprīlis   _____

7. _____   Jūlius   _____

8. _____   Octōber   _____

7   You should now be able to understand the following familiar saying:

Trīgintā diēs habet September,
Aprīlis, Jūnius et November.
Omnēs aliī habent trīgintā et ūnum   **aliī** *others*
Praeter Februārium, quī habet   **praeter** *except*
duodētrīgintā.   **quī** *which*

8   The four seasons of the year are:

vēr, vēr*is* n   **aestās -*ātis* f**   **autumn*us* -*ī* m**   **hiem*s* -*is* f**
 (*spring*)   (*summer*)   (*autumn*)   (*winter*)

The Romans did not have a single word for "season"; instead, they said **tempus annī** (*time of the year*).

Activitātēs

L.   Write the Latin name of the season after each month:

1. Mārtius _____   **4.** Jānuārius _____

2. Jūlius _____   **5.** December _____

3. Octōber _____   **6.** Māius _____

7. Augustus _____   10. Jūnius _____

8. Aprīlis _____   11. September _____

9. November _____   12. Februārius _____

M. Fill in the Latin names of the months for each season:

vēr	aestās	autumnus	hiems
M_____	J_____	S_____	D_____
A_____	J_____	O_____	J_____
M_____	A_____	N_____	F_____

9 Now you should be able to understand the teacher's questions and the students' answers:

MAGISTER: Quid est tuum tempus annī grātiōsissimum? Quis est tuus mēnsis grātiōsissimus? Cūr?

TERENTIUS: Hiems. Mēnsis Jānuārius. In nive lūděre amō.

OCTĀVIA: Aestās. Mēnsis Augustus, quia in stāgnō natāre amō.

MAXIMUS: Autumnus. Mēnsis Octōber, quia folia sunt pulchra.

folium -ī *n leaf*

ANTŌNIA: Aestās. Mēnsis Jūnius, quia schola fīnem habet.

fīnem habēre *to come to an end*

CLAUDIA: Vēr. Mēnsis Aprīlis, quia pluviam spectāre amō.

MARCELLUS: Vēr. Mēnsis Māius, quia flōrēs pulchrī mihi placent.

Āctivitātēs

N. Match the person with his or her favorite month. Write the matching letter in the space provided:

1. Antōnia _____

2. Octāvia _____

3. Maximus _____

4. Claudia _____

5. Marcellus _____

6. Terentius _____

a. Māius
b. Octōber
c. Aprīlis
d. Jānuārius
e. Jūnius
f. Augustus

O. Give the reason in Latin why each person prefers his or her month. (Be sure to change the verb to the third person where necessary.):

1. Marcellus: _____

2. Terentius: _____

3. Claudia: _____

4. Octāvia: _____

5. Maximus: _____

6. Antōnia: _____

THE LATIN CONNECTION

Look over the list of Latin words and the list of English words (called derivatives) that come from the Latin words. Then write the English word in the space next to the Latin word that is connected with it in meaning:

1. Mercurius	_____	temporal
		March
2. hōra	_____	lunatic
		mercury
		hour
3. tempus	_____	annual
		labor
4. decim	_____	second
		autumn
		decimal
5. lūna	_____	
6. secundus	_____	
7. annus	_____	
8. autumnus	_____	
9. Mārtius	_____	
10. labōrāre	_____	

VOCĀBULA

māne, merīdiē, noctū *morning, noon, and night*
incipĕre *to begin*
prīmā lūce *at first light, at dawn*
jentāculum -ī *n breakfast*
id est *that is*
quiēs -ētis *f rest, nap*

brevis -is -e *brief, short*
quiētam capĕre *to take a nap*
pōmerīdiē *in the afternoon*
vespere *in the evening*
miser -a -um *poor*
herus -ī *m boss*

COLLOQUIUM

Complete the dialog with expressions chosen from the following list:

pōmerīdiē quiētem brevem   vespere
merīdiē   sūmis   māne, merīdiē, noctū
hodiē   jentāculum   labōrāre
herus   ad tertiam noctis hōram prīmā lūce

QUAESTIŌNĒS PERSŌNĀLĒS

1. Quotā hōrā ā lectō māne surgis (*you get up*)?

   _____

2. Quotā hōrā jentāculum sūmis?

   _____

3. Quandō prandium sūmis?

   _____

4. Quiētem brevem pōmerīdiē capis?

   _____

5. Quotā hōrā schola fīnem habet?

   _____

6. Quotā hōrā ā scholā domum venis?

   _____

7. Quotā hōrā cēnam sūmis?

   _____

8. Labōrāsne an lūdis post cēnam?

   _____

9. Quotā hōrā noctis ad lectum īs?

   _____

10. Ad quotam hōram diē Sāturnī dormīs?

    _____

Recōgnitiō IV (Lectiōnēs XIII-XVI)

Lectiō XIII

a. To conjugate an **-ĕre** verb, drop **-ĕre** from the infinitive and add the proper endings:

    EXAMPLE: **facĕre**

If the subject is **ego**   and **iō**   to the remaining stem: **fac*iō***
               tū   **is**   **fac*is***
               is, ea, id   **it**   **fac*it***
               nōs   **imus**   **fac*imus***
               vōs   **itis**   **fac*itis***
               eī, eae, ea   **iunt**   **fac*iunt***

b. Verbs of the **-iō** family:

         capiō   **capĕre**   *to take*
         faciō   **facĕre**   *to make, do*
         fugiō   **fugĕre**   *to flee*
         rapiō   **rapĕre**   *to grab, seize*

Lectiō XIV

a. Nouns of the fourth declension end in **-us** and are mostly masculine:

	SINGULAR		PLURAL
NOMINATIVE	**lac*us***	NOMINATIVE	**lac*ūs***
GENITIVE	**lac*ūs***	GENITIVE	**lac*uum***
ACCUSATIVE	**lac*um***	ACCUSATIVE	**lac*ūs***
ABLATIVE	**lac*ū***	ABLATIVE	**lac*ibus***

b. The dative case of nouns:

SINGULAR					
	FIRST DECLENSION	SECOND DECLENSION		THIRD DECLENSION	FOURTH DECLENSION
NOMINATIVE	**silv*a***	**camp*us***	**stāgn*um***	**fōns**	**lacus**
DATIVE	**silv*ae***	**camp*ō***	**stāgn*ō***	**font*ī***	**lac*uī***
ABLATIVE	**silv*ā***	**camp*ō***	**stāgn*ō***	**font*e***	**lac*ū***

PLURAL					
	FIRST DECLENSION	SECOND DECLENSION		THIRD DECLENSION	FOURTH DECLENSION
NOMINATIVE	**silv*ae***	**camp*ī***	**stāgn*a***	**font*ēs***	**lac*ūs***
DATIVE	**silv*īs***	**camp*īs***	**stāgn*īs***	**font*ibus***	**lac*ibus***
ABLATIVE	**silv*īs***	**camp*īs***	**stāgn*īs***	**font*ibus***	**lac*ibus***

c. The dative case of pronouns:

NOMINATIVE	DATIVE	NOMINATIVE	DATIVE
ego	mihi	nōs	nōbīs
tū	tibi	vōs	vōbīs
is	eī	eī	eīs
ea	eī	eae	eīs
id	eī	ea	eīs

d. (1) The most common use of the dative is to indicate the indirect object, to whom something is given or said:

> **Fīlia flōrēs *mātri* dat.** *The daughter is giving her mother flowers.*
> *The daughter is giving flowers to her mother.*

(2) The dative is used after certain verbs:

> ***Parentibus* pareō.** *I obey my parents.*

(3) The dative is used to show possession:

> **Pecūnia *Marcō* est.** *Marcus has money.*

(4) The dative is used with certain adjectives:

> **Senātor *mihi nōtus* est.** *The senator is familiar to me.*

Lectiō XV

a. The noun **domus** has some endings like nouns of the second declension and some endings like nouns of the fourth declension:

	SINGULAR	PLURAL
NOMINATIVE	domus	domūs
GENITIVE	domī (-ūs)	domōrum (-uum)
ACCUSATIVE	domum	domōs (-ūs)
DATIVE	domō (-uī)	domibus
ABLATIVE	domō (-ū)	domibus

Special meanings: **domī** *at home*; **domum** *home(ward)*; **domō** *from home*.

b. Possessive adjectives:

me*us -a -um*	*my*
tu*us -a -um*	*your*
ejus	*his, her, its*
nost*er -tra -trum*	*our*
vest*er -tra -trum*	*your*
eōrum (referring to masculine nouns)	*their*
eārum (referring to feminine nouns)	*their*
eōrum (referring to neuter nouns)	*their*

There is no true possessive adjective in Latin for *his, her, its*. The genitive case of the pronoun is used: **ejus** (literally, "of him," "of her," "of it").

Lectiō XVI

Nouns of the fifth declension end in **-ēs** and are mostly feminine:

	SINGULAR	PLURAL
NOMINATIVE	**diēs**	**diēs**
GENITIVE	**diēī**	**diērum**
ACCUSATIVE	**diem**	**diēs**
DATIVE	**diēī**	**diēbus**
ABLATIVE	**diē**	**diēbus**

Āctivitātēs

A. Write the Latin word under each picture you see. Then circle the word in the puzzle on page 262:

1. _____

4. _____

2. _____

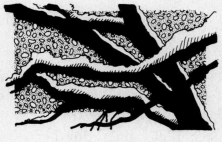

5. _____

3. _____

6. _____

7. _____

12. _____

8. _____

13. _____

9. _____

14. _____

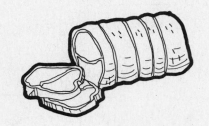

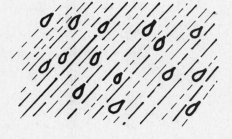

10. _____

15. _____

11. _____

16. _____

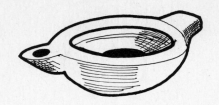

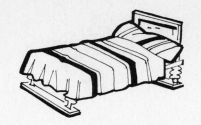

17. _____

19. _____

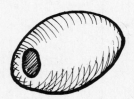

18. _____

20. _____

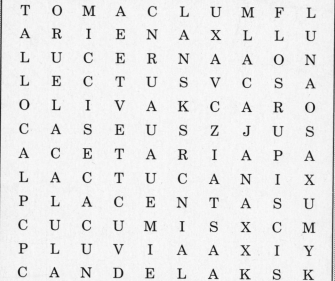

T	O	M	A	C	L	U	M	F		L
A	R	I	E	N	A	X	L	L		U
L	U	C	E	R	N	A	A	O		N
L	E	C	T	U	S	V	C	S		A
O	L	I	V	A	K	C	A	R		O
C	A	S	E	U	S	Z	J	U		S
A	C	E	T	A	R	I	A	P		A
L	A	C	T	U	C	A	N	I		X
P	L	A	C	E	N	T	A	S		U
C	U	C	U	M	I	S	X	C		M
P	L	U	V	I	A	A	X	I		Y
C	A	N	D	E	L	A	K	S		K

B. Appius has just served a meal in a restaurant. But he has forgotten a few things. Can you help him out? Here is his checklist:

	Sānē	Nōn
1. ōva		
2. piscis		
3. asparagus		
4. olīvae		
5. tomāclum		
6. persica		
7. vīnum		
8. lactūca		

	Sānē	Nōn
9. aqua		
10. acētāria		
11. perna		
12. pira		
13. panis		
14. ariēnae		
15. placenta		
16. māla		

C. Write the time in Latin. The first three clocks show the time of *day*. The next three clocks show the time of *night*:

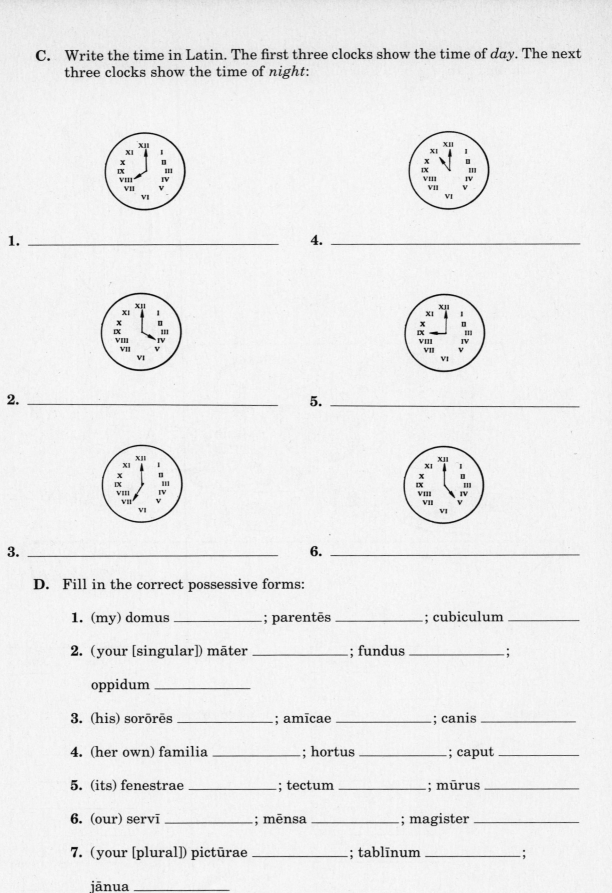

1. _____

4. _____

2. _____

5. _____

3. _____

6. _____

D. Fill in the correct possessive forms:

1. (my) domus _____; parentēs _____; cubiculum _____

2. (your [singular]) māter _____; fundus _____;

   oppidum _____

3. (his) sorōrēs _____; amīcae _____; canis _____

4. (her own) familia _____; hortus _____; caput _____

5. (its) fenestrae _____; tectum _____; mūrus _____

6. (our) servī _____; mēnsa _____; magister _____

7. (your [plural]) pictūrae _____; tablīnum _____;

   jānua _____

8. (their [masculine]) culīna _____; frātrēs _____;

tabernae _____

9. (their [feminine]) pānis _____; fābulae _____;

officīna _____

10. (their own) vīnum _____; holera _____; tempus _____

E. Picture Story. Can you read this story? Much of it is in picture form. Whenever you come to a picture, read it as if it were a Latin word:

Hodiē est diēs [S L M M J V S]. Claudia cum

[image] et [image] et [image] ad magnum

macellum (market) it, ubi emunt [image] et

[image] et [image] et [image] et [image]

et [image] et [image]. Deinde tabernam

pomāriam intrant et emunt [image]

et [image] et [image] et [image]. et [image]

In taberna laniēna emunt et et
pro . Si restat *(is left)*,

tabernam crūstulāriam intrant, ubi emunt.

Tum domum redeunt, circum sedent

et cēnam magnificam sūmunt.

Pars Quinta

XVII | Numerī

Imperfect Tense

1   Here are some more numbers in addition to those you have already learned. It may be a good idea to review first the numbers in Lesson VIII:

40	XL	quadrāgintā
41	XLI	quadrāgintā ūnus
42	XLII	quadrāgintā duo
43	XLIII	quadrāgintā trēs
44	XLIV	quadrāgintā quattuor
45	XLV	quadrāgintā quīnque
46	XLVI	quadrāgintā sex
47	XLVII	quadrāgintā septem
48	XLVIII	duodēquīnquāgintā
49	XLIX	ūndēquīnquāgintā
50	L	quīnquāgintā
60	LX	sexāgintā
70	LXX	septuāgintā
80	LXXX	octōgintā
90	XC	nōnāgintā
100	C	centum
500	D	quīngentī
1000	M	mīlle

Activitātēs

A.   Read the following numbers aloud and write the correct Roman numeral in the space provided:

1. vīgintī quīnque   _____   7. octōgintā duo   _____

2. trīgintā trēs   _____   8. duodēseptuāgintā   _____

3. quīnquāgintā   _____   9. ūndēnōnāgintā   _____

4. quattuor   _____   10. centum trīgintā ūnus   _____

5. decem   _____   11. quadrāgintā quattuor   _____

6. sexāgintā duo   _____   12. duodētrīgintā   _____

B. Give the Arabic numerals for the following Roman numerals:

1. CCC _____

2. XLV _____

3. DCC _____

4. XC _____

5. LXXX _____

6. DC _____

7. CIV _____

8. CCLIII _____

9. MDCCLXXVI _____

10. MCDXCII _____

11. MCMXVI _____

12. MCMLXXXIX _____

C. Write out the Latin numbers for the following Roman numerals:

1. L _____

2. C _____

3. M _____

4. D _____

5. X _____

6. V _____

7. XLV _____

8. XCV _____

9. LX _____

10. CIX _____

11. XLIX _____

12. MDVIII _____

2 Here is a story about an auction. Auctions can be fun, but one has to be careful:

AUCTIONĀRIUS: Ecce pictūra magnifica! Est opus pictōris clārī. Nōmen pictōris est Maximus Pūpiēnus. Nōmen pictūrae est "Canis quī edit placentam in lectō." Ecce intellegēns faciēs canis! Ecce ejus oculī pulchrī! Quālis nasus! Quālēs dentēs! Quālis vultus!

auctionārius -ī *m auctioneer*
ecce *see, look at*
opus -eris *n work*
clārus -a -um *famous*

OMNĒS: Aaaaaaah!

CORNĒLIUS: Pictūra est rīdicula!

OCTĀVIA: Est mōnstruōsa!

mōnstruōsus -a -um *monstrous*

AUCTIONĀRIUS: Quantum offertis prō hāc pictūrā magnificā? Quis dat mihi quīnquāgintā denāriōs?

quantum *how much*
offertis *do you offer*
hāc *this*
denārius -ī *m denarius (dollar)*
licitātor -ōris *m bidder*

LICITĀTOR I: Quīnquāgintā denāriōs!

LICITĀTOR II: Sexāgintā denāriōs!

CORNĒLIUS: Eī sunt insānī!

OCTĀVIA: Ego nōn darem ūnum denārium prō illō miserābilī cane!

nōn darem *wouldn't give*
illō *that*
miserābilis -is -e *miserable*
neque *nor (would)*

CORNĒLIUS: Neque ego. Pictūra est rīdicula.

LICITĀTOR I: Septuāgintā quīnque denāriōs!

LICITĀTOR II: Octōgintā denāriōs!

LICITĀTOR I: Nōnāgintā denāriōs!

AUCTIONĀRIUS: Nōnāginatā semel; nōnāgintā bis, ... Quis dabit mihi centum denāriōs?

semel *once*
bis *twice* dabit *will give*

Tunc maximē Lucrētia intrat. Octāvia tollit bracchium ut amīcam suam Lucrētiam salūtet.

tunc maximē *just then*
tollĕre *to raise*
ut *in order to*

AUCTIONĀRIUS: Vendita puellae in stolā rubrā centum denāriīs! Pictūra est ejus!

vendita *sold*

Āctivitātēs

D. Respondē ad quaestiōnēs:

1. Quis est pictor?

_____

2. Quid est titulus (*the title*) pictūrae?

_____

3. Quid Cornēlius dē pictūrā dīcit?

_____

4. Quid Octāvia dē pictūrā dīcit?

_____

5. Quid canis in pictūrā edit?

_____

6. Ubi canis jacet?

_____

7. Quot licitātōrēs pictūram emĕre optant?

_____

8. Quot denāriōs Octāvia prō pictūrā expendit (*pay*)?

_____

E. Rearrange the following list of numbers so that they are in order, the lowest first and the highest last:

1. vīgintī _____   6. mīlle _____

2. centum _____   7. quīngentī _____

3. nōnāgintā _____   8. sexāgintā _____

4. quattuordecim _____   9. duodētrīgintā _____

5. quadrāgintā _____   10. septendecim _____

F. Problem solving. Read the Latin carefully and then give your answer in a complete Latin sentence:

1. Pater nōnāgintā denāriōs habet. Tabernam tignāriam (*carpenter shop*) intrat. Quīnquāgintā denāriōs prō mēnsā et vīgintī denāriōs prō sellā expendit. Quot denāriī restant?

   _____

2. Māter laniēnam cum centum denāriīs intrat, ubi carnem emĕre optat. Tomācla decem denāriīs cōnstant et perna quīnque denāriīs cōnstat. Quot denāriōs māter nunc habet?

   _____

3. Jūlia tabernam pōmāriam intrat. Quīnquāgintā denāriōs habet. Ariēnae quattuor denāriīs cōnstant. Asparagus quīnque denāriīs cōnstat, et persica quīnque denāriīs cōnstant. Quot denāriī restant Jūliae?

   _____

4. Marīa sexāgintā quīnque denāriōs habet. Tabernam vestiāriam (*clothing*) intrat. Duae tunicae rubrae vīgintī denāriīs cōnstant. Stola caerulea quīndecim denāriīs cōnstat. Quot denāriī nunc Marīae sunt?

   _____

5. Familia Scīpiō amīcōs vīsitat. Decem mēnsēs apud (*at the house of*) Marcum manet. Decem mēnsēs apud Gaium manet, et quattuor mēnsēs apud Cornēlium manet. Quot annōs apud variōs amīcōs manet familia Scīpiō?

   _____

6. Aprīlis, Jūnius, September et November habent trīgintā diēs. Sī Cassius per Aprīlem, Jūnium, Septembrem, et Novembrem Rōmam vīsitat, quot diēs in urbe manet?

   _____

G. Imagine yourself once again sitting on a bench in a school in ancient Rome learning arithmetic. You learned Roman numbers up to thirty earlier. Now see whether you can do equally well with higher numbers:

   EXAMPLE: Quot sunt quadrāgintā et trīgintā?
   Quadrāgintā et trīgintā sunt septuāgintā.

   1. Quot sunt quīngentī et quīngentī?

   _____

   2. Quot sunt trīgintā et trīgintā?

   _____

3. Quot sunt quadrāgintā quīnque et decem?

_____

4. Quot sunt nōnāgintā et vīgintī?

_____

5. Quot sunt duōdēsexāgintā et duo?

_____

6. Quot sunt sexāgintā et sexāgintā?

_____

7. Quot sunt vīgintī quattuor et septuāgintā sex?

_____

8. Quot sunt vīgintī quīnque et vīgintī quīnque?

_____

9. Quot sunt quadrāgintā quattuor et quadrāgintā octō?

_____

10. Quot sunt duodēsexāgintā et duodecim?

_____

H. **Magnificē!** Now try your skill at subtraction:

EXAMPLE: Quot sunt quīnquāgintā dē centum?
Quīnquāgintā dē centum sunt quīnquāgintā.

1. Quot sunt quīndecim dē centum?

_____

2. Quot sunt vīgintī quīnque dē quīnquāgintā?

_____

3. Quot sunt quīngentī dē mīlle?

_____

4. Quot sunt decem dē centum?

_____

5. Quot sunt septuāgintā quīnque dē centum?

_____

6. Quot sunt quadrāgintā quīnque dē nōnāgintā?

_____

7. Quot sunt quīndecim dē octōgintā?

_____

8. Quot sunt octōgintā sex dē nōnāgintā?

_____

9. Quot sunt vīgintī de sexāgintā?

_____

10. Quot sunt trīgintā quīnque dē septuāgintā?

_____

3 Up to now, you have used verbs only in the present tense. The IMPERFECT TENSE describes an action that was continued or repeated in the past. Compare these sentences:

Hodiē in culīnā _labōrāmus._ [Present Tense]
Today we are working in the kitchen.

Herī in culīnā _labōrābāmus._ [Imperfect Tense — continued action]
Yesterday we were working in the kitchen.

In culīnā saepe _labōrābāmus._ [Imperfect Tense — repeated action]
We often used to work in the kitchen.
We often worked in the kitchen.

The following table will help you form the imperfect tense of all verb families:

I		**portā**		**-bam**
II		**tenē**		**-bās**
III		**dīcē**		**-bat**
III	**-iō**	**capiē**	**+**	
IV		**audiē**		**-bāmus**
				-bātis
				-bant

Āctivitātēs

I. Write out the imperfect tense of the following verbs:

	portāre	**tenēre**	**dīcĕre**	**capĕre**	**audīre**
ego	_____	_____	_____	_____	_____
tū	_____	_____	_____	_____	_____
is, ea, id	_____	_____	_____	_____	_____

nōs   _____   _____   _____   _____   _____

vōs   _____   _____   _____   _____   _____

eī, eae, ea   _____   _____   _____   _____   _____

J. The endings of the imperfect tense of **īre** are regular. The stem is simply **-i-**. Write out the imperfect tense:

ego   _____   nōs   _____

tū   _____   vōs   _____

is, ea, id _____   eī, eae, ea _____

K. Rewrite the sentences with the verb in the imperfect tense:

1. Coquus cibum gustat.   _____

2. Tōnsor comam tondet.   _____

3. Pōma sub arbore jacent.   _____

4. Ego manē semper sitiō.   _____

5. Āthlēta sē exercet.   _____

6. Caput meum semper dolet.   _____

7. Puerī in flūmine natant.   _____

8. In scholā studēmus.   _____

9. In lūdō sileō.   _____

10. Vēnditor nummōs ēnumerat.   _____

11. Īnfāns dormit.   _____

12. Avēs trāns domum volant.   _____

13. Cūr vīnum pōtās?   _____

14. Quandō librōs legis?   _____

15. Quid tibi placet?   _____

16. Servae dīligenter labōrant.   _____

17. Āthlēta per stadium currit.   _____

18. Quid dīcis? _____

19. Puerī, salūtātisne senātōrēs? _____

20. Avum et aviam vīsitāmus. _____

4 The imperfect tense of **esse** is quite different from the other verbs:

ego eram   **nōs erāmus**

tū erās   **vōs erātis**

is, ea, id erat   **eī, eae, ea erant**

Āctivitātēs

L. Rewrite the following sentences with the verb in the imperfect tense:

1. Trīgintā discipulī in classe meā sunt.

_____

2. Tristēs sumus quandō tū hīc nōn es.

_____

3. Suntne servae in culīnā?

_____

4. Avus fēlix est quandō in vīllā sum.

_____

5. Puellae, cūr in āreā estis?

_____

6. Advocātī in forō sunt.

_____

7. Vēnditor in macellō (*produce market*) est.

_____

8. Claudia, esne in cubiculō tuō?

_____

9. Pecūnia mihi nōn est.

_____

10. Fabius mihi benignus est.

_____

M. Read the following sentences. See whether you can tell the difference between continued action and repeated action. Write "continued" or "repeated" in the space provided:

1. Pīstor pānem herī torrēbat.

_____

2. Puerī in stāgnō saepe natābant.

_____

3. Canis noster in culīnā semper dormiēbat.

_____

4. Cūr canis latrābat?

_____

5. Interdum apud amīcum manēbam.

_____

N. The imperfect tense of **posse** is formed by adding the past forms of **esse** to the root **pot-** (**poteram, poterās, poterat,** etc.). Rewrite the following sentences with the verb in the imperfect tense:

1. Quis astra et lūnam vidēre potest?

_____

2. Potesne nōbīscum lūdĕre?

_____

3. Lac bibĕre possum.

_____

4. Pugilēs bene pugnāre possunt.

_____

5. Rūs īre semper possumus.

_____

QUAESTIŌNĒS PERSŌNĀLĒS

Respondē Latīnē (*Write out all numbers*):

1. Quot membra in familiā tuā sunt?

   _____

2. Quot puerī in classe tuā sunt?

   _____

3. Quot puellae in classe tuā sunt?

   _____

4. Quot annōs nātus est pater tuus?

   _____

5. Quot annōs nāta est māter tua?

   _____

6. Quot annōs nātus/nāta es tū?

   _____

7. Quid est numerus domūs tuae?

   _____

8. Quot lectiōnēs sunt in librō Latīnō tuō?

   _____

CONVERSĀTIŌ

VOCĀBULA

hominēs -um *mpl people*   **tantummodo** *only*
circa (+ accusative case) *about, approximately*

COLLOQUIUM

Complete the dialog with expressions chosen from the following list:

tantummodo	inter gladiātōrēs	Minimē vērō
pugnābant	vēnditābam	circa
circa mīlle	gladiātōrēs	amphitheātrō
hominēs	pugilēs	vēnditor
hodiē manē		

Adverbs

1   The Romans believed in many gods and goddesses. Statues and paintings showed them with certain symbols so that people could recognize them. For example, Saturn was shown with a big scythe (like Father Time), Diana with bow and arrow because she loved to hunt. Jupiter was shown with lightning bolts and an eagle, Juno with a peacock. Note the symbols with each god or goddess:

Juppiter, Jovis *m*

Jūnō *-ōnis f*

Jānus *-ī m*

Apollō *-inis m*

Diāna *-ae f*

Minerva *-ae f*

Venus -eris *f*

Cupīdō -inis *m*

Neptūnus -ī *m*

Mercurius -ī *m*

Cerēs -ēris *f*

Bacchus -ī *m*

Sāturnus -ī *m*

Mārs -tis *m*

Vulcānus -ī *m*

Activitās

A. Look carefully at the symbols and identify the gods and goddesses in Latin:

1. _____

5. _____

2. _____

6. _____

3. _____

7. _____

4. _____

8. _____

9. _____

10. _____

13. _____

11. _____

14. _____

12. _____

15. _____

2 Now that you have seen what the gods and goddesses looked like, let's learn something about them:

Domus deōrum deārumque erat in Monte Olympō, ubi in rēgiā splendidā habitābant. Via aurea ad rēgiam dūcēbat. Deī deaeque erant immortālēs, quia ambrosiam edēbant et nectar bibēbant. Vītam bonam et fēlīcem in Monte Olympō dūcēbant.

deus **-ī** *m god* **dea -ae** *f goddess*
  -que *and*
rēgia -ae *f palace*
aureus **-a -um** *golden, of gold*
immortālis **-is -e** *immortal*
  ambrosia -ae *f ambrosia*
nectar -is *n nectar*

Juppiter erat rēx deōrum deārumque. In cathedrā aureā sedēbat. Aquila ad pedēs Jovis semper stābat. Fulmina manū tenēbat. Juppiter pluviam ad terram mittēbat. Ā rēgiā tōtam terram spectāre poterat. Omnēs deī et hominēs Jovem timēbant.

Juppiter; Jovis *m Jupiter*
  rēx, rēgis *m king*
aquila **-ae** *f eagle*
fulmen **-minis** *n lightning bolt*

Pater Jovis erat Sāturnus; avus Jovis erat Ūranus. Plūtō, frāter Jovis, erat rēx mortuōrum in regiōne subterrāneā.

mortuus **-a -um** *dead;* **mortuī**
  -ōrum *mpl the dead*
regiō -ōnis *f region*
  subterrāneus **-a -um** *below
  the earth*

Jūnō erat rēgīna deōrum deārumque. Fēminae Rōmānae Jūnōnem amābant et adōrābant. Jūnō ārās in urbibus magnīs et in oppidīs parvīs habēbat. Mēnsis Jūnius erat sacer Jūnōnī. Avis Jūnōnis erat pāvō.

rēgīna **-ae** *f queen*

āra **-ae** *f altar*

sacer, sacra, **sacr**um *sacred*
  pāvō -ōnis *m peacock*

Diāna erat dea lūnae et silvārum et bestiārum. Diāna noctū in caelō habitābat sed interdiū in terrā habitābat. Per silvās obscūrās ambulāre amābat. Arcum et sagittās manū semper tenēbat. Bestiae Diānam nōn timēbant, et Diāna bestiās nōn timēbat. Diāna bestiīs semper benigna erat.

bestia -ae *f wild beast*
  noctū *at night*
interdiū *during the day*
obscūrus **-a -um** *dark*
  arcus -ūs *m bow*
sagitta **-ae** *f arrow*

Frāter Diānae erat Apollō, deus sōlis et mūsicae. Ut Diāna erat dea lūnae, sīc Apollō erat deus sōlis. Ut sōl omnia vidēbat, sīc Apollō omnia vidēbat. Quia omnia vidēbat, Apollō erat deus prophēticus. Apollō futūram praedīcere poterat.

mūsica **-ae** *f music*
  ut . . . sīc *as . . . so*
sōl, -is *m sun*

prophēticus -a -um *prophetic*
praedīcere *to predict*

Activitās

B. Respondē ad quaestiōnēs:

1. Ubi erat domus deōrum deārumque?

_____

2. Quid deī deaeque edēbant?

_____

3. Quid deī deaeque bibēbant?

_____

4. Quis erat rēx deōrum deārumque?

_____

5. Quid Juppiter manū tenēbat?

_____

6. Quid ad pedēs Jovis stābat?

_____

7. Quis pater Jovis erat?

_____

8. Quis avus Jovis erat?

_____

9. Quis erat rēgīna deōrum deārumque?

_____

10. Quis erat rēx mortuōrum?

_____

11. Quid ad pedēs Jūnōnis stābat?

_____

12. Quis erat dea lūnae et silvārum?

_____

13. Quis erat deus sōlis et mūsicae?

_____

14. Quis deus habēbat duās faciēs?

_____

The Latin word **planēta -ae** *f* gives us our English word *planet*. All the planets except Earth (**Terra**) were named after Roman gods:

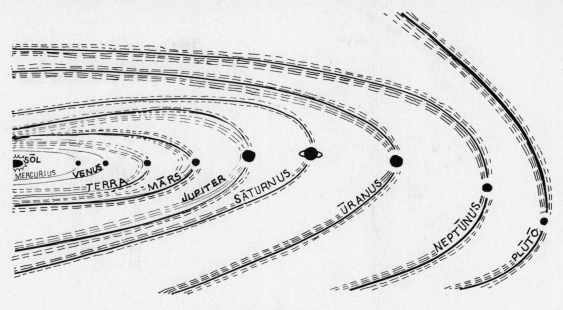

Activitās

C. Look at the symbols below and write the name of the god or goddess they represent:

1. _____

3. _____

2. _____

4. _____

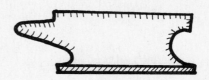

5. _____   7. _____

6. _____   8. _____

3 Now let's get better acquainted with some of the other gods and goddesses:

Neptūnus erat rēx maris et flūminum. Tridentem manū tenēbat. Nautae Rōmānī Neptūnum adōrābant. In aquīs Ōceanī domum habēbat. Neptūnus nautīs benignus erat.

tridēns -tis *m trident*
Ōceanus -ī *m ocean*

Mārs erat deus bellī. Mīlitēs Mārtem praecipuē adōrābant. Mēnsis Mārtius erat sacer Mārtī. Mārs erat deus ferōx, sed uxor sua erat dea pulchra et ēlegāns, nam uxor sua erat Venus.

bellum -ī *n war*
praecipuē *especially*
uxor -ōris *f wife*
nam *for, since*

Avis Veneris erat columba. Fīlius parvus, Cupīdō, Venerī erat. Puellae Rōmānae Venerem et Cupīdinem praecipuē adōrābant. Cupīdō manibus arcum et sagittās tenēbat. Ālās in dorsō habēbat.

columba -ae *f dove*

āla -ae *f wing* **dorsum -ī** *n back*

Mercurius erat nuntius deōrum deārumque. In pedibus sandalia cum ālīs habēbat. In capite petasum cum alīs habēbat. Inter caelum et terram saepe iter faciēbat.

nuntius -ī *m messenger*

petasus -ī *m (broad-brimmed) hat*
iter itineris *n trip;* **iter facĕre** *to travel, take a trip*

Jānus duās faciēs habēbat. Jānus erat deus annī novī. Mēnsis Jānuārius erat sacer Jānō. Statua ejus ante jānuam saepe stābat.

statua -ae *f statue*

Bacchus erat deus vīnī, et Cerēs erat dea frūmentī. Bacchus ūvās manū tenēbat et Cerēs frūmentum manū tenēbat.

frūmentum -ī *n grain*

Vulcānus erat faber ferrārius. Officīna Vulcānī sub monte erat, ubi fulmina Jovis fabricābat.

faber ferrārius *m blacksmith*

fabricō -āre *to make*

Minerva erat dea sapientiae et bellī. Tamquam Mārs, Minerva galeam in capite gerēbat et scūtum manū sinistrā tenēbat. Būbō erat avis sacra Minervae. Minerva erat patrōna discipulōrum.

sapientia -ae *f wisdom*
tamquam *just as*
galea -ae *f helmet*
scūtum -ī *n shield*
būbō -ōnis *m owl*
patrōna -ae *f patroness*

Āctivitātēs

D. Respondē ad quaestiōnēs:

1. Quis erat rēx maris et flūminum? _____

2. Quis Neptūnum adōrābat? _____

3. Quis erat deus bellī? _____

4. Quis Mārtem adōrābant? _____

5. Quis erat uxor Mārtis? _____

6. Quid erat avis Veneris? _____

7. Quis erat fīlius Veneris? _____

8. Quid Cupīdō manibus tenēbat? _____

9. Quis erat nuntius deōrum? _____

10. Quid in capite gerēbat? _____

11. Quid in pedibus gerēbat? _____

12. Quis duās faciēs habēbat? _____

13. Quis erat deus vīnī? _____

14. Quis erat dea frūmentī? _____

15. Ubi erat officīna Vulcānī? _____

16. Quis erat dea sapientiae? _____

E. Do you remember the Latin days of the week from Lesson XVI? Give the days of the week in English for the following:

1. diēs Mārtis _____   **4.** diēs Sāturnī _____

2. diēs Veneris _____   **5.** diēs Mercuriī _____

3. diēs Jovis _____

F. From what you have read about the gods and goddesses, you should be able to make one statement about each of the following:

1. Plūtō _____

2. Neptūnus _____

3. Ūranus _____

4. Sāturnus _____

5. Juppiter _____

6. Mārs _____

7. Venus _____

8. Mercurius _____

4 Now let's learn Latin adverbs. English adverbs end in -*ly* (*surely*, *quickly*). Latin adverbs end in **-ē** if the adverb comes from an adjective ending in **-us -a -um**:

sincēr*us* *-a* *-um* *sincere*   **sincēr*ē*** *sincerely*

Latin adverbs end in **-iter** if the adverb comes from an adjective with the ending in **-is -is -e**:

fidēl*is* *-is* *-e* *faithful*   **fidēl*iter*** *faithfully*

An important exception to the rule is **facilis** (*easy*); its adverbial form is **facilē** (*easily*). **Difficilis** (*difficult*) may have the regular adverbial form **difficil*iter*** or the irregular form **difficilē** (*with difficulty*).

Remember that not all adjectives of the third declension end in **-is -is -e**: **ēlegāns, intellegēns.** These adjectives drop the **-s** from the nominative ending and add **-ter.**

ēlegāns *elegant*   **ēlegan*ter*** *elegantly*

Activitās

G. Form adverbs from the following adjectives and give their meanings:

ADJECTIVE	ADVERB	MEANING
sevērus	_____	_____
tacitus	_____	_____
splendidus	_____	_____
ēnormis	_____	_____
nobilis	_____	_____
prūdēns	_____	_____
obēdiēns	_____	_____
pius	_____	_____
laetus	_____	_____
malus	_____	_____
obstinātus	_____	_____

5 There are many Latin adverbs that have none of these endings, just as there are English adverbs that don't end in -*ly* (*there, also, ever, sometimes*). Here are some Latin adverbs that do not follow any pattern of endings. You have already met several of them in previous lessons:

ibi	*there*	**paulātim**	*little by little*
diū	*for a long time*	**tandem**	*finally*
nūper	*recently*	**cito**	*quickly*

THE LATIN CONNECTION

Look over the list of Latin words and the list of English words (called derivatives) that come from the Latin words. Then write the English word in the space next to the Latin word that is connected with it in meaning:

1. Plūtō _____

2. Mercurius _____

3. Ūranus _____

4. Vulcānus _____

5. mortuus _____

6. subterrāneus _____

7. sacer _____

8. bestia _____

9. noctū _____

10. obscūrus _____

11. arcus _____

12. sagitta _____

13. prophēticus _____

14. dorsum _____

15. iter, itineris _____

16. patrōna _____

17. planēta _____

18. praedīcere _____

beast
patron
obscure
itinerary
arch
dorsal
nocturnal
subterranean
planet
plutonium
predict
volcano
Sagittarius
mercury
mortal
prophetic
uranium
sacred

CONVERSĀTIŌ

ubi *when*
hāc nocte *tonight*
facilē *easily*

nimis remōt*us -a -um* *too far away*
fortasse *maybe*
aliquandō *someday*

COLLOQUIUM

Complete the dialog with expressions chosen from the following list:

aliae planētae	lūnam vīsitāre
vidēre possum	astra
dormīre	fenestram

XIX Nāvigātiō

Imperative

1 Can you guess the meanings of the new words?

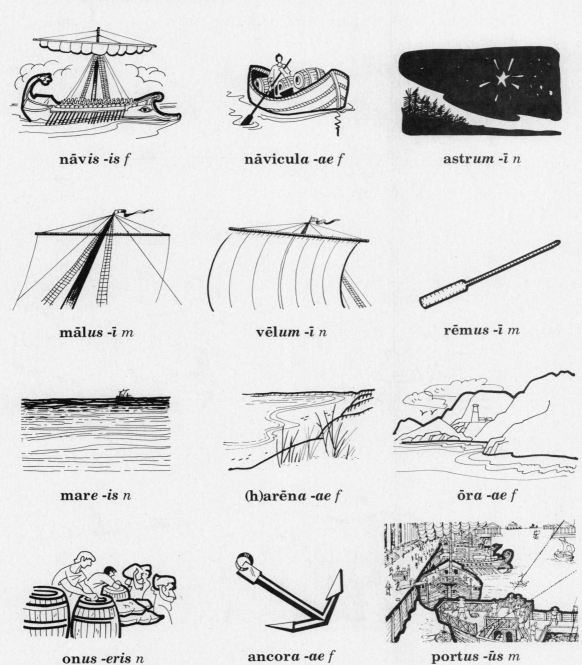

nāv*is -is* f   **nāvicul***a -ae* f   **astr***um -ī* n

māl*us -ī* m   **vēl***um -ī* n   **rēm***us -ī* m

mar*e -is* n   **(h)arēn***a -ae* f   **ōr***a -ae* f

on*us -eris* n   **ancor***a -ae* f   **portus** *-ūs* m

pristis -is *f*

bālaena -ae *f*

flūctus -ūs *m*

Āctivitās

A. Identify and write the Latin name, genitive, and gender of the following:

1. _____

2. _____

3. _____

4. _____

5. _____

6. _____

7. _____

12. _____

8. _____

13. _____

9. _____

10. _____

14. _____

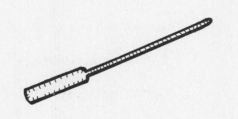

11. _____

15. _____

2 Pitfalls. Among the new words you have just met, there is one that looks like a word you had before: **mālus -ī** m (*mast*). Do you remember the word for apple?

_____. Note the long vowel in some of the following words:

māl*um* **-ī** *n*	*apple*	**māl***us* **-a -um**	*evil, bad*
māl*us* **-ī** *f*	*apple tree*	**mal***a* **-ōrum** *npl*	*evils*
māl*us* **-ī** *m*	*mast*		

3 A verb form that expresses a command is in the IMPERATIVE MOOD. The IMPERATIVE form is easily recognized. Here are the imperative forms for all the verbs. Look carefully at the following examples:

	I	II	III	III -iō	IV
SINGULAR	**portā** (*carry!*)	**tenē** (*hold!*)	**mitte** (*send!*)	**cape** (*take!*)	**audī** (*hear!*)
PLURAL	**portāte** (*carry!*)	**tenēte** (*hold!*)	**mittite** (*send!*)	**capite** (*take!*)	**audīte** (*hear!*)

The imperative forms of the verb **īre** (*to go*) are: **ī** (*go!* [singular]), **īte** (*go!* [plural]).

The imperative forms of the verb **esse** (*to be*) are: **es** (*be!* [singular]), **este** (*be!* [plural]).

There are four verbs with an irregular form in the singular imperative. The plural is normal:

SINGULAR		PLURAL	
dīc	*say!, speak!*	**dīcite**	*say!, speak!*
dūc	*lead!*	**dūcite**	*lead!*
fac	*do!, make!*	**facite**	*do!, make!*
fer	*bring!*	**ferte**	*bring!*

Look over the plural forms. Which of the plural imperatives is different?

_____. Which letter was omitted in that form? _____. Look at the first column. What is the letter that was dropped at the end of the singular imperatives that makes them irregular? _____.

Āctivitātēs

B. Rewrite the sentences, changing the imperative from singular to plural:

1. Tenē manum meam! _____

2. Stā ante classem! _____

3. Gustā placentam! _____

4. Exspectā mē! _____

5. Lūde in āreā! _____

6. Studē dīligenter! _____

7. Narrā mihi fābulam! _____

8. Dīc mihi! _____

9. Portam aperī! _____

10. Respondē Latīnē! _____

11. Venī statim! _____

12. Salī in stāgnum! _____

13. Dūc mē ad forum. _____

14. Fer aquam ad balneum. _____

C. In the following sentences, use the singular or plural imperative of the indicated verb. The noun in the vocative case determines whether to use the singular or plural imperative:

1. (tondēre)   Tōnsor, _____ comām meām!

2. (cōnsīdĕre)   Discipulī, _____!

3. (manēre)   Nautae, _____ in navibus!

4. (dūcĕre)   Serve, _____ mē ad dominum tuum!

5. (edĕre)   Puerī, _____ holera vestra!

6. (parāre)   Coquae, _____ cēnam meam!

7. (spectāre)   Claudia, _____ astra in caelō!

8. (emĕre)   Māter, _____ mihi crūstulum!

9. (gerĕre)   Senātōrēs, _____ hodiē togās vestrās albās!

10. (facĕre)   Faber tignārī, _____ mihi subsellium!

11. (dare)   Vēnditor, _____ mihi octō ariēnas.

12. (exuĕre)   Līberī, _____ calceōs vestrōs.

4 Negative Latin commands are expressed by **nōlī** (singular) or **nōlīte** (plural), followed by the infinitive of the verb. (**Nōlī** and **nōlīte** literally mean "be unwilling."):

SINGULAR:	**Nōlī timēre!** *Do not fear!*
PLURAL:	**Nōlīte timēre!** *Do not fear!*

Āctivitātēs

D. Complete the following negative commands with **nōlī** or **nōlīte**:

1. Discipulī, _____ dormīre in scholā!

2. Claudī, _____ salīre in aquam!

3. Medice, _____ nocēre mihi!

4. Puellae, _____ jacēre sub arbore!

5. Clēmēns, _____ frangĕre fenestram nostram!

6. Vēnditōrēs, _____ clāmāre in macellō!

E. Change the following positive commands to negative commands:

1. Mī amīce, ī in nāviculam. _____

2. Nautae, ferte ancoram. _____

3. Puerī, lūdite in āreā. _____

4. Nauta, portā onus in nāvem. _____

5. Nautae, spectāte astra. _____

6. Frātercule, ede cerasa mea. _____

5 Now enjoy this story:

Duo puerī, Claudius et Terentius, in ōrā maritimā sedēbant et in arēnā lūdēbant. Nāvem magnam in portū spectābant. Nāvis mālum altum et vēla alba habēbat. Multae nāviculae cum rēmīs circum nāvem magnam nāvigābant.

maritim*us* -*a* -*um* *sea, of the sea*

Nautae onus ā terrā in nāvem portābant. Erat nāvis onerāria. Magister nāvem cōnscendēbat. Magister nautīs clāmābat:

nāvis onerāria *f cargo ship*
magis*ter* -*trī* *m captain*
cōnscendĕre *to climb aboard*

"Tollite ancoram! Vēla ventīs date!"

Claudius et Terentius mare amābant. Flūctūs altōs vidēre optābant. Dum magister nāvis et nautae occupātī sunt, puerī nāvem clam cōnscendunt et post onus latent.

Nunc nāvis ē portū ad mare altum nāvigābat. Puerī laetī erant, nam pristēs vidēbant. Etiam bālaenae inter flūctūs natābant.

Sed tempestās subitō surgit. Ventī strident. Caelum nōn jam clārum et caeruleum est sed ātrum. Flūctūs altī nāvem pulsant. "Ō Neptūne, deus maris, servā nōs!" puerī clāmant.

Post multās horās tempestās paulātim subsīdit et nāvis ad portum redit. Claudius et Terentius dē nāve dēscendunt. Puerī laetī sunt, quia iterum in terrā firmā sunt.

tollĕre *to lift, weigh*
vēla ventīs dare *to set sail*
(literally, *to give the sails to the winds*)
dum *while*

clam *secretly*

mare altum *high seas*
etiam *even, also*

stridēre *to howl*
nōn jam *no longer*
clārus -a -um *clear*
pulsāre *to beat against*

paulātim *little by little*
subsīdĕre *to subside, calm down*
dēscendĕre *to get off, climb down*
firmus -a -um *firm*

Āctivitātēs

F. Respondē ad quaestiōnēs:

1. Ubi Claudius et Terentius sedēbant?

_____

2. Quid spectābant?

_____

3. Quid habēbat nāvis?

_____

4. Quid circum nāvem magnam nāvigābat?

_____

5. Quid nautae ā terrā in nāvem portābant?

_____

6. Ubi puerī in nāve latēbant?

_____

7. Quid puerī in marī vidēbant?

_____

8. Quid subitō surgit?

_____

9. Quid nāvem pulsat?

_____

10. Cūr puerī laetī sunt?

_____

G. Complete the sentences with the expression in parentheses that best fits the sense:

1. Bālaenae _____ natābant.
   (in marī / in ōrā)

2. Puerī parvī _____ lūdēbant.
   (in arēnā / in flūctibus)

3. Pristēs sunt piscēs _____.
   (benignae / ferōcēs)

4. Tempestās puerōs _____.
   (timēbat / terrēbat)

5. Nāvis onerāria _____ trānsportat.
   (onus / piscēs)

6. Bālaena est _____.
   (piscis / nāvicula)

7. Mālus _____ tenet.
   (rēmōs / vēla)

8. Nautae _____ tollunt.
   (arēnam / ancoram)

9. Magister nāvis _____ cōnscendēbat.
   (mālum / nāvem)

10. _____ nāvem pulsābant.
    (Rēmī / Flūctūs)

11. Pristēs _____ habent.
    (dentēs ēnormēs / comam longam)

12. Nāvis _____ nāvigat.
    (per ārenam / per flūctūs)

6 Ancient sailors did not know of the compass. They sailed close to land whenever possible. On the open sea, they sailed by the sun by day and by the stars at night. Here are the directions in which they might sail:

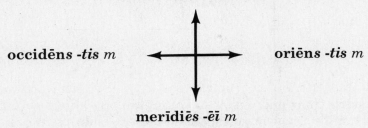

septentriōnēs *-um mpl*

occidēns *-tis m*　　　**oriēns** *-tis m*

merīdiēs *-ēī m*

Āctivitātēs

H. Write the English directions indicated in Latin:

1. Nāvicula ab oriente ad occidentem nāvigābat. _____

2. Sōl in oriente surgit. _____

3. Sōl in occidente occidit (*sets*). _____

4. Nāvis onerāria ā merīdiē ad septentriōnēs nāvigābat. _____

5. Fenestra mea ad occidentem spectat (*faces*). _____

6. Templum Minervae ad orientem spectat. _____

7. Ventus ex occidente surgit. _____

8. Ad septentriōnēs urbis habitō. _____

I. Rewrite the following sentences, but reverse the direction given in each sentence:

1. Cubiculum meum ad orientem spectat.

_____

2. Pristēs in septentriōnēs natābant.

_____

3. Nāvis onerāria in occidentem nāvigābat.

_____

4. Bālaenae in merīdiem natābant.

_____

5. Pater meus ab oriente ad occidentem per Ītaliam iter facit.

_____

J. Scrambled sentences. You can usually tell which words belong together by observing their endings. Can you figure out which words belong to which? Unscramble the sentences, observing the endings. Write out the sentences in Latin, putting the verb at the end. Then give the English meanings:

    EXAMPLE: Parvī nāvem cōnscendunt puerī magnam.
                 Puerī parvī nāvem magnam cōnscendunt.

1. Alba habēbant nāvēs vēla onerāriae.

_____

_____

2. Multae circum nāvem nāvigābant nāviculae magnam.

_____

_____

3. Ē nunc nāvigat portū nāvicula ad septentriōnēs parva.

_____

_____

4. In pristēs bālaenaeque natābant marī altō ēnormēs.

_____

_____

5. Habet cūr magnam nāvis ancoram parva?

_____

_____

CONVERSĀTIŌ

VOCĀBULA

rēmigāre *to row*
nescīre *not know (how to)*
vēlificāre *to operate the sails*

Magna rēs nōn est. *It's not important.*
magis *more*

COLLOQUIUM

Complete the dialog with expressions chosen from the following list:

mihi   in arēnā
tempestās surgit   vēlificāre nesciō
Nōlī timēre!   rēmōs
firmam magis   ōram maritimam
rēmigāre

THE LATIN CONNECTION

Look over the list of Latin words and the list of English words that derive from the Latin words. Then write the English derivative next to its Latin origin:

1. tempestās   _____

2. ancora   _____

3. maritima   _____

4. flūctus   _____

5. vēlum   _____

6. nāvis   _____

7. portus   _____

8. arēna   _____

9. nāvigāre   _____

10. firmus   _____

11. dēscendĕre   _____

12. oriēns   _____

13. subsīdĕre   _____

14. pulsāre   _____

15. astrum / nauta   _____

firm
orient
arena
naval
subside
anchor
astronaut
navigate
descend
fluctuate
veil
maritime
port
pulse
tempest

QUAESTIŌNĒS PERSŌNĀLĒS

1. Delectatne tē ōra maritima?

   _____

2. Habetne familia tua casam in ōrā maritimā?

   _____

3. Vīsitāsne ōram maritimam aestāte?

   _____

4. Amāsne in arēnā an in flūctibus lūdĕre?

   _____

5. Amāsne mare magis quam terram?

   _____

6. Scīsne (*do you know how to*) rēmigāre?

   _____

7. Scīsne vēlificāre?

   _____

8. Timēsne pristēs ubi in marī natās?

   _____

RĒS PERSŌNĀLĒS

Imagine that you are a Roman youngster who will take a trip on a ship for the first time. Name in Latin three persons and three things that you would take with you:

_____   _____

_____   _____

_____   _____

Animālia

The Verb ferre

1 You have already learned the names of some animals. Can you guess the meanings of these words?

leō -ōnis *m*

tigris -*is f*

avis -*is f*

ovis -*is f*

lupus -*ī m*

vulpēs -*is f*

sīmia -*ae f*

ursus -*ī m*

camēlus -*ī m*

anas -*atis f*

gallus -*ī m*

aquila -*ae f*

cunīcul*us* -*ī* *m*

taur*us* -*ī* *m*

Āctivitātēs

A. Identify. Indicate the nominative case, genitive case, and the gender of each animal:

1. _____

4. _____

2. _____

5. _____

3. _____

6. _____

7. _____

11. _____

8. _____

12. _____

9. _____

13. _____

10. _____

14. _____

B. There are other animals that you have met earlier. Match the descriptions with the pictures:

equus	asinus	gallīna
canis	porcus	elephantus
fēlēs	vacca	mūs

1. _____

4. _____

7. _____

2. _____

5. _____

8. _____

3. _____

6. _____

9. _____

C. For convenience, we can group animals as domestic animals (**domesticus -a -um**), country or farm animals (**rūsticus -a -um**), wild animals (**ferus -a -um**), animals that live in water (**aquāticus -a -um**), and animals that fly (**volāns -antis**). Look over the following list of animals and then write their names under the proper heading:

anas	cunīculus	lupus	taurus
avis	equus	mūs	tigris
aquila	fēlēs	ovis	ursus
asinus	gallīna	piscis	vacca
bālaena	gallus	porcus	vulpēs
canis	leō	sīmia	

animālia domestica	animālia rūstica	animālia fera	animālia aquātica	animālia volantia
_____	_____	_____	_____	_____
_____	_____	_____	_____	_____
	_____	_____		_____
	_____	_____		_____
	_____	_____		_____
	_____			
	_____			

D. Now that you know the Latin names of many animals, can you figure out their identity from their descriptions. Write the name of the animal in the space provided:

1. Ego sum parva. In cavō habitō. Frūmentum et cāseum amō. Fēlēs timeō.

   cav*um* -*ī* n *hole*

   Sum _____.

2. Ego sum animal rūsticum. In fundō habitō. Herbam multam in prātō cotīdiē edō et lac agricolīs dō.

   prāt*um* -*ī* n *meadow*

   Sum _____.

3. Ego in campō et in silvā habitō. Interdum in montibus habitō. Omnēs bestiae mē timent, nam rēx bestiārum sum.

   interdum *sometimes*

   Sum _____.

4. Ego domum custōdiō. Cito currĕre possum. Fēlēs nōn amō. Magnā vocē saepe latrō.

   custōdīre *to guard* **cito** *fast*
   magnā voce *in a loud voice*
   latrāre *to bark*

   Sum _____.

5. Ego plūmas habeō, sed numquam per caelum volō. Ōva alba pariō. Hominēs ōva mea edunt.

   plūm*a* -*ae* f *feather*
   parĕre *to lay*

   Sum _____.

6. Ego in cavō habitō. Caudam longam et pilōsam habeō. Animal astūtum sum. Gallīnās et cunīculōs petĕre amō.

cauda -ae f tail
pilōsus -a -um bushy, hairy
  astūtus -a -um sly
petĕre to chase after

Sum _____.

7. Ego sum animal ferōx tremendae vēlōcitātis. Familiae fēlīnae pertineō. Sunt līneae in pelle.

tremendus -a -um tremendous
vēlōcitās -ātis f speed
  fēlīnus -a -um feline, cat
pertinēre to belong to
  līnea -ae f line, stripe
  pellis -is f fur

Sum _____.

8. Ego sum animal ēnorme sed clēmēns. Memoria excellēns mihi est. Duōs dentēs ēburneōs habeō. Manus longa mihi est.

clēmēns -tis gentle
  memoria -ae f memory
dēns -tis m tusk
  ēburneus -a -um of ivory
manus -ūs f trunk

Sum _____.

9. Ego sum animal ferum. In specū habitō. Mel edĕre amō. Pellis mea est atra aut fusca. Per tōtam hiemem dormiō.

specus -ūs m cave

Sum _____.

10. Ego caudam longam habeō. In arboribus saepe sum. Ab arbore ad arborem salīre possum. Ariēnās praecipuē amō.

praecipuē especially

Sum _____.

11. Ego cito currĕre possum. Aurēs longae mihi sunt. Canēs et vēnātōrēs mē frequenter petunt. Carōtās maximē amō.

vēnātor -ōris m hunter
maximē very much

Sum _____.

12. Ego nōn magnus sum sed onera magna portāre possum. Aurēs longae mihi sunt. Interdum obstinātus sum.

onus -eris n weight, load

Sum _____.

13. Ego animal rūsticum sum. Quattuor crūra mihi sunt. Herbam edō. Lānam dēnsam habeō.

lāna -ae *f wool*
dēnsus -a -um *dense, thick*

Sum _____.

14. Ego animal desertōrum sum. Multōs diēs per arēnās sine aquā īre possum. Duo tūbera in dorsō habeō.

deserta -ōrum *npl desert*

tūber -eris *n hump*

Sum _____.

15. Ego parvum animal cum plūmīs sum. Alās habeō. Per caelum volō. Pīpilāre amō. Nīdum in arbore fabricō.

pīpilāre *to chirp*
nīdus -ī *m nest*

Sum _____.

16. Ego sum animal crassum. In fundō habitō. In lūtō jacēre amō. Pernae et tomācla ā mē veniunt. Ego grunniō.

crassus -a -um *fat*
lūtum -ī *n mud*

grunnīre *to grunt*

Sum _____.

E. Match the products with the animals they come from. Write the matching letters in the spaces:

1. vacca _____

2. gallīna _____

3. ovis _____

4. porcus _____

a. ōva
b. lāna
c. lac
d. perna
e. cāseus

F. In the spaces provided, list the animals according to size, beginning with the largest and ending with the smallest. Give also the genitive form and the gender of each:

lupus   **gallus**   **leō**
elephantus   **taurus**

1. _____

2. _____

3. _____

4. _____

5. _____

2 In the previous lesson, you saw that the imperative forms of the verb **ferre** (*to bring, bear, carry*) — **fer!** (singular) and **ferte!** (plural) — are irregular. In fact, most of its forms in the present tense, including the infinitive **ferre,** are irregular. Here is the present tense:

ferō	ferimus
fers	fertis
fert	ferunt

Can you pick out the three forms that are irregular? (Compare this verb with the regular forms of the third family of verbs, like **dūcĕre.**):

_____ _____ _____

What is the letter that was dropped from these three forms? _____ The imperfect tense of **ferre** is regular: **ferēbam, ferēbās, ferēbat, ferēbāmus, ferēbātis, ferēbant.**

3 In the following description of a scene in a Roman kitchen, all the forms of the present tense of **ferre** occur. See whether you can find them all:

Cornēlius cum familiā suā in trīclīniō est.
Dāvus et Glaucus, servī domesticī, cēnam in
trīclīnium **ferunt.** Cornēlius Davō et Glaucō
dīcit:

"Dāve et Glauce, iam tempus est cibum
ferre."

"Bene, domine," respondet Dāvus; "ego ipse
jūs **ferō** et Glaucus acētāria **fert.**

"**Fertis**ne etiam vīnum?" quaerit Cornēlius.

"Ita, domine," respondet Dāvus; "sed vīnum
post cibum **ferimus.**"

"Dāve, cūr nōn vīnum rubrum hodiē **fers?**"
quaerit Cornēlius.

"Quia solum vīnum album in cellā est,   **solum** *only*
domine," dīcit Dāvus.   **cella -ae** *f storeroom*

Activitās

G. Respondē ad quaestiōnēs:

1. Quis cēnam in trīclīnium fert? _____

2. Quid fert Dāvus ipse? _____

3. Quid fert Glaucus? _____

4. Quando servī vīnum ferunt? _____

5. Cūr servī vīnum rubrum nōn ferunt? _____

4 You can form many new verbs with **ferre** by adding prefixes. With each prefix, the meaning of the verb changes. Remember that the last letter of a prefix often changes to become the same as the first letter of the verb. Here are some examples:

PREFIX		ROOT			
ab-	+	**ferre**	=	**auferre**	*to bring away, take away, remove*
ad-	+	**ferre**	=	**afferre**	*to bring to, fetch, bring along*
circum-	+	**ferre**	=	**circumferre**	*to bring around*
in-	+	**ferre**	=	**inferre**	*to bring in, infer*

Āctivitātēs

H. Now see whether you can provide the English derivatives, following the example:

PREFIX	ROOT			LITERAL MEANING	ENGLISH DERIVATIVE
dē-	+ **ferre**	=	**deferre**	*to bring (or bear) away*	*to defer*
con-	+ **ferre**	=	**conferre**	*to bring together, gather*	_____
ob-	+ **ferre**	=	**offerre**	*to bring to, present*	_____
prae-	+ **ferre**	=	**praeferre**	*to bring before*	_____
re-	+ **ferre**	=	**referre**	*to bring back*	_____
sub-	+ **ferre**	=	**sufferre**	*to bear up under*	_____
trāns-	+ **ferre**	=	**trānsferre**	*to bring across*	_____

I. Rewrite the following sentences, changing the subject and verb to the plural:

EXAMPLE: **Pōmārius** māla ariēnīs **praefert.**
The fruitseller prefers apples to bananas.

Pōmāriī māla ariēnīs **praeferunt.**
The fruitsellers prefer apples to bananas.

1. Serve, fer togam meam!

_____

2. Discipule, refer librum meum!

_____

3. Magister dolōrem capitis suffert.

_____

4. Puella flōrēs confert.

_____

5. Equum camēlō praeferō.

_____

6. Vēnātor leōnēs et tigrēs confert.

_____

7. Nauta onus in nāvem trānsfert.

_____

8. Cūr fēlem ā culīnā aufers?

_____

5 Read the following story of how animals in the wild get along:

Leō, lupus, vulpēs, ursus societātem faciunt. Multam praedam capĕre optant. Per silvās et campōs, per montēs et vallēs praedam petunt. Omnem praedam in unum locum conferunt. Tum in quattuor partēs praedam dīvidunt.

societās -ātis *f partnership*
praeda -ae *f prey*

petĕre *to chase after*
pars -tis *f part, quarter*
dīvidĕre *to divide*

"Prīma pars," lupus inquit, "mea est, nam ego eram vēnātor rapidus."

nam *for*
vēnātor -ōris *m hunter*

"Minimē vērō!" dīcit leō; "prīma pars est mea, nam leō est rex animālium."

Vulpēs autem dīcit: "Secunda pars est mea, nam vēnātor astūtus eram."

autem *now, but*

"Minimē vērō!" dīcit leō; "secunda pars est mea, nam appetentiam magnam habeō."

"Tertia pars," ursus timidē inquit, "est mea, nam ego eram vēnātor dīligēns."

timidē *timidly*

"Minimē vērō!" rudit leō; "tertia mea est, nam famem habeō. Et sī quis partem quārtam vindicat, ego eum dēvorābō."

Āctivitātēs

J. Can you name all the animals in the barnyard? End each sentence with **videō** (*I see*):

1. _____

2. _____

3. _____

4. _____

5. _____

6. _____

7. _____

8. _____

9. _____

10. _____

11. _____

K. Find the hidden animals. There are 10 animals hidden in this picture. Find them and list their Latin names below. Give the nominative and genitive cases and the gender:

1. _____   6. _____

2. _____   7. _____

3. _____   8. _____

4. _____   9. _____

5. _____   10. _____

VOCĀBULA

praeferō praeferre *to prefer*   **sciō scīre** *to know*
rūrī *in the country*

COLLOQUIUM

Complete the dialog with suitable expressions chosen from the following list:

Amphitheātrum aut forum frequentō.
Nōn habeō. In parvō cēnāculō habitō.
Ita. Ūnā cum multīs amīcīs studeō et ludō.
Quia multās rēs ibi vidēre et facĕre possum.

RĒS PERSŌNĀLĒS

Animals share our world with us. Write the Latin names for:

1. Your favorite domestic animal _____

farm animal _____

wild animal _____

2. Name five other animals in Latin that live on the farm or in the country:

_____

_____

_____

_____

_____

3. Name five animals that you can see in the zoo:

_____   _____

_____   _____

_____

THE LATIN CONNECTION

Look over the list of Latin words and the list of English words that are derived from the Latin words. Then write the English derivative in the space next to its Latin origin:

1. cavum   _____

2. plūma   _____

3. astūtus   _____

4. vēlōcitās   _____

5. custodīre   _____

6. cella   _____

7. dīvidĕre   _____

8. societās   _____

9. pars, partis   _____

10. linea   _____

society
line
astute
cell
divide
plume
part
custodian
cave
velocity

Recōgnitiō V (Lectiōnēs XVII-XX)

Lectiō XVII

40	XL	quadrāgintā		50	L	quīnquāgintā
41	XLI	quadrāgintā ūnus		60	LX	sexāgintā
42	XLII	quadrāgintā duo		70	LXX	septuāgintā
43	XLIII	quadrāgintā trēs		80	LXXX	octōgintā
44	XLIV	quadrāgintā quattuor		90	XC	nōnāgintā
45	XLV	quadrāgintā quīnque		100	C	centum
46	XLVI	quadrāgintā sex		500	D	quīngentī
47	XLVII	quadrāgintā septem		1000	M	mīlle
48	XLVIII	duodēquīnquāgintā				
49	XLIX	ūndēquīnquāgintā				

Formation of the imperfect tense of all verbs:

$$
\left.
\begin{array}{ll}
\text{I} & \textbf{portā} \\
\text{II} & \textbf{habē} \\
\text{III} & \textbf{dīcē} \\
\text{III -iō} & \textbf{capiē} \\
\text{IV} & \textbf{audiē}
\end{array}
\right\}
+
\left\{
\begin{array}{l}
\textbf{-bam} \\
\textbf{-bās} \\
\textbf{-bat} \\
\textbf{-bāmus} \\
\textbf{-bātis} \\
\textbf{-bant}
\end{array}
\right.
$$

Lectiō XVIII

Formation of adverbs:

a. The ending of the adverb in Latin is **-ē** if the adverb comes from an adjective with endings **-us -a -um**:

sevēr*us* **-*a* -*um*** *severe*   **sevēr***ē* *severely*

b. The ending of the adverb in Latin is **-iter** if the adverb comes from an adjective with endings **-is -is -e**:

fidēl*is* **-*is* -*e*** *faithful*   **fidēl***iter* *faithfully*

c. The ending of the adverb in Latin is **-ter** if the adverb comes from an adjective of the third class with endings other than **-is -is -e**:

prūdēn*s* *prudent*   **prūden***ter* *prudently*

d. Many other adverbs have various endings: **nunc** (*now*), **deinde** (*then*), **interdum** (*sometimes*).

Lectiō XIX

a. A verb expressing a command is called an imperative. The imperative forms of the various families of verbs are:

	I	II	III	III -iō	IV
SINGULAR:	portā	tenē	mitte	cape	audī
	} carry!	} hold!	} send!	} take!	} hear!
PLURAL:	portāte	tenēte	mittite	capite	audīte

b. Four verbs of the third family of verbs have no imperative ending in the singular:

dīc	say!
dūc	lead!
fac	do!
fer	bring!

The plural of **fer** is also irregular: **ferte.**

c. Negative commands are expressed by **nōlī** (singular) and **nōlīte** (plural) and the infinitive of the verb:

SINGULAR:	**Nōlī timēre!**	*Do not fear!*
PLURAL:	**Nōlīte timēre!**	*Do not fear!*

Lectiō XX

The present tense of **ferre** (*to bring, bear, take*) has several irregular forms in the present tense:

ferō	ferimus
fers	fertis
fert	ferunt

Āctivitātēs

A. Write the Latin word under the picture you see. Then circle the Latin word in the puzzle on page 329:

1. _____   2. _____

3. _____

8. _____

4. _____

9. _____

5. _____

10. _____

6. _____

11. _____

7. _____

12. _____

13.  _____

18. _____

14. _____

19. _____

15. _____

20. _____

16. _____

21. _____

17. _____

22. _____

328   *RECOGNITIO V*

```
B  A  C  C  H  U  S  D  V  M  F  N
A  S  T  R  U  M  I  I  U  I  L  A
L  U  P  U  S  G  M  A  L  N  U  V
A  N  C  O  R  A  I  N  P  E  C  I
E  Q  U  U  S  L  A  A  E  R  T  C
N  A  V  I  S  L  E  O  S  V  U  U
A  N  A  S  M  U  O  R  A  A  S  L
U  R  S  U  S  S  V  E  N  U  S  A
F  A  S  I  N  U  S  K  A  V  I  S
E  L  E  P  H  A  N  T  U  S  A  R
```

B. After filling in all the horizontal slots, look at the vertical box to find the mystery word that ties all the other words together:

1. duck   ___ ___ ___ ___

2. rabbit   ___ ___ ___ ___ ___ ___ ___ ___ ___

3. monkey   ___ ___ ___ ___

4. mouse   ___ ___ ___

5. camel   ___ ___ ___ ___ ___

6. lion   ___ ___ ___

7. chicken   ___ ___ ___ ___ ___ ___

8. bird   ___ ___ ___

C. Write out the numbers in Latin and then fit them correctly into the puzzle. Numbers that are followed by an (H) fit into horizontal blocks; numbers that are followed by a (V) fit into vertical blocks:

3 letters

II (H) _____

VI (H) _____

4 letters

I (H) _____

VIII (V) _____

III (H) _____

5 letters

X (H) _____

IX (H) _____

M (V) _____

6 letters

C (H) _____

VII (V) _____

7 letters

XX (H) _____

XI (H) _____

V (V) _____

XVI (V) _____

8 letters

XIII (V) _____

IV (H) _____

XXX (V) _____

XII (V) _____

12 letters

XVIII (V) _____

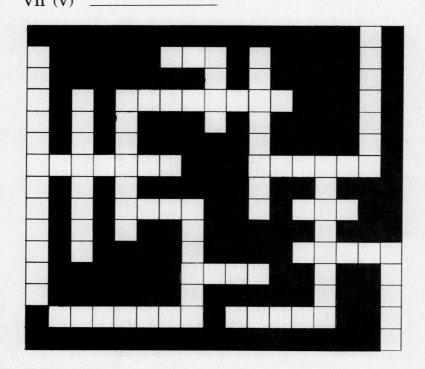

D. After filling in all the horizontal slots, look at the vertical boxes to find the mystery word:

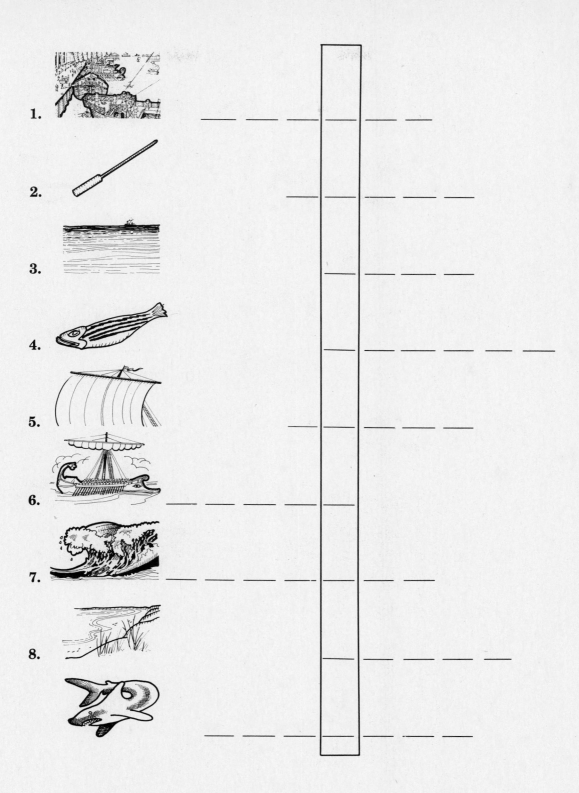

1. ___ ___ ___ ___ ___

2. ___ ___ ___ ___

3. ___ ___ ___

4. ___ ___ ___ ___ ___

5. ___ ___ ___

6. ___ ___ ___ ___

7. ___ ___ ___ ___

8. ___ ___ ___ ___

___ ___ ___ ___

E. Picture Story. Can you read this story. Much of it is in picture form. Whenever you come to a picture, read it as if it were a Latin word:

Ego et [woman] et per [forest] saepe errāmus, ubi multa animālia habitant. [bird] in [tree] sedet et pīpilat. [wolf] et [bear] et [fox] ad [water] veniunt et [spring] bibunt. [eagle] per [sky] volat. [lion] et [elephant] et [monkey] in hāc silvā non habitant.

Ultra silvam est [road], ubi animālia rūstica habitant. [sheep] et [cow] in prātō edunt. [rabbit] per agrum currit. [hen] et [rooster] ubīque sunt. [farmer] ē [farmhouse] venit et nōs ad cēnam invītat.

Pars
Sexta

XXI

Vestīmenta et ornāmenta

Perfect Tense

1 As you have seen in the pictures throughout this book, the Roman style of clothes was quite different from our own. Men and boys never wore pants. In Roman times, only "barbarians" wore pants. And Romans rarely wore hats. They wore stockings only in winter to keep warm; in the Rome area, winters were never long or very cold. All Romans—men, women, boys, and girls—wore a loose-fitting, knee-length garment without sleeves, called a tunic. If the weather got chilly, they might wear several tunics one on top of the other. Boys and men wore similar clothes, and girls and women wore similar clothes. The clothes of women and girls were more colorful than those of men and boys. The ordinary Roman owned so few clothes that there were no built-in closets in bedrooms.

Can you guess the meanings of these new words?

tunica -ae *f*

toga -ae *f*

stola -ae *f*

vēlum -ī *n*

solea -ae *f*

calceus -ī *m*

335

cingulum -ī *n*

paenula -ae *f*

lacerna -ae *f*

petasus -ī *m*

monīle -is *n*

gemma -ae *f*

anulus -ī *m*

inaurēs -ium *fpl*

fībula -ae *f*

armilla -ae *f*

Activitās

A. **Quid id est?** Write the name of each item in the space provided:

1. _____

2. _____

3. _____

4. _____

5. _____

6. _____

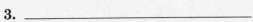

7. _____

8. _____

9. _____

10. _____

11. _____

12. _____

13. _____

15. _____

14. _____

16. _____

2 You have learned how to express a repeated or continuous action in the past with the imperfect tense. Now you will learn how to express a single action in the past with the PERFECT TENSE. You might say that the imperfect tense represents a moving picture, while the PERFECT TENSE represents a snapshot. The endings of the PERFECT TENSE are the same for all verbs. But the endings are added, not to the present stem, but to the perfect stem:

I	**portāv**		**-ī**
II	**tenu**		**-istī**
III	**dīx**	+	**-it**
III -iō	**cēp**		**-imus**
IV	**audīv**		**-istis**
			-ērunt

The verb in the perfect tense is equivalent to the simple past in English:

portāvī	_I carried_
tenuī	_I held_
dīxī	_I said_
cēpī	_I took, caught_
audīvī	_I heard_

Occasionally, the perfect tense may be equivalent to an English present perfect (**portāvī** _I have carried_) if the sentence as a whole suggests such a meaning.

Āctivitātēs

B. Write out the perfect tense of the following verbs, using the perfect stems:

ego	portāv_____	tenu_____	dīx_____	cēp_____	audīv_____
tū	_____	_____	_____	_____	_____
is, ea, id	_____	_____	_____	_____	_____
nōs	_____	_____	_____	_____	_____
vōs	_____	_____	_____	_____	_____
eī, eae, ea	_____	_____	_____	_____	_____

C. Which of these endings are used only for the perfect tense? Circle them and then write them in the correct order:

1. -istī **4.** -bam **7.** -ērunt
2. -ō **5.** -it **8.** -istis
3. -imus **6.** -tis **9.** -ī

SINGULAR _____ PLURAL _____

_____ _____

_____ _____

D. Most of the verbs of the **-āre** family have the same stem in the perfect tense: **-āv.** You have met all of the following verbs in earlier lessons. Change each of the verbs from the present to the perfect tense, but keep the verb in the same person. Then write the English meaning for the perfect tense:

EXAMPLE: **labōrat** *he is working, he works* **labōrāvit** *he worked*

1. natō _____ _____

2. ambulant _____ _____

3. habitāmus _____ _____

4. gustās _____ _____

5. narrat _____ _____

6. clāmātis _____ _____

E. Give the infinitive and the perfect tense of the following verbs:

    Example: volō   **volāre**   **volāvī**

1. nāvigō   _____   _____

2. optō   _____   _____

3. rogō   _____   _____

4. cantō   _____   _____

5. vēnditō   _____   _____

4   Here are a few important verbs of the **-āre** family that have an irregular perfect stem, but their endings are regular:

dō	*I give, am giving*	**dare**	**dedī**	*I gave*
cōnstō	*I cost*	**cōnstāre**	**cōnstitī**	*I cost*
juvō	*I help, am helping*	**juvāre**	**jūvī**	*I helped*
lavō	*I wash, am washing*	**lavāre**	**lāvī**	*I washed*
stō	*I stand, am standing*	**stāre**	**stetī**	*I stood*

The perfect stem of the verb **esse** is irregular:

    sum *I am*   **esse**   **fuī** *I was*

Āctivitātēs

F. Complete with the correct form of the perfect tense:

1. (lāvit, lāvērunt)   Māter fenestrās herī _____.

2. (jūvī, jūvimus)   Ego et Caecilia mātrem _____.

3. (stetistī, stetistis)   Cūr tū in stāgnō _____.

4. (cōnstitit, cōnstitērunt) Stola mea duodecim dēnāriīs _____.

5. (dedī, dedit)   Pater mihi pecūniam _____.

6. (fuī, fuērunt)   Multī amīcī mihi in Siciliā _____.

7. (fuistī, fuistis)   Puerī, discipulī dīligentēs semper _____.

8. (dedit, dedērunt)   Avia mea mihi crūstulum _____.

G. In the following story, change the verb from the present tense to the perfect tense:

Claudia et Tullia in tabernā vestiāriā

taberna vestiāria *f clothing store*

_____. Tunicās et stolās novās
(stant)

emĕre _____. Tunica quīnque
(optant)

denāriīs _____ et stola novem
(cōnstat)

denāriīs _____. Satis pecūniae
(cōnstat)

satis pecuniae *enough money*

Claudiae nōn _____, sed Tullia
(est)

Claudiam _____, nam Tullia trēs
(juvat)

denāriōs Claudiae _____. Claudia
(dat)

_____ laeta, quia satis pecūniae
(est)

eī _____. Puellae deinde
(est)

eī *to her*

pecūniam vestiāriō _____ et
(dant)

vestiārius -ī *m (clothes) salesman*

vestiārius vestīmenta puellīs

vestīmenta -ōrum *npl clothes*

_____.
(vēnditat)

5 Many verbs of the **-ēre** family have the perfect stem ending in **-u:**

habeō *I have*   **habēre**   **habuī** *I had*

Activitās

H. In the space provided, write the perfect tense (first person) of the following verbs:

1. doceō   docēre   _____

2. doleō   dolēre   _____

3. exerceō	exercēre	_____
4. jaceō	jacēre	_____
5. lateō	latēre	_____
6. mereō	merēre	_____
7. sileō	silēre	_____
8. studeō	studēre	_____
9. teneō	tenēre	_____
10. timeō	timēre	_____
11. terreō	terrēre	_____

6 Other verbs of the **-ēre** family do not have perfect stems ending in **-u.** Note the different perfect stems:

moveō	*I move, am moving*	**movēre**	**mōvī**	*I moved*
respondeō	*I answer, am answering*	**respondēre**	**respondī**	*I answered*
videō	*I see*	**vidēre**	**vīdī**	*I saw*
maneō	*I stay, am staying*	**manēre**	**mānsī**	*I stayed*
rīdeō	*I laugh, am laughing*	**rīdēre**	**rīsī**	*I laughed*
subrīdeō	*I smile, am smiling*	**subrīdēre**	**subrīsī**	*I smiled*

You will see the perfect tense of other verbs as you go along. But before you read the next story, here are a few verbs of the **-ēre** family that you need to know:

dīcō	*I say, am saying*	**dīcĕre**	**dīxī**	*I said*
gerō	*I wear, am wearing*	**gerĕre**	**gessī**	*I wore*
induō	*I put on, am putting on*	**induĕre**	**induī**	*I put on*
exuō	*I take off, am taking off*	**exuĕre**	**exuī**	*I took off*

7 Now read the following story, noting particularly the use of the perfect tense:

Ego sum Claudius. Amīcus meus, Fabius, in proximō vīcō habitat. Herī nātālem sēdecimum celebrāvit. Fabius mē et sorōrem meam ad convīvium suum invītāvit.

proximus -a -um *next*
  vīcus -ī *m street, block*
  nātālis -is *m birthday*
celebrāre *to celebrate*
convīvium -ī *n party*
invītāre *to invite*

Ego ipse tunicam fuscam cum cingulō caeruleō induī; deinde calceōs novōs induī. Circum collum bullam meam gessī.

bulla -ae *f charm*

Claudia, soror mea, tam superba est! Tunicam roseam pulchram induit; deinde stolam super tunicam induit. Inaurēs cum gemmīs dē auribus pendēbant. In bracchiō sinistrō armillam gessit. Circum ejus collum

superbus -a -um *proud*

sinister -tra -trum *left*

gessit monīle pulchrum. Anulum aureum in digitō gessit.

Ut in speculum spectavit, exclāmāvit, "Ō, quam bella sum!"

speculum -ī *n mirror*
quam *how*

"Ita, ita!" murmurāvī.

murmurāre *to murmur*

Deinde Claudia dīxit: "Ō, stola mea nimis longa est. Nēmō meās soleās pulchrās vidēre potest." Itaque stolam roseam exuit et stolam flāvam induit. Iterum animum mūtāvit et stolam viridem induit. Vēlum super comam gessit.

nēmō -inis *m no one*

animus -ī *m mind*
mūtāre *to change*

Dēnique exclāmāvī: "Jam tempus est discēdĕre, Claudia. Nōndum parāta es? Tardī sumus."

dēnique *finally*
discēdō discēdĕre discessī *to leave*   **nōndum** *not yet*
tardus -a -um *late*

"Patientia, patientia, cāre frāter," dīxit Claudia.

patientia -ae *f patience*
cārus -a -um *dear*

Ut ego jānuam aperuī, Claudia exclāmāvit: "Dī superī! Ecce, pluit! Ubi est paenula mea?"

aperiō aperīre aperuī *to open*
Dī superī! *Ye gods above!*
pluit *it is raining*

"Bene!" ego respondī; "hodiē nātālem domī celebrāmus."

"Super meum corpus mortuum," exclāmāvit Claudia et per pluviam ambulāvit, et ego dīrēctō post cāram sorōrem meam.

dīrēctō *directly*

Activitās

I.   Respondē ad quaestiōnēs:

1. Quis nātālem celebrāvit?

_____

2. Quot annōs nātus est?

_____

3. Ubi Fabius habitāvit?

_____

4. Quid Claudius circum collum gessit?

_____

5. Quālem (*what kind of*) tunicam Claudia prīmum induit?

_____

6. Quid Claudia in auribus gessit?

_____

7. Quid Claudia in bracchiō sinistrō gessit?

_____

8. Quid Claudia in digitō gessit?

_____

9. Cūr Claudia stolam roseam exuit?

_____

10. Quālem stolam Claudia deinde induit?

_____

11. Quālem stolam dēnique gessit?

_____

THE LATIN CONNECTION

Look over the list of Latin words and the list of English words that derive from the Latin words. Then write the English word in the space next to the Latin word that is connected with it in meaning:

celebrate
natal, prenatal, postnatal
sinister
gem
sole (of the shoe)
veil
tardy
stole
patience
vestment
superb
ornament

1. solea _____

2. gemma _____

3. stola _____

4. vēlum _____

5. vestīmentum _____

6. ornāmentum _____

7. nātālis _____

8. sinister _____

9. tardus _____

10. celebrāre _____

11. patientia _____

12. superbus _____

CONVERSĀTIŌ

VOCĀBULA

necessārius -a -um *necessary*
dōnum -ī *gift*
lūdificāre *to kid, fool*

ipsa *myself*
jam *already*

COLLOQUIUM

Complete the dialog with expressions chosen from the following list:

gerĕre

mē paenitet

trēdecim annōs

convīvium nātāle

tē lūdificāre

mihi nōn est

dōnum

mihi placent

nōn necessāria est

quot annōs

calceī meī

QUAESTIŌNĒS PERSŌNĀLĒS

1. Convīvia nātālia amās?

   _____

2. Vestīmenta nova tibi placent?

   _____

3. Habēsne multa ornāmenta?

   _____

4. Gerisne anulum in digitō tuō?

   _____

5. Geritne māter tua inaurēs?

   _____

6. Gerisne tū an māter tua monīle circum collum?

   _____

7. Praefersne calceōs novōs an calceōs veterēs?

   _____

8. Amīcī tuī tē saepe lūdificant?

   _____

9. Lūdificāsne amīcōs tuōs saepe?

   _____

10. Quandō nātālem tuum celebrās?

    _____

Pronouns

1   Can you guess the meanings of these new words?

urbs *-is f*

templum *-ī n*

amphitheātrum *-ī n*

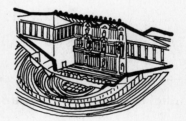

theātrum *-ī n*

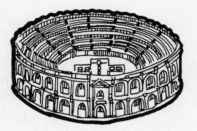

hortī publicī *mpl*

schola *-ae f*

forum *-ī n*

Circus Maximus *-ī m*

348

thermae -ārum *fpl*

cūria -ae *f*

popīna -ae *f*

īnsula -ae *f*

macellum -ī *n*

aquaeductus -ūs *m*

bibliothēca -ae *f*

lectīca -ae *f*

raeda -ae *f*

mūrus -ī *m*

Āctivitās

A. Identify the pictures and give the genitive case and gender:

1. _____

2. _____

3. _____

4. _____

5. _____

6. _____

7. _____

8. _____

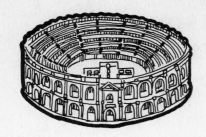

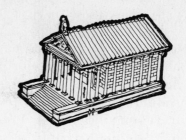

9. _____

14. _____

10. _____

15. _____

11. _____

16. _____

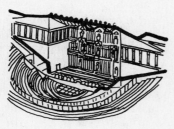

12. _____

17. _____

13. _____

18. _____

2 Now read the following story about an ancient Roman city:

Nōmen mihi est Caecilius. In magnā urbe habitō. Lūcius, cōnsōbrīnus meus, rūrī habitat. Abhinc duōs diēs Lūcius urbem prīmum vīsitāvit. Per portam in mūrō urbem intrāvimus. Ego ipse Lūcium per urbem dūxī. Per hortōs pūblicōs ambulāvimus, ubi flōrēs rubrōs et albōs et flāvōs vīdimus. Multa et magna aedificia vīdimus. Vehicula in viīs ubīque festīnābant: lectīcae, raedae, plaustra.

> **cōnsōbrīn*us* -*ī* m** *cousin*
> **abhinc** *ago*
> **prīmum** *for the first time*
>   **port*a* -*ae* f** *gate*

> **aedifici*um* -*ī* n** *building*
>   **vehicul*um* -*ī* n** *vehicle*
> **ubīque** *everywhere*
>   **festīnāre** *to rush (about)*

"Quis," quaesīvit Lūcius, "in illā lectīcā est?"

> **quaerō quaerĕre quaesīvī** *to ask*

"Est senātor," respondī. "Ad cūriam festīnat, ubi ōrātiōnem habēre optat."

> **cūri*a* -*ae* f** *senate building*
> **ōrātiō -ōnis f:** **ōrātiōnem habēre** *to give a speech*

"Senātor nōn festīnat," dīxit cōnsōbrīnus meus et subrīsit, "sed quattuor servī festīnant quī senātōrem in lectīcā portant."

> **quī** *who*

"Rectē dīcis," respondī.

> **rectē dīcis** *you are right*

"Cūr tot templa in forō sunt?" quaesīvit cōnsōbrīnus meus.

"Quia Rōmānī multōs deōs deāsque adōrant," explicuī, "et quisque templum suum habet."

> **explicō explicāre explicuī** *to explain*
>   **quisque** *each one*

Ē forō excessimus et popīnam intrāvimus, ubi jūs calidum et pānem et cāseum et acētāria ēdimus. Post cibum thermās intrāvimus, ubi nōs lāvimus et in piscīnā magnā natāvimus.

> **excēdō excēdĕre excessī** *to go out*
> **edō esse ēdī** *to eat*
> **cib*us* ī m** *meal*
> **lavō lavāre lāvī** *to wash*
>   **piscīn*a* -*ae* f** *swimming pool*

Dēnique domum īvimus et somnum pōmerīdiānum cēpimus.

> **eō īre īvī** *to go*
>   **somn*um* -*ī* n** *sleep;*
>   **pōmerīdiān*us* -*a* -*um*** *afternoon:* **somnum pōmerīdiānum** *siesta*
> **magnificēns -entis** *magnificent*
> **crās** *tomorrow*

"Vita in urbe est magnificēns!" exclāmāvit cōnsōbrīnus meus. "Crās sperō vidēre theātrum et amphitheātrum et macellum et aquaeductum et . . ."

"Satis, satis!" ego respondī, "pedēs meī jam dolent."

Activitātēs

B. Respondē ad quaestiōnēs:

1. Ubi Lūcius habitat?

_____

2. Cūr tot templa in forō fuērunt?

_____

3. Quis senātōrem in lectīcā portāvit?

_____

4. Quid senātor in cūriā fēcit?

_____

5. Ubi Caecilius et cōnsōbrīnus ēdērunt?

_____

6. Quid in thermīs fēcērunt puerī?

_____

C. Various activities of the Romans are described in the left column. The right column indicates where the activities took place. Write the matching letter in the space next to the activity:

1. Rōmānī deōs deāsque adōrāvērunt. _____
2. Rōmānī gladiātōrēs spectant. _____
3. Rōmānī āctōrēs et āctrīcēs spectant. _____
4. Magister discipulōs docuit. _____
5. Rōmānī sē lāvērunt. _____
6. Rōmānī habitāvērunt. _____
7. Senātōrēs ōrātiōnēs habuērunt. _____
8. Puerī puellaeque lūdēbant. _____
9. Rōmānī cibum ēdērunt. _____
10. Rōmānī librōs lēgērunt. _____
11. Rōmānī equōs spectāvērunt. _____
12. Rōmānī pōma et holera ēmērunt. _____

a. in īnsulā
b. in scholā
c. in āreā
d. in cūriā
e. in macellō
f. in popīnā
g. in templō
h. in amphitheātrō
i. in Circō Maximō
j. in theātrō
k. in bibliothēcā
l. in thermīs

3 In Lesson 14, you learned the dative case of the pronouns **ego, tu,** etc. In Lesson 15, you learned possessive adjectives. Now is a good time to review them. In the spaces provided, write out the possessives of the pronouns:

			MASCULINE	FEMININE	NEUTER
SINGULAR:	**ego**	*my:*	_____	_____	_____
	tū	*your:*	_____	_____	_____
	is	*his:*	_____	_____	_____
	ea	*her:*	_____	_____	_____
	id	*its:*	_____	_____	_____

			MASCULINE	FEMININE	NEUTER
PLURAL:	**nōs**	*our:*	_____	_____	_____
	vōs	*your:*	_____	_____	_____
	eī	*their:*	_____	_____	_____
	eae	*their:*	_____	_____	_____
	ea	*their:*	_____	_____	_____

Now learn the rest of the forms of the pronouns:

SINGULAR

NOMINATIVE	**ego**	**tū**	**is**	**ea**	**id**
GENITIVE	**meī**	**tuī**	**ejus**	**ejus**	**ejus**
ACCUSATIVE	**mē**	**tē**	**eum**	**eam**	**id**
DATIVE	**mihi**	**tibi**	**eī**	**eī**	**eī**
ABLATIVE	**mē**	**tē**	**eō**	**ea**	**eō**

PLURAL

NOMINATIVE	**nōs**	**vōs**	**eī**	**eae**	**ea**
GENITIVE	**nostrum**	**vestrum**	**eōrum**	**eārum**	**eōrum**
ACCUSATIVE	**nōs**	**vōs**	**eōs**	**eās**	**ea**
DATIVE	**nōbīs**	**vōbīs**	**eīs**	**eīs**	**eīs**
ABLATIVE	**nōbīs**	**vōbīs**	**eīs**	**eīs**	**eīs**

The combination of the preposition **cum** with the ablative of certain pronouns becomes **mēcum, tēcum, nōbīscum, vōbīscum;** but **cum eō, cum eā, cum eīs.**

Āctivitātēs

D. In the following phrases, substitute the pronoun for the noun. Remember that, if the noun is masculine or feminine, even though it refers to a thing, the pronoun also must be masculine or feminine:

1. in lectīcā   in _____
2. sine macellō   sine _____
3. per portam   per _____
4. ob scholam   ob _____
5. inter īnsulās   inter _____

6. intra mūrōs   intra _____
7. in bibliothēcā in _____
8. prō templō   prō _____
9. post popīnam post _____
10. in theātrō   in _____

E. Rewrite the following sentences, substituting the pronoun for the noun in bold type:

1. Aulus cum **amīcīs** lūdēbat.   _____
2. Pater cum **fīliō** labōrāvit.   _____
3. Īnfāns in **lectō** dormiēbat.   _____
4. Cūr **raedam** spectābās?   _____
5. Tōnsor in **tōnstrīnā** comam tondet.   _____
6. **Astra** spectābāmus.   _____
7. Leō cum **ursō** pugnābat.   _____
8. **Templum** vīsitāvimus.   _____
9. Appius **Jūliam** amat.   _____
10. Mūrus **urbis** est altus.   _____
11. Dōnum **puellae** dedī.   _____
12. Leōnēs in **montibus** sunt.   _____

F. Reverse the following sentences, making the subject the object and the object the subject. Be sure to make the verb agree with the new subject:

EXAMPLE: Ego consōbrīnum meum exspectō.
            I am waiting for my cousin.

            Consōbrīnus meus mē exspectat.
            My cousin is waiting for me.

1. Ego avum meum amō.   _____

2. Is aviam vīsitāvit. _____

3. Eae ursum timent. _____

4. Tū magistrum nōn vīdistī. _____

5. Nōs senātōrem salūtāmus. _____

G. In the following sentences, reverse the subject with the object of the preposition:

EXAMPLE: Ego cum puerīs ludēbam.   Puerī mēcum ludēbant.
I was playing with the boys.   _The boys were playing with me._

1. Tū cum frātre studēbās. _____

2. Nōs cum patre ēdimus. _____

3. Vōs cum puellīs cantābātis. _____

4. Tūne sine parentibus venīs? _____

5. Ego cum cane ambulābam. _____

6. Eae cum amīcīs rīsērunt. _____

4 Now enjoy this story about the city mouse and the country mouse:

Ōlim mūs rūsticus in cavō in margine silvae habitābat. Pauper erat sed contentus et līber. Amīcum suum, mūrem urbānum, in cavum excēpit. Cēnam simplicem hospitī parāvit: grāna hordeī et trīticī. Mūrēs in lectīs strāmentī jacuērunt. Sed hospes superbus cēnā simplicī nōn contentus erat.

"Quōmodo contentus esse potes," quaesīvit mūs urbānus, "rūrī sīc habitāre? Venī mēcum in urbem. Ibi tamquam rēgēs in domō spatiōsā vīvĕre possumus."

Itaque ē cavō saliērunt et mediā nocte sub urbis mūrum rēpsērunt et domum spatiōsam intrāvērunt. In triclīniō magnō accubuērunt. Mūs urbānus amīcum suum super lectum purpureum locāvit. Ē culīnā fercula dē cēnā

rūstic_us -a -um_ country
  margō _-inis f_ edge
content_us -a -um_ content(ed)
  līber lībera līber_um free_
urbān_us -a -um_ city, from the city
excipiō excipĕre excēpī _to welcome_
  hospes _-itis m_ guest
grān_um -ī n_ grain
  horde_um -ī n_ barley
  trītic_um -ī n_ wheat
strāment_um -ī n_ straw
quōmodo _how_
sīc _like this_
tamquam _like, as_
vīvō vīvĕre vīxī _to live_

saliō salīre saliī _to jump_
  mediā nocte _in the middle of the night_
rēpō rēpĕre rēpsī _to creep_
accumbō accumbĕre accubuī _to recline at table_
lect_us -ī m_ dining couch
locāre _to place_
  fercul_um -ī n_ tray

hesternā afferēbat. Mūs rūsticus carnem et carōtās et lactūcam et cucumerēs cupidē gustābat, cum subitō canis ēnormis per jānuam vēnit et latrāvit. Mūs rūsticus, perterritus, dē lectō saliit et dīxit, "Tālis vīta mihi nōn placet. Valē. Silva cavumque mē magis delectant. Ibi vīta est simplex, sed utque tūtus et līber sum."

hestern*us -a -um* yesterday's
  afferō afferre attulī *to bring*
cupidē *eagerly*
cum subitō *when suddenly*

perterrit*us -a -um* very scared
  tāl*is -is -e *such a*
magis *more*
utque *at least*

Activitās

H. Respondē ad quaestiōnēs:

1. Ubi mūs rūsticus habitābat?

_____

2. Quis mūrem rūsticum vīsitāvit?

_____

3. Quid mūs rūsticus prō mūre urbānō parāvit?

_____

4. Ubi jacuērunt mūrēs?

_____

5. Placuitne cēna simplex mūrō urbānō?

_____

6. Quandō mūrēs sub urbis mūrōs rēpsērunt?

_____

7. Ubi accubuērunt mūrēs in domō spatiōsā?

_____

8. Ubi mūs urbānus amīcum locāvit?

_____

9. Quid mūs rūsticus cupidē gustāvit?

_____

10. Quis mūrem rūsticum et mūrem urbānum terruit?

_____

11. Quid mūrem rūsticum dēlectāvit magis quam domus spatiōsa?

_____

12. Cūr mūs rūsticus vītam rūsticam amāvit?

_____

THE LATIN CONNECTION

Look over the list of Latin words and the list of English derivatives. Then write the English derivative in the space next to the Latin origin:

1. urbānus _____

2. rūsticus _____

3. ubīque _____

4. ōrātiō _____

5. cavum _____

6. margō _____

7. simplex _____

8. grānum _____

9. porta _____

10. vehiculum _____

11. aquaeductus _____

12. mūrus _____

oration
ubiquitous
vehicle
portal
grain
cave
margin
urbane
mural
aqueduct
simple
rustic

CONVERSĀTIŌ

VOCĀBULA

rūrī *in the country*
trānseō trānsīre trānsiī *to move*
praeferō praeferre praetulī *to prefer*
plēnus -a -um *full*
dē quibus *from which*

carpō carpĕre carpsī *to pick*
nōn sōlum . . . sed etiam *not only . . . but also*
equitāre *to ride horseback*
strepitus -ūs *m noise*
quiēs -ētis *f quiet*

COLLOQUIUM

Complete the dialog by writing Rufus' replies, choosing them from the list below:

Rūrī sunt fontēs et flūviī et stāgna.

Rūrī sunt multī equī. Ego nōn sōlum equōs vidēre possum sed etiam cotīdiē in prātō equitāre possum.

Ita. Sed rūrī strepitum vehiculōrum nōn habēmus. Quiētem rūris praeferō.

Rūrī sunt prāta plēna flōrum pulchrōrum.

Quia ego rūs urbī praeferō, Quīnte.

Rūrī sunt arborēs dē quibus ego māla et persica et pira et cerasa carpēre possum.

QUAESTIŌNĒS PERSŌNĀLĒS

Quid praefers tū?

1. Rūs an urbem? _____

2. Piscīnam an stāgnum? _____

3. Īnsulam in urbe an vīllam rūrī? _____

4. Strepitum vehiculōrum an quiētem rūris? _____

5. Tabernās pōmārias an arborēs plēnās fructūs? _____

6. Scholam in urbe an labōrem in agrīs? _____

7. Equōs vidēre an equitāre in prātō? _____

8. Aquam ex aquaeductū an aquam ē flūviō? _____

XXIII | Mīlitia

Superlative

1 Can you guess the meaning of these words?

mīles *-itis m*

imperātor *-ōris m*

scūtum *-ī n*

gladius *-ī m*

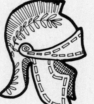

galea *-ae f*

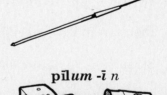

pīlum *-ī n*

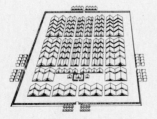

curriculum *-ī n*

centuriō *-ōnis m*

lōrīca *-ae f*

castra *-ōrum npl*

balteus *-ī m*

caliga *-ae f*

362

eques -itis _m_

exercitus -ūs _m_

signum -ī _n_

Activitās

A. Quid id est? Write the correct Latin name below each picture. Give the genitive case and the gender of each:

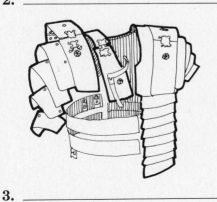

1. _____

2. _____

3. _____

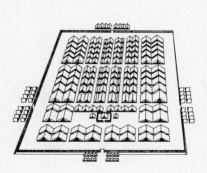

4. _____

5. _____

6. _____

7. _____

11. _____

8. _____

12. _____

9. _____

13. _____

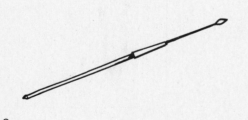

10. _____

14. _____

15. _____

364   *LECTIO XXIII*

2　So far, all the adjectives that you have used were in the simple form called the positive degree. Latin indicates the highest degree, called the SUPERLATIVE degree, by a special ending. For an adjective that ends in **-us -a -um,** the endings of the superlative degree are **-issim*us* -*a* -*um*:**

POSITIVE	SUPERLATIVE
clār*us* -*a* -*um* clear	clār*issimus* -*a* -*um* clearest, very clear
nov*us* -*a* -*um* new	nov*issimus* -*a* -*um* newest, very new

Adjectives in **-er** end in **-*rimus* -*a* -*um*** to form the superlative:

POSITIVE	SUPERLATIVE
pulch*er* pulchr*a* pulchr*um* beautiful	pulcher*rimus* -*a* -*um* most beautiful, very beautiful
miser miser*a* miser*um* poor, wretched	miser*rimus* -*a* -*um* most wretched, very wretched
celer celer*is* celer*e* fast	celer*rimus* -*a* -*um* fastest, very fast

Adjectives of the third declension have **-issim*us* -*a* -*um*** in the superlative:

POSITIVE	SUPERLATIVE
fort*is* -*is* -*e* brave	fort*issimus* -*a* -*um* bravest, very brave

A few adjectives ending in **-ilis** have **-lim*us* -*a* -*um*** in the superlative:

POSITIVE	SUPERLATIVE
facil*is* -*is* -*e* easy	facil*limus* -*a* -*um* easiest, very easy
difficil*is* -*is* -*e* difficult	difficil*limus* -*a* -*um* most difficult, very difficult
simil*is* -*is* -*e* similar	simil*limus* -*a* -*um* most similar, very similar

Āctivitās

B.　Complete the sentences with the correct superlative form of the adjective:

1. Mīles Rōmānus galeam _____ gessit. (pulcher)

2. Jūlius Caesar erat imperātor _____. (fortis)

3. Pater et fīlius togās _____ gerēbant. (similis)

4. Puerī sine amīcīs sunt _____. (miser)

5. Īnsulae in urbe sunt _____. (altus)

6. Astra in caelō sunt _____. (clārus)

7. Puella Rōmāna est _____. (bellus)

8. Vīta in mīlitiā est _____. (difficilis)

3 Pay special attention to superlative endings of third-declension adjectives that have the same nominative ending for masculine, feminine, and neuter. For these adjectives, the superlative endings are added to the genitive stem:

POSITIVE		SUPERLATIVE
ferōx *wild*	**ferōcis** (genitive case)	**ferōcissimus -a -um** *wildest, very wild*
fēlīx *happy*	**fēlīcis** (genitive case)	**fēlīcissimus -a -um** *happiest, very happy*
ēlegāns *elegant*	**ēlegantis** (genitive case)	**ēlegantissimus -a -um** *most elegant, very elegant*
audāx *bold*	**audācis** (genitive case)	**audācissimus -a -um** *boldest, very bold*
vetus *old*	**veteris** (genitive case)	**veterrimus -a -um** *oldest, very old*

Āctivitās

C. Complete the sentences with the superlative of the adjective in parentheses. (Note that the nominative and genitive cases are supplied):

1. (audāx, audācis) Centuriō Rōmānus est _____ .

2. (ēlegāns, ēlegantis) Caecilia stolam _____ gessit.

3. (prūdēns, prūdentis) Avus meus erat homō _____ .

4. (intellegēns, intellegentis) Gaius Marius erat imperātor

   _____ .

5. (vetus, veteris) Gladius meus est _____ .

6. (obēdiēns, obēdientis) Parentēs līberōs _____ amant.

7. (fēlīx, fēlīcis) Ego sum _____ ubi nōn in scholā sum.

8. (ferōx, ferōcis) Suntne leōnēs animālia _____ ?

4 Just as some adjectives in English have an irregular form in the superlative degree (*good — best*), so also some Latin adjectives have an irregular form in the superlative. Here are some of the common Latin adjectives with irregular superlatives:

POSITIVE	SUPERLATIVE
bonus -a -um *good*	**optimus -a -um** *best, very good*
magnus -a -um *big*	**maximus -a -um** *biggest, very big*
malus -a -um *bad*	**pessimus -a -um** *worst, very bad*
multus -a -um *much* (plural: *many*)	**plūrimus -a -um** *most, very many*
parvus -a -um *small*	**minimus -a -um** *smallest, very small*

Activitās

D. Supply the superlative degree of the adjective in parentheses:

1. (bonus) Claudius est mīles _____ in exercitū.

2. (magnus) Imperātor gladium _____ habet.

3. (parvus) Centuriō caligās _____ gerit.

4. (malus) Mīlitēs fortūnam _____ habuērunt.

5. (multī) _____ mīlitēs trāns montem et vallem iter fēcērunt.

6. (malī) Hodiē discipulī erant _____ in lūdō.

7. (magnus) Bālaenae sunt _____ piscēs in ōceanō.

8. (bonus) Caecilius dōnum amīcō _____ dedit.

9. (magna) Castra Rōmāna sunt _____.

10. (parvus) Horātius est centuriō _____ in exercitū.

5 Now read the following story about Roman valor:

MARCUS: Heus, pater, ubi es?
PATER: Hīc in tablīnō. Quid optās?
MARCUS: Quid facis, pater?
PATER: Epistulās scrībō.
MARCUS: Nārrā, quaesō, mihi, dē mīlitiā Rōmānā, nam tū erās mīles in exercitū.
PATER: Occupātus sum. Ī et rogā mātrem. Ea multās fābulās scit.
MARCUS: Māter quoque occupāta est. Praetereā, nihil dē mīlitiā scit.
PATER: Bene. Cōnsīdē. Ab ipsō initiō Rōmānī erant pugnātōrēs optimī. In Campō Mārtiō prope flūmen Tiberim mīlitēs et equitēs cotīdiē sē exercēbant. Centuriōnēs erant sevērissimī sed aequī. Urbem Rōmam et ejus cīvēs adversus omnēs hostēs dēfendērunt. Mīlitēs erant validissimī et fortissimī.

heus! *hey!*

epistul*a -ae* f *letter*
mīliti*a -ae* f *military service*

occupāt*us -a -um* *busy*

praetereā *besides*
  nihil *nothing*
bene *O.K.*
  ab ipsō initiō *from the very beginning*
pugnāt*or -ōris* m *fighter*
Campus Mārtius *Field of Mars*
  Tiber*is -is* m *Tiber*
sevēr*us -a -um* *stern*
  aequ*us -a -um* *fair*
cīv*is -is* m *citizen*
adversus (+ acc.) *against*
host*is -is* m *enemy*
  dēfendō dēfendĕre dēfendī *to defend*
valid*us -a -um* *strong*

Ūnus fortissimōrum mīlitum fuit Horātius Coclēs. Urbs in maximō perīculō erat, quia exercitus hostium castra dīrectē trāns Tiberim locāvit. Ūnō diē hostēs ē castrīs vēnērunt et pontem Rōmānum trānsīre temptāvērunt. Imperātor hostium erat Porsenna, rēx Etrūscus. Etrūscī erant hostēs Rōmānōrum. Porsenna exercitum suum ē castrīs ēdūxit et ad rīpam Tiberis cum omnibus cōpiīs ruit. Terror in urbe erat maximus. Erat terror etiam in exercitū Rōmānō.

Multī mīlitēs Rōmānī, quī ultrā flūmen erant, trāns pontem fūgērunt; sed ūnus, Horātius Coclēs, trāns pontem nōn fūgit. In capite galeam gessit et in pedibus caligās gessit. Lōrīca pectus ejus prōtexit. Dextrā manū pīlum tenuit; sinistrō bracchiō scūtum portāvit. Gladius dē balteō dēpendit. In ejus corde erat fortitūdō. Ut hostēs et Rōmānī stābant attonitī,

locāre *to place, put*
pōns -tis *m bridge*
temptāre *to try*
Etrūscus -a -um *Etruscan*

rīpa -ae *f bank*
cōpiae -ārum *fpl troops, forces*
 ruō ruĕre ruī *to rush*

ultrā (+ acc.) *on the other side of*
fugiō fugĕre fūgī *to flee*
pectus -oris *n chest*
 prōtegō prōtegĕre prōtexī *to protect*
dēpendō dēpendĕre dēpendī *to hang down*
fortitūdō -inis *f fortitude, courage*
attonitus -a -um *astonished, in astonishment*

"Pontem dēlēte, commīlitēs," exclāmāvit Horātius. Diū et acriter Horātius cum hostibus pugnāvit. Plūrimōs hostēs vulnerāvit. Subitō erat magnus fragor ut pōns in flūmen cecidit. Tum Horātius ūnā cum armīs suīs in flūmen dēsiluit et ad alteram rīpam natāvit. Sīc Horātius Coclēs urbem nostram servāvit."

MARCUS: Gratiās tibi agō, pater. Illa fābula erat mīrābilis. Aliquandō sperō esse mīles.

dēleō dēlēre dēlēvī *to destroy*
   commīles -*itis* m *fellow soldier*
diū et acriter *long and hard*
magnus fragor *loud crash*
cadō cadĕre cecidī *to fall*
   arm*a -ōrum* npl *arms*
ūnā cum *together with*
   dēsiliō dēsilīre dēsiluī *to
   jump down*
alter altera alterum *the other*

mīrābilis -*is* -*e wonderful*
   aliquandō *someday*

Āctivitātēs

E. Respondē ad quaestiōnēs:

1. Ubi Marcus patrem comperit?

_____

2. Quid pater faciēbat?

_____

3. Cūr pater fābulās nārrāre nōn optāvit?

_____

4. Ubi mīlitēs equitēsque Rōmānī sē exercēbant?

_____

5. Ubi est Campus Mārtius?

_____

6. Quis erat ūnus fortissimōrum mīlitum?

_____

7. Cūr urbs Rōma in maximō perīculō erat?

_____

8. Quis erat imperātor hostium?

_____

9. Quid mīlitēs Rōmānī fēcērunt, ubi imperātor hostium exercitum ē castrīs ēdūxit?

_____

10. Quid Horātius Coclēs in capite gessit?

_____

11. Quid in pedibus gessit?

_____

12. Quid pectus ejus prōtēxit?

_____

13. Quid dextrā manū tenēbat?

_____

14. Quid sinistrō bracchiō portābat?

_____

15. Quid dē balteō dēpendēbat?

_____

16. Quid in ejus corde fuit?

_____

17. Quid Horātius exclāmāvit?

_____

18. Quid Horātius fēcit postquam pōns in flūmen cecidit?

_____

F. Fill in the names of the objects worn by the Roman soldier:

6 Adverbs in the superlative degree end in **-ē**:

maximus **-a -um** *biggest, largest*
minimus **-a -um** *smallest*
audācissimus **-a -um** *boldest, very bold*

maximē *most; especially*
minimē *least, to the smallest degree*
audācissimē *most boldly, very boldly*

Āctivitās

G. Complete the sentences with the superlative forms of the adverbs in parentheses:

1. (**fort**_iter_)   Centuriōnēs Rōmānī _____ pugnāvērunt.

2. (**pulchr**_ē_)   Soror mea _____ cantat.

3. (**audāc**_ter_)   Horātius Coclēs urbem Rōmam _____ dēfendit.

4. (**ēlegan**_ter_)   Senātōrēs _____ vīvunt.

5. (**timid**_ē_)   Discipulus magistrō _____ respondit.

6. (**grav**_iter_)   Hostis imperātōrem nostrum _____ vulnerāvit.

7. (**rapid**_ē_)   Tigris per silvās _____ ruit.

8. (**ferōc**_iter_)   Leō cum vulpe _____ pugnāvit.

QUAESTIŌNĒS PERSŌNĀLĒS

1. Quis est amīcus tuus optimus?

_____

2. Quis est amīca tua fidēlissima?

_____

3. Quis est magister tuus sevērissimus (an magistra sevērissima)?

_____

4. Suntne parentēs tuī veterrimī?

_____

5. Quod tempus annī maximē amās?

_____

6. Quod tempus annī minimē amās?

_____

7. Praefersne bellum an pācem?

_____

8. Optāsne esse mīles aliquandō?

_____

THE LATIN CONNECTION

Look over the list of Latin words and the list of English words that derive from the Latin words. Then write the English word in the space next to the Latin word that is connected with it in meaning:

1. fābula	_____	arms
		delete
2. occupātus	_____	admirable
		defend
3. sevērus	_____	valid
		maximum
4. dēfendĕre	_____	locate
5. validus	_____	tempt
		fortitude
6. temptāre	_____	occupied
		fable
7. maximus	_____	belt
		severe
8. fortitūdō	_____	hostile
9. dēlēre	_____	
10. arma	_____	
11. balteus	_____	
12. mīrābilis	_____	
13. hostis	_____	
14. locāre	_____	

CONVERSĀTIŌ

etiam *even* **iter facĕre** *to march*

COLLOQUIUM

Complete the dialog with expressions chosen from the following list:

iter facĕre	in castrīs
dūra est	etiam centuriō
adultus	sperās
prō cōnsiliō tuō	minimē vērō

Mundus Rōmānus

Conjunctions

1   Here are some of the important countries and inhabitants of the Roman world (**mundus Rōmānus**). You should easily recognize most of them:

Āfrica *-ae f*	**Āfricānus** *-a -um*
Asia *-ae f*	**Asiāticus** *-a -um*
Aegyptus *-ī f*	**Aegyptus** *-a -um*
Britannia *-ae f*	**Britannus** *-a -um*
Eurōpa *-ae f*	**Eurōpaeus** *-a -um*
Gallia *-ae f*	**Gallus** *-a -um*
Germānia *-ae f*	**Germānus** *-a -um*
Graecia *-ae f*	**Graecus** *-a -um*
Hispānia *-ae f*	**Hispānus** *-a -um*
Ītalia *-ae f*	**Ītalicus** *-a -um*
Sarmātia *-ae f*	**Sarmāticus** *-a -um*
Sicilia *-ae f*	**Siculus** *-a -um*
Syria *-ae f*	**Syrius** *-a -um*

You probably had some difficulty in recognizing two of the countries: **Gallia** (*France*) and **Sarmātia** (*Russia*). International borders have changed over the centuries, and the borders of **Gallia** and **Sarmātia** are not exactly those of modern France and Russia.

What is the gender of all of the countries listed above? _____. All but one of the names of the countries end in **-a**. Which country does not end in **-a**?

_____. Actually, there are also three continents: **Āfrica, Asia, Eurōpa.** Only small portions of these continents were ever controlled by Rome.

2   The masculine and feminine adjectives referring to countries are also used for the inhabitants (**incolae**) of the countries. For example, **Āfricānus** may mean *African* (*man*) and **Āfricāna** *African* (*woman*); **Āfricānī** means *Africans*. So also, **Gallus** may mean *Gaul* (*male*), **Galla** *Gaul* (*female*), and **Gallī** *Gauls*. There is one exception: the people of **Sarmātia** were not **Sarmāticī**, but **Sarmātae** *-ārum mpl* (*Sarmatians*).

Activitātēs

A. Study carefully this map of the Roman Empire. Then, with Rome as your point of reference, name the countries in Latin in each direction from Rome:

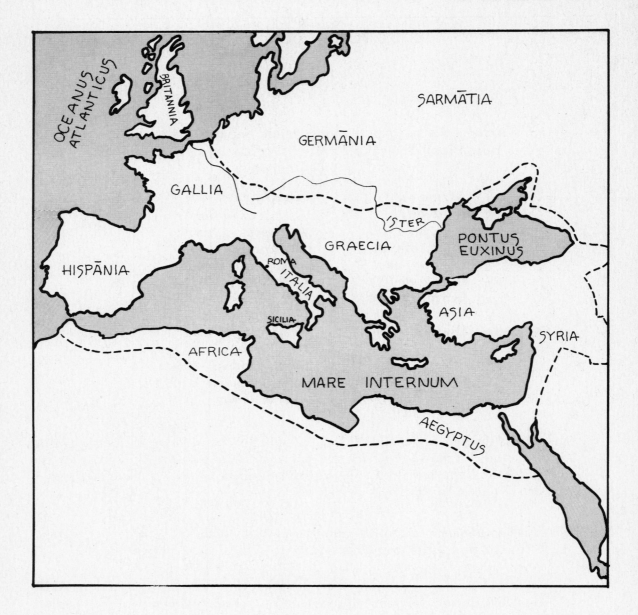

In merīdiē	In septentriōnibus	In oriente	In occidente
_____	_____	_____	_____
_____	_____	_____	_____
_____	_____		
	_____		

B. Fill in the name of the country or the inhabitants:

EXAMPLES: Germānī in Germāniā habitābant.
The Germans lived in Germany.

Hispānia erat terra Hispanōrum.
Spain was the country of the Spanish.

1. Āfricānī in _____ habitābant.

2. _____ in Graeciā habitābant.

3. Britannī in _____ habitābant.

4. Eurōpaeī in _____ habitābant.

5. Asia erat terra _____.

6. Syriī in _____ habitābant.

7. Gallia erat terra _____.

8. Siculī in _____ habitābant.

9. Sicilia erat terra _____.

10. _____ in Hispānia habitābant.

11. Ītalicī in _____ habitābant.

12. Germānia erat terra _____.

13. Aegyptī in _____ habitābant.

14. Eurōpa erat terra _____.

15. Britannia erat terra _____.

C. Identify the inhabitants of the following countries:

1. Incolae Hispāniae sunt _____.

2. Incolae Galliae sunt _____.

3. Incolae Graeciae sunt _____.

4. Incolae Āfricae sunt _____.

5. Incolae Siciliae sunt _____.

6. Incolae Sarmātiae sunt _____.

3   Conjunctions are words that connect other words or groups of words. You have already seen four important conjunctions: **et** (*and*), **aut** or **an** (*or*), and **sed** (*but*). You have also seen a few conjunctions that join dependent clauses to independent (or main) clauses. These are called subordinating conjunctions:

Discipulī rīsērunt *quia* Caecilius tardus vēnit.
The pupils laughed because Caecilius came late.

In this example, the subordinate or dependent clause is **quia Caecilius tardus vēnit**. Note that in Latin the dependent clause begins with the subordinating conjunction (in this example, **quia**) and ends with the verb (in this example, **vēnit**). In Latin, it's easy to see where the dependent (or subordinate) clause begins and ends. This fact is very important in understanding Latin sentences.

Here are some of the common subordinating conjunctions:

antequam	*before*	**dum** ⎫	
postquam	*after*	**quoad** ⎬	*as long as*
quod ⎫		**nam**	*for, since*
quia ⎬	*because*	**dōnec**	*until*
quoniam ⎭		**dum**	*while*
cum prīmum ⎫		**ubi**	*when; where*
simul ac ⎬	*as soon as*	**ut**	*as*
simul atque ⎭		**quamquam**	*although*

Activitās

D.   Read over the Latin sentences carefully. Then choose the conjunction that best fits the sense of the sentence:

1. (antequam, quamquam) _____ Rōma magna urbs fuit, oppidum parvum fuit.

2. (simul ac, antequam) _____ magister lūdum intrāvit, discipulī siluērunt.

3. (ubi, quamquam) _____ pluit, paenulam gerō.

4. (dum, postquam) _____ amīcōs habeō, fēlīx sum.

5. (postquam, quoniam) _____ āthlēta dūrus est, saepe vincit.

6. (quamquam, quoniam) _____ mīles fortis est, nōn ferox est.

7. (postquam, dōnec) Nōlī discēdĕre _____ veniō.

8. (quamquam, ut) _____ puella ē fenestrā spectāvit, trēs avēs in arbore vīdit.

9. (antequam, quia) _____ magister benignus mihi erat, grātiās eī dedī.

10. (ubi, dōnec) Rōmānī pugnāvērunt _____ tōtam Eurōpam vīcērunt.

4   Now let's read something about the Roman world:

Ab initiō Rōma erat oppidum parvum in mediā Ītaliā in rīpā flūminis Tiberis. Mūrus altus oppidum prōtēxit. Cīvēs Rōmānī erant agricolae. Agrōs extrā mūrōs arāvērunt. Sed Rōmānī etiam mīlitēs dūrī erant. Cōtīdiē in Campō Mārtiō sē exercuērunt. Sīc parātī bellō semper erant.

initium -ī *n beginning;* **ab initiō** *in the beginning*
oppidum -ī *n town*
medius -a -um *central*
arāre *to plough*

Simul ac fīnitimī agrōs Rōmānōs invāsērunt, exercitus Rōmānus hostēs fugāvit. Hōc modō Rōma paulātim tōtam Ītaliam vīcit. Postquam Rōmānī Ītaliam vīcērunt, Siciliam quoque vīcērunt. Sicilia est īnsula nōn procul ab Ītaliā. Sicilia erat prīma prōvincia Rōmae.

fīnitimus -ī *m neighbor*
invādō invādĕre invāsī *to invade*
fugāre *to drive away*
hōc modō *in this way*
paulātim *little by little*
vincō vincĕre vīcī *to conquer*
prōvincia -ae *f province*
victor -ōris *m victor*

Postquam Rōmānī Siciliam vīcērunt, cum Hispānīs pugnāvērunt; deinde cum Gallīs et Germānīs pugnāvērunt. Quoniam mīlitēs Rōmānī fortēs et dūrī erant, semper victōrēs in bellō erant. Mox Rōma multās prōvinciās habuit.

Mīlitēs Rōmānī viās per tōtam Ītaliam mūnīvērunt. Sīc exercitus Rōmānus in omnēs partēs celeriter iter facĕre potuit. Prīma via, nōmine Via Appia, in merīdiem dūxit. Alia via in septentriōnēs dūxit ad Galliam et Germāniam et Sarmātiam. Alia via in occidentem dūxit ad Hispāniam et Britanniam. Alia via in orientem dūxit ad Graeciam et Asiam et Syriam.

mūniō mūnīre mūnīvī *to build*
in omnēs partēs *in all directions*
celeriter *swiftly*
possum posse potuī *to be able*
dūcō ducĕre dūxī *to run, lead*
alia *another*

Cum prīmum Rōmānī gentēs externās vīcērunt, pācem cum eīs fēcērunt. Gentēs externae mox mōrēs Rōmānōs et linguam Latīnam didicērunt. Omnēs gentēs jūs Rōmānum accēpērunt. Pāx Rōmāna erat ubīque.

externus -a -um *foreign*
pāx pācis *f peace*
mōs mōris *m custom*
lingua -ae *f language*
discō discĕre didicī *to learn*
jūs jūris *n law*

Āctivitās

E. Respondē ad quaestiōnēs:

   1. Ubi est Rōma?

   _____

   2. Quid oppidum prōtēxit?

   _____

   3. Ubi agrī Rōmānōrum agricolārum erant?

   _____

   4. Ubi erat prīma prōvincia Rōmāna?

   _____

   5. Cūr mīlitēs Rōmānī semper victōrēs in bellō erant?

   _____

   6. Quid est nōmen prīmae viae Rōmānae?

   _____

   7. Ad quās (*which*) terrās dūxit via in septentriōnēs?

   _____

   8. Ad quās terrās dūxit via in occidentem?

   _____

   9. Ad quās terrās dūxit via in orientem?

   _____

  10. Quid gentēs externae didicērunt?

   _____

  11. Quid accēpērunt omnēs gentēs?

   _____

  12. Ubi erat pāx Rōmāna?

   _____

CONVERSĀTIŌ

VOCĀBULA

peregrīnus -ī *m stranger, foreigner*
unde *where (from)*
longē *far*
sub caelō calidō *in a warm climate*
patria -ae *f country, native land*

nebulōsus -a -um *misty*
brācae -ārum *fpl pants*
sōlus -a -um *alone, only*
Latīnē dīcěre *to speak Latin*
mīrus -a -um *strange*

COLLOQUIUM

Complete the dialog with expressions chosen from the following list:

Deīs grātiās agō
puellae sōlae
Latīnē dīcunt
tunicam
sub caelō calidō

brācās
longē trāns mare
minimē
unde

QUAESTIŌNĒS PERSŌNĀLĒS

1. Quās terrās vīsitāre maximē optās?   Quās terrās vīsitāre minimē optās?

   _____   _____

   _____   _____

   _____   _____

   _____   _____

   _____   _____

   _____   _____

2. Unde veniunt avus et avia? _____

3. Unde veniunt parentēs tuī? _____

4. Potesne dīcĕre Latīnē? _____

5. Optāsne dīcĕre Latīnē? _____

Recōgnitiō VI (Lectiōnēs XXI-XXIV)

Lectiō XXI

The perfect tense expresses a single action in the past. The endings of the perfect tense are the same for all verbs. The endings are added to the perfect stem, not to the present stem. The perfect stem varies from verb to verb and must be memorized. Samples of the perfect stems of typical verbs of each family of verbs and the perfect endings are as follows:

I	portāv	-ī
II	tenu	-istī
III	dīx	-it
III -iō	cēp	-imus
IV	audīv	-istis
		-ērunt

Lectiō XXII

Formation of pronouns:

	FIRST PERSON	SECOND PERSON	THIRD PERSON		
SINGULAR:					
NOMINATIVE	ego	tū	is	ea	id
GENITIVE	meī	tuī	ejus	ejus	ejus
ACCUSATIVE	mē	tē	eum	eam	id
DATIVE	mihi	tibi	eī	eī	eī
ABLATIVE	mē	tē	eō	eā	eō
PLURAL:					
NOMINATIVE	nōs	vōs	eī	eae	ea
GENITIVE	nostrum	vestrum	eōrum	eārum	eōrum
ACCUSATIVE	nōs	vōs	eōs	eās	ea
DATIVE	nōbis	vōbis	eīs	eīs	eīs
ABLATIVE	nōbis	vōbis	eīs	eīs	eīs

384

Lectiō XXIII

Formation of the adjective in the superlative degree:

a. Adjectives ending in **-us -a -um** have superlatives that end in **-issimus -issima -issimum:**

POSITIVE DEGREE	SUPERLATIVE DEGREE
clārus -a -um *clear*	**clārissimus -a -um** *clearest, very clear*

b. Adjectives ending in **-er** have superlatives that end in **-rimus -rima -rimum:**

POSITIVE DEGREE	SUPERLATIVE DEGREE
pulcher pulchra pulchrum *beautiful*	**pulcherrimus -a -um** *most beautiful, very beautiful*
celer -is -e *swift*	**celerrimus -a -um** *swiftest, very swift*

c. Adjectives of the third declension ending in **-is -is -e** have superlatives that end in **-issimus -issima -issimum:**

POSITIVE DEGREE	SUPERLATIVE DEGREE
fortis -is -e *brave*	**fortissimus -a -um** *bravest, very brave*

d. A few adjectives of the third declension ending in **-ilis -ilis -ile** have superlatives that end in **-limus -lima -limum:**

POSITVE DEGREE	SUPERLATIVE DEGREE
facilis -is -e *easy*	**facillimus -a -um** *easiest, very easy*
difficilis -is -e *difficult*	**difficillimus -a -um** *most difficult, very difficult*
similis -is -e *similar*	**simillimus -a -um** *most similar, very similar*

e. Adjectives of the third declension with only one ending for the masculine, feminine, and neuter do not show their complete stem in the nominative case. The complete stem appears in the genitive case:

POSITIVE DEGREE	SUPERLATIVE DEGREE
ferōx (genitive: **ferōcis**) *wild*	**ferōcissimus -a -um** *fiercest, very fierce*
fēlix (genitive: **fēlīcis**) *happy*	**fēlīcissimus -a -um** *happiest, very happy*
ēlegāns (genitive: **ēlegantis**) *elegant*	**ēlegantissimus -a -um** *most elegant, very elegant*

f. Some adjectives have irregular forms in the superlative:

POSITIVE DEGREE	SUPERLATIVE DEGREE
bonus -a -um *good*	**optimus -a -um** *best, very good*
magnus -a -um *big*	**maximus -a -um** *biggest, very big*
malus -a -um *bad*	**pessimus -a -um** *worst, very bad*
multus -a -um *much* (plural: *many*)	**plūrimus -a -um** *most, very much* (plural: *very many*)
parvus -a -um *small*	**minimus -a -um** *smallest, very small*

g. Adverbs in the superlative degree end in **-ē:**

POSTIVE DEGREE	SUPERLATIVE DEGREE
bene *well*	**optimē** *best, very well*
magnopere *greatly*	**maximē** *most, especially*
male *badly*	**pessimē** *worst, very badly*
multum *much, a lot*	**plūrimē** *most, very much*
parum *a little*	**minimē** *least, very little*
lātē *widely*	**lātissimē** *most widely, very widely*
ēleganter *elegantly*	**ēlegantissimē** *most elegantly, very elegantly*

Lectiō XXIV

Conjunctions are words that connect other words or groups of words.

a. Coordinating conjunctions in Latin that correspond to the three coordinating conjunctions in English are as follows:

$$\left.\begin{array}{l}\textbf{et}\\\textbf{atque}\\\textbf{-que}\end{array}\right\} and \qquad \left.\begin{array}{l}\textbf{aut}\\\textbf{an}\end{array}\right\} or \qquad \textbf{sed}\ but$$

b. Subordinating conjunctions connect one or more dependent (subordinate) clauses to an independent (main) clause. Some common subordinating conjunctions are:

antequam	*before*	**dum**	*as long as*
postquam	*after*	**quoad**	
quod		**nam**	*for, since*
quia	*because*	**dōnec**	*until*
quoniam		**dum**	*while*
cum prīmum		**ubi**	*when*
simul ac	*as soon as*	**ut**	*as*
simul atque		**quamquam**	*although*

Āctivitātēs

A. Write the Latin word under each picture. Then circle the word in the puzzle on page 387:

1. _____   2. _____   3. _____

4. _____

7. _____

10. _____

5. _____

8. _____

11. _____

6. _____

9. _____

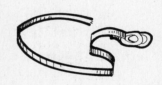

12. _____

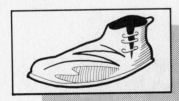

C	A	L	C	E	U	S		P		R
I	N	A	U	R	E	S		A		P
N	T	O	G	A	H		T	E		E
G	E	M	M	A	V		U	N		T
U	S	O	L	E	A		N	U	L	A	S
L	V	E	L	U	M		I	L		A
U	H	Q	H	V	K		C	A		S
M	O	N	I	L	E		A	D		U
K	A	R	M	I	L	L	A	L	A	Y

B. After filling in all the horizontal slots look at the vertical box to find the mystery word:

1. soldier

2. breastplate

3. sword

4. boots

5. belt

6. javelin

7. camp

C. Place the Latin names of these countries correctly in the puzzle. (H) means "horizontal" and (V) means "vertical":

4 letters	5 letters	6 letters	7 letters	8 letters	9 letters
Asia (H)	Syria (V)	Africa (H)	Greece (V)	Germany (H)	England (H)
		Europe (V)	Sicily (H)	Spain (V)	
		France (H)		Russia (V)	
		Italy (V)			

D. A Roman merchant is taking a business trip around the Roman Empire. List the countries in the order in which he visits them, including, of course, the country from which he sets out:

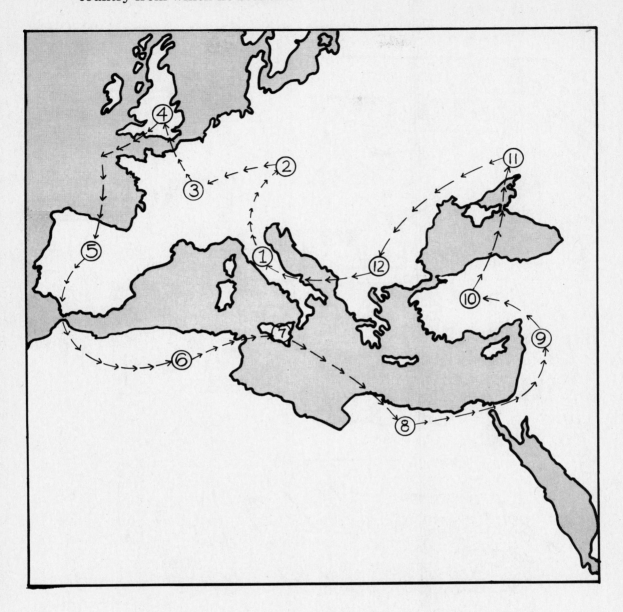

1. _____

2. _____

3. _____

4. _____

5. _____

6. _____

7. _____

8. _____

9. _____

10. _____

11. _____

12. _____

E. Claudius' cousin, Rufus, has just come from his farm in the country to visit the city for a few days. Claudius proudly shows Rufus around town. In the spaces provided, explain what the two cousins might see or do at each of the numbered stops:

1. _____

2. _____

3. _____

4. _____

5. _____

6. _____

7. _____

8. _____

9. _____

10. _____

11. _____

12. _____

13. _____

14. _____

15. _____

16. _____

17. _____

18. _____

19. _____

20. _____

F. Jumble. Unscramble the words, all of which are names of constructions. Then unscramble the letters in the circles to give you the answer to the question.

SUMUR

SCHALO

RIACU

EMPTLMU

Ubi sunt aedificia? _____

G. Picture Story. Can you read this story? Whenever you come to a picture, read it as if it were a Latin word:

Caecilius erat ⬚ Rōmānus. Nōn ⬚ sed ⬚ gerēbat. Nōn ⬚ sed ⬚ gerēbat. Nōn ⬚ sed ⬚ gerēbat. Dum in urbe Rōmā est, ⬚ et ⬚ et ⬚ et ⬚ et ⬚ vīsitāvit. In ⬚ vīnum potābat et ⬚ edēbat. Sed nōn diū in urbe Rōmā manēbat. Mox ad Āfricam in ⬚ longā nāvigāvit, ubi Caecilius ⬚ et ⬚ et etiam ⬚ vīdit. Nōn ⬚ et ⬚ sed ⬚ ēdit. Quam mīra terra erat Āfrica!

Achievement Test II
(Lessons XIII-XXIV)

1 Vocabulary [15 points]

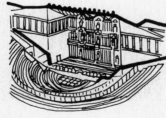

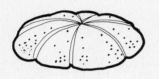

1. _____

2. _____

3. _____

4. _____

5. _____

6. _____

7. _____

8. _____

9. _____

10. _____

11. _____

12. _____

393

13. _____   14. _____   15. _____

2 Possessive adjectives [10 points]

Choose the correct possessive and write it in the space provided:

1. patria (noster, nostra)   _____

2. cubiculum (meus, meum)   _____

3. domus (ejus, ea)   _____

4. dentēs (tuī, tuae)   _____

5. māter (suus, sua)   _____

6. nāvicula (ea, eārum)   _____

7. īnsulae (nostrum, nostrae)   _____

8. templum (vestrum, vestrī)   _____

9. canis (suī, suus)   _____

10. amīcī (meī, meus)   _____

3 Numbers [10 points]

Write out the following numbers in Latin:

1. XLIV   _____

2. LXXX   _____

3. C   _____

4. M   _____

5. L   _____

6. LXV   _____

7. XC   _____

8. D _____

9. LXXIII _____

10. XXXIX _____

4 Roman numerals [5 points]

Give the Arabic numerals for the following Roman numerals:

1. CMLVI _____

2. MCDXCII _____

3. MLXVI _____

4. MDCCCLXV _____

5. MCMLXXXIX _____

5 Imperative [5 points]

Give the imperative singular and plural of the following verbs:

1. laborāre _____ _____

2. tenēre _____ _____

3. sumĕre _____ _____

4. dormīre _____ _____

5. ferre _____ _____

6 Perfect tense [10 points]

Change the following verbs from the present tense to the perfect tense:

1. dīcimus _____

2. faciō _____

3. cantātis _____

4. docet _____

5. habent _____

6. rogās _____

7. audīmus _____

8. teneō _____

9. nāvigāmus _____

10. exercet _____

7 Opposites [5 points]

Find the five pairs of words that have opposite meanings and write them side by side in the spaces provided:

1. _____ _____

2. _____ _____

3. _____ _____

4. _____ _____

5. _____ _____

mare	astrum
hortus	tandem
urbs	vallēs
ūnus	rēmus
mōns	pāx
popīna	terra
bellum	caput
lupus	ovis
prīmum	rūs
taberna	armilla

8 The Latin connection [10 points]

Look over the list of Latin words and the list of English derivatives. Then write the English word in the space next to the Latin word from which it is derived:

1. lacus _____

2. bestia _____

3. vēlum _____

4. gemma _____

5. hōra _____

6. Ūranus _____

7. herba _____

8. canis _____

9. domus _____

10. planēta _____

hour
herb
domicile
lake
veil
canine
uranium
planet
beast
gem

9 Countries of the Roman world [5 points]

Give the Latin names of the countries in which the following inhabitants live:

1. Germānī _____

2. Hispānī _____

3. Siculī   _____

4. Āfricānī   _____

5. Aegyptī   _____

10   Imperfect tense [10 points]

Change the following verbs to the imperfect tense:

1. optō   _____

2. dīcis   _____

3. dormiunt   _____

4. facimus   _____

5. capit   _____

6. sum   _____

7. īmus   _____

8. exspectās   _____

9. sunt   _____

10. tenētis   _____

11   Reading comprehension [10 points]

Read over the following story carefully. Then circle the letter for the expression that best completes the statement:

Erat mēnsis Augustus. Claudius et soror sua, Cornēlia, cum parentibus iter longum fēcērunt. Prīmum in Siciliam nāvigāvērunt, ubi fundum avī aviaeque vīsitāvērunt. In fundō Claudius et soror per collēs et vallēs equitāvērunt. Deinde ā Siciliā in Aegyptum nāvigāvērunt. In Aegyptō multōs camēlōs in dēsertīs vīdērunt et pȳramidēs vīsitāvērunt. Ibi ariēnās ēdērunt. Deinde in Graeciam nāvigāvērunt, ubi templa pulchra vīdērunt et pater cum Claudiō theātrum frequentāvit. Māter et Cornēlia ad tabernās vestiāriās īvērunt et multa vestīmenta pulchra ēmērunt. Post quattuor diēs ā Graeciā vēla dedērunt et in Ītaliam contentī rediērunt.

1. Tempus annī est (a) hiems; (b) vēr; (b) autumnus; (d) aestās.

2. Quis iter longum fēcit? (a) Claudius et Cornēlia; (b) pater et māter; (c) fīlius et fīlia cum parentibus; (d) Claudius cum patre.

3. In Siciliā in fundō avī aviaeque Claudius et soror (a) in hortō lūdēbant; (b) per collēs et vallēs equitābant; (c) in flūmine natābant; (d) florēs in agrīs carpēbant.

4. In Aegyptō familia (a) pȳramidēs ascendit; (b) ariēnās et uvās·vēndidit; (c) camēlōs in dēsertīs vīdit et pȳramidēs vīsitāvit; (d) templa pulchra vīsitāvit.

5. In Graeciā (a) pater et māter theātrum frequentāvērunt; (b) Claudius et Cornēlia in templīs deōs adorāvērunt; (c) Cornēlia et māter ad tabernās vestiāriās īvērunt; (d) pater et māter multa vestīmenta pulchra ēmērunt.

12 Slot Completion [5 points]

Underline the expression that best completes the sentence:

Est aestās. Claudia avum et ___(1)___ in fundō vīsitat. Avus est ___(2)___ et in agrīs labōrat. Claudia in fundō multās ___(3)___ videt. Claudiae avia est ___(4)___ sed semper in hortō ___(5)___ .

1. (a) aviam
   (b) avem
   (c) viam
   (d) navem
2. (a) nauta
   (b) magister
   (c) āctor
   (d) agricola
3. (a) simiās
   (b) camēlōs
   (c) vaccās
   (d) leōnēs
4. (a) vetus
   (b) angusta
   (c) nova
   (d) acris
5. (a) salit
   (b) gustat
   (c) natat
   (d) labōrat

Vocābula Latīna-Anglica

The nominative and genitive endings and the gender are given for nouns: **actor -oris** *m.*

The first person present, the present infinitive, and the first person perfect are given for verbs: **expendo expendere expendi.**

The masculine, feminine, and neuter forms are given for adjectives: **clarus -a -um.** Adjectives of the third declension with one ending are followed by a semicolon and the genitive singular: **vetus; veteris.**

In words of three or more syllables, a dot is under the stressed syllable: **convivium.** A stressed syllable containing a diphthong is indicated as follows: **Europaeus.**

Italicized endings indicate the point at which other endings are attached. The following abbreviations occur:

abl	= ablative	*interj*	= interjection
acc	= accusative	*m*	= masculine
conj	= conjunction	*n*	= neuter
dat	= dative	*pl*	= plural
f	= feminine	*pref*	= prefix
indecl	= indeclinable	*prep*	= preposition

A

a, ab *prep* (+ *abl*) from; by
a-, ab- *pref* from, away
abhinc *adv* ago
accipio accipere accepi to accept, receive
acer acris acre sharp
acetaria -orum *npl* salad
acetum -i *n* vinegar
activitas -atis *f* activity
actor -oris *m* actor
actrix -icis *f* actress
ad *prep* (+ *acc*) to
ad- *pref* to, toward
adjectivum -i *n* adjective
adjuvo -juvare -juvi to help
admirabilis -is -e wonderful
adulescentulus -i *m* young man
adultus -a -um grown-up, adult
adverbium -i *n* adverb
adversus *prep* (+ *acc*) against
advocatus -i *m* lawyer
aedificium -i *n* building

aegrotus -a -um sick
Aegyptus -i *f* Egypt
Aegyptus -a -um Egyptian
aequuus -a -um fair
aestas -atis *f* summer
affero afferre attuli to bring to, bring along, fetch
Africa -ae *f* Africa
Africanus -a -um African
ager agri *m* field
agricola -ae *m* farmer
ala -ae *f* wing
albus -a -um white
aliquando *adv* someday
aliquid *pron* something
aliquot *indecl* some
alius -a -ud another
alter altera alterum the other
altus -a -um high
amabilis -is -e lovable
amarus -a -um bitter
ambitiosus -a -um ambitious
Ambrosia -ae *f* Ambrosia (*food of the gods*)

ambulo -are -avi to walk
amica -ae *f* (female) friend
amicus -i *m* (male) friend
amo -are -avi to love
amphitheatrum -tri *n* amphitheater
an *conj* or
ancora -ae *f* anchor
angustus -a -um narrow
animal -alis *n* animal
animus -i *m* mind
ante *prep* (+ *acc*) in front of
antequam *conj* before
antiquuus -a -um ancient
Antonia -ae *f* Antonia
Antonius -i *m* Anthony
anulus -i *m* ring
aperio -ire aperui to open
Apollo Apollinis *m* Apollo
appetentia -ae *f* appetite
Appius -i *m* (*male name*) Appius
Aprilis -is *m* April
apud *prep* (+ *acc*) at the house of

aqua -ae f water
aquaeductus -us m aqueduct
aquaticus -a um aquatic, living in water
aquila -ae f eagle
ara -ae f altar
arbor arboris f tree
arcus -us m bow
Ardea -ae f Ardea (*small town near Rome*)
area -ae f playground
arena -ae f sand
ariena -ae f banana
arma -orum npl arms
armilla -ae f bracelet
aro -are -avi to plough
Asia -ae f Asia
Asiaticus -a -um Asiatic
asinus -i m donkey
asparagus -i m asparagus
astrum -i n star
astutus -a -um sly
ater atra atrum black
athleta -ae m athlete
atramentum -i n ink
atrium -i n atrium, reception room
attonitus -a -um astonished
auctionarius -i m auctioneer
audax; audacis bold
audio -ire -ivi to hear
auffero auferre abstuli to bring away, take away, remove
Augustus -i m August
Aulus -i m (*male name*) Aulus
Aurelia -ae f (*female name*) Aurelia
aureus -a -um golden, of gold
auris -is f ear
ausculto -are -avi to listen to; to hear
aut conj or
autem adv however
autumnus -i m fall, autumn
avia -ae f grandmother
avis -is f bird
avus -i m grandfather
auxilium -i n help

B

Bacchus -i m Bacchus
badius -a -um chestnut (color)

balaena -ae f whale
balneum -i n bath
balteus -i m sword belt
barba -ae f beard
bellum -i n war
bellus -a -um pretty
bene adv fine, O.K.; **bene paratus** well prepared
benignus -a -um kind
bestia -ae f beast
bibliotheca -ae f library
bonus -a -um good
bracae -arum fpl pants
bracchium -i n arm
brevis -is -e short
Britannia -ae f Britain
Britannus -a -um British
bubo -onis m owl
bulla -ae f charm (*worn around the neck by boys*)

C

cadaver -eris n cadaver, corpse
Caecilius -i m Cecil
cado cadere cecidi to fall
caelum -i n sky; **sub caelo calido** in a warm climate
caeruleus -a -um blue
calamus -i m pen
calceus -i m shoe
calidus -a -um hot
caliga -ae f boot
calvus -a -um bald
camelus -i m camel
campus -i m field, plain; **Campus Martius** Field of Mars (*in Rome*)
candela -ae f candle
candidus -a -um white
caninus -a -um canine; **domus canina** doghouse
canis -is m dog
canto -are -avi to sing
cantor -oris m singer
cantrix -icis f singer
canus -a -um grey
capio capere cepi to take, accept
capto -are -avi to catch
caput -itis n head
carcer carceris n starting gate; **e carceribus** out of the starting gate

carissimus -a -um very expensive, very dear
carmen carminis n song
caro -nis f meat
carota -ae f carrot
carpo carpere carpsi to pick
carus -a -um dear
casa -ae f house, cottage
crudus -a -um crude
caseus -i m cheese
castra -orum npl camp
cathedra -ae f chair
cavum -i n hole
charta -ae f sheet
cauda -ae f tail
cedo cedere cessi to go
celebro -are -avi to celebrate
celeriter adv swiftly
cella -ae f cellar
cena -ae f dinner
cenaculum -i n apartment
centum indecl hundred
centurio -onis m centurion
cerasum -i n cherry
Ceres Cereris f Ceres (*goddess of grain*)
certe adv certainly
cibus -i m food; meal
cingulum -i n belt
circa prep (+ acc) about, approximately
circum prep (+ acc) around
circum- pref around
circumfero circumferre circumtuli to bring around
Circus -i m racetrack; **Circus Maximus** Circus Maximus (*main racetrack*)
cito adv quickly
civis -is m citizen
clam adv secretly
clamo -are -avi to shout
clamor -oris m shout
clarus -a -um famous
classis -is f class
Claudia -ae f Claudia
Claudius -i m Claudius
claudo claudere clausi to close
Clemens Clementis m Clement
clemens; clementis gentle
collis -is m hill
colloquium -i n dialog
collum -i n neck
color -oris m color
columba -ae f dove

coma -ae f hair
combinatio -onis f combination
commiles -itis m fellow soldier
commodus -a -um comfortable, cozy
comperio comperire comperi to find out
compluvium -i n skylight
computo -are -avi to count, do figures
con-, com- pref with; together; completely, up
concedo -cedere -cessi to go along with, concede
concipio -cipere -cepi to conceive
conclave -is n room
concludo -cludere -clusi to close up, conclude
confero conferre contuli to bring together, gather
conficio -ficere -feci to do completely, complete, accomplish
confido -fidere (+ dat) to trust
conscendo -scendere -scendi to climb aboard, climb up
consido -sidere -sedi to sit down
consilium -i n advice
consobrinus -i m cousin
contentus -a -um content(ed)
contra- pref against
conversatio -onis f conversation
convivium -i n party
copiae -arum fpl troops, forces
coqua -ae f (female) cook
coquus -i m (male) cook
cor cordis n heart
Cornelia -ae f (female name) Cornelia
Cornelius -i m (male name) Cornelius
cotidie adv daily
cras adv tomorrow
crassus -a -um fat
crudus -a -um crude
crustularius -a -um pastry; **crustularius -i** m pastry baker
crustulum -i n cookie
creatio -onis f creation
credo credere credidi (+ dat) to believe

crus cruris n leg
cubiculum -i n bedroom
cucumis cucumeris m cucumber
culina -ae f kitchen
cum prep (+ abl) with
cum primum adv as soon as possible
cum subito conj when suddenly
cuniculus -i m rabbit
cupide adv eagerly
Cupido -inis m Cupid
cupidus -a -um eager
cur adv why; **cur autem** why then
curia -ae f senate building
curriculum -i n chariot
curro currere cucurri to run
cursus -us m race; **in quoque cursu** in each race
curtus -a -um short
custodio custodire custodii to guard

D

de prep (+ abl) down from; about, concerning
de- pref down; away from
dea -ae f goddess
decem indecl ten
December -bris m December
decimus -a -um tenth
decipio decipere decepi to deceive
defendo defendere defendi to defend
defero deferre detuli to bring away; to defer
deficio deficere defeci to run low, be deficient
deformis -is -e ugly
deinde adv then, next
deleo delere delevi to destroy
demonstro -are -avi to point out
denarius -i m denarius, "dollar"; **mille denariis constat** it costs a thousand dollars
denique adv finally
dens dentis m tooth
densus -a -um dense, thick

dependeo dependere dependi to hang from; to depend
deporto -are -avi to bring down; to deport
descendo descendere descendi to get off, climb down; to come down
descriptio -onis f description
deserta -orum npl desert
desilio desilire desilii to jump down
deus -i m god
devoro -are -avi to devour
di mpl gods; **di superi!** ye gods above!
Diana -ae f Diana (goddess of the hunt and the moon)
dico dicere dixi to say; to speak
dies diei m day; **dies festus** holiday; **dies Jovis** Thursday; **dies Lunae** Monday; **dies Martis** Tuesday; **dies Mercurii** Wednesday; **dies Saturni** Saturday; **dies Solis** Sunday; **dies Veneris** Friday
difficilis -is -e difficult
difficiliter adv with difficulty
digitus -i m finger
diligenter adv diligently, hard
diligo diligere dilexi to like
directo adv directly
discedo discedere discessi to leave
discipula -ae f pupil, school girl
discipulus -i m pupil, school boy
disco discere didici to learn
diu adv long; **diu et acriter** long and hard
diversus -a -um various, different
dives; divitis rich
divido dividere dividi to divide
do dare dedi to give; **dabit** (he/she/it) will give; **non darem** I wouldn't give
doceo docere docui to teach
doleo dolere dolui to ache, hurt
dolor -oris m ache
domesticus -a -um doméstic

domina -ae f Miss

Domitilla -ae f (female name) Domitilla

donec conj until

donum -i n gift

dormio dormire dormivi to sleep

dorsum -i n back

domus -us f home; **domi** at home; **domum** home(ward)

duco ducere duxi to lead; (of a road) to run

dulcis -is -e sweet; **dulcia** npl sweets, candy

Drusilla -ae f (female name) Drusilla

dum conj while; as long as

duo duae duo two

duodecim indecl twelve

duodecimus -a -um twelfth

duodequinquaginta indecl forty-eight

duodesexaginta indecl fifty-eight

duodetriginta indecl twenty-eight

duodeviginti indecl eighteen

durus -a -um hard

E

e, ex prep (+ abl) out of, from

e-, ex- pref out of, from

ea pron she; npl they, them

eae pron fpl they

earum pron fpl their

eburneus -a -um of ivory

ecce interj see, look!

edo edere (or **esse**) **edi** to eat

effugio effugere effugi to flee out of, escape

ego pron I

ei pron to him, to her, to it; mpl they

ejus pron his, her, its

electricus -a -um electrical

elegans; elegantis elegant

eleganter adv elegantly

emo emere emi to buy

enormis -is -e enormous

enormiter adv enormously

enumero -are -avi to count (out); **eos enumerabo** I'll count them

eo ire i(v)i to go; **eamus** let's go

eorum pron mpl and npl their

epistula -ae f letter

eques equitis m cavalryman

equito -are -avi to ride horseback

equus -i m horse

esse see **sum**

esurio esurire to be hungry

et conj and; **et cetera** and so forth

etiam adv also; even

Etruscus -a -um Etruscan; **Etrusci** mpl Etruscans

eum pron him

Europa -ae f Europe

Europaeus -a -um European

excedo excedere excessi to go out; to exceed

excellens; excellentis excellent

excipio excipere excepi to welcome

excludo excludere exclusi to exclude

exerceo exercere exercui to practice; **se exercere** to practice

exercitus -us m army

expecto -are -avi to wait for

expello expellere expuli to chase out

expendo expendere expendi to pay (out)

explico -are -avi to explain

exporto -are -avi to export, carry out

externus -a -um external

extra prep (+ acc) outside

exuo exuere exui to take off

F

faber -bri m craftsman; **faber ferrarius** blacksmith, ironworker; **faber tignarius** carpenter

Fabius -i m (male name) Fabius

fabrico -are -avi to make

fabula -ae f story, tale

facies -ei f face

facile adv easily

facio facere feci to make, do; **facio ut oculi quiescant** I'm resting my eyes

falsus -a -um false

famis -is m hunger; **famem habere** to be starved

familia -ae f family

familiaris -is -e familiar

famosus -a -um famous

fascia -ae bandage

Februarius -i m February

feles -is f cat

felinus -a -um feline; **cibus felinus** cat food

felix; felicis happy

femina -ae f woman

fenestra -ae f window

ferculum -i n tray

fero ferre tuli to bring, bear, carry

ferox; ferocis fierce

fertilis -is -e fertile

ferus -a -um wild

festino -are -avi to rush, rush about

fibula -ae f safety pin

fidelis -is -e faithful

fideliter adv faithfully

fides -ei f faith, trust; **per deorum fidem!** for heaven's sake!

filia -ae f daughter

filius -i m son

finis -is m finish, finish line; **finem habere** to come to an end

finio finire finivi to finish

finitimus -i m neighbor

firmus -a -um firm, solid

Flavia -ae f (female name) Flavia

flavus -a -um yellow

flos floris m flower

fluctus -us m wave

flumen -inis n river

folium -i n leaf

fons -tis m spring, fountain

fortasse adv maybe

fortitudo -inis f fortitude, courage

fortunatus -a -um fortunate

forum -i n forum, marketplace

fragilis -is -e fragile

fragor -oris m crash; **magnus fragor** loud crash

frango frangere fregi to break

Frankenpetrus -i *m* Frankenstein

frater -tris *m* brother

fraterculus -i *m* little brother

frequento -are -avi to go regularly to, attend; to use

frigidus -a -um cold

fructus -us *m* fruit

frumentum -i *n* grain

fugio fugere fugi to flee, run away

fugo -are -avi to drive away

fulmen -inis *n* lightning bolt

fundus -i *m* farm

furnus -i *m* oven

fuscus -a -um brown

G

galea -ae *f* helmet

Gallia -ae *f* Gaul (France)

gallina -ae *f* chicken

gallus -i *m* rooster

Gallus -a -um Gallic

gaudium -i *n* joy

gemma -ae *f* gem

Germania -ae *f* Germany

Germanus -a -um German

gero gerere gessi to wear

gladiator -oris *m* gladiator

gladiatorius -a -um gladiatorial

gladius -i *m* sword

Graecia -ae *f* Greece

Graecus -a -um Greek

granum -i *n* grain

gratias *interj* thanks!

gratus -a -um pleasing, welcome, pleasant

gravis -is -e heavy

grunnio -ire -ivi to grunt

gusto -are -avi to taste

H

habeo habere habui to have; **habesne?** do you have?

haec *f* this; *npl* these

(h)arena -ae *f* sand

herba -ae *f* grass

herus -i *m* boss

hesternus -a -um yesterday's

heus! *interj* hey!

hic *adv* here

hiems hiemis *f* winter

Hispania -ae *f* Spain

Hispanus -a -um Spanish

hodie *adv* today

holus holeris *n* vegetable

homo hominis *m* man, person; **homines** *mpl* people

honestus -a -um honest

hora -ae *f* hour

Horatius -i *m* Horace

hordeum -i *n* barley

hortus -i *m* garden; **horti publici** *mpl* park

hospes hospitis *mf* guest

hostis -is *m* enemy

humidus -a -um humid

I

id *pron* it; **id est** that is

igitur *adv* therefore

ignosco ignoscere ignovi (+ *dat*) to pardon

ille -a -ud that; *pron* he, that man; she, that woman; it, that thing

immisceo immiscere immiscui to mix in

immortalis -is -e immortal

impatiens; impatientis impatient

imperator -oris *m* commander; emperor

imperfectus -a -um imperfect

impluvium -i *n* rain basin

importo -are -avi to bring in, import

in *prep* (+ *abl*) in; on; (+ *acc*) into

in-, im- *pref* in, into

inaures -ium *fpl* earrings

incipio incipere incepi to begin

includo includere inclusi to enclose, include

incola -ae *m* inhabitant

incredibilis -is -e incredible

induco inducere induxi to lead in, induce

infans infantis *mf* baby, infant

infero inferre intuli to bring in, infer

infidelis -is -e unfaithful

infirmus -a -um infirm, weak

inhabito -are -avi to live in, inhabit

initium -i *n* beginning; **ab initio** from the beginning; **ab ipso initio** from the very beginning

inquit he/she says

inrideo inridere inrisi to laugh at

insanus -a -um insane, mad, crazy

insula -ae *f* apartment building; island

inter *prep* (+ *acc*) between

inter- *pref* between

intercedo -cedere -cessi to go between, intercede

interdiu *adv* during the day

interdum *adv* sometimes

intro -are -avi to enter

intro- *pref* in, inward

introduco -ducere -duxi to lead in, introduce

invado invadere invasi to invade

invideo invidere invidi (+ *dat*) to envy

invito -are -avi to invite

irritabilis -is -e irritable

is *pron* he

ita *adv* yes

itaque *adv* and so, therefore

iter itineris *n* trip; **iter facere** to travel, take a trip; to march

Italia -ae *f* Italy

Italicus -a -um Italian

J

jam *adv* already

janua -ae *f* door

Januarius -i *m* January

Janus -i *m* Janus (*two-headed Roman god*)

jaceo jacere jacui to lie down

jentaculum -i *n* breakfast

jubeo jubere jussi to order

judicium -i *n* courthouse

Julia -ae *f* Julia

Julius -i *m* July

Junius -i *m* June

Juno -onis f Juno (*queen of the gods*)

Juppiter, Jovis m Jupiter (*king of the gods*)

jus juris n soup; law

justus -a -um just

L

labor -oris m work, labor

laboratorium -i n laboratory

laboro -are -avi to work

labrum -i n lip

lac lactis n milk

lacerna -ae f cape

lactuca -ae f lettuce

lacus -us m lake

laete adv happily

laetus -a -um happy

lambo lambere to lick

lana -ae f wool

laniena -ae f butcher shop

lanius -i m butcher

lateo latere latui to hide

Latine adv (in) Latin; **Latine dicere** to speak Latin; **Latine loquitur** he speaks Latin

latro -are -avi to bark

latus -a -um broad, wide

lavo -are -avi to wash

lectica -ae f litter

lectio -onis f lesson

lectus -i m bed; dining couch

lego legere legi to read

legislator -oris m legislator

lente adv slowly

leo -onis m lion

levis -is -e light

libenter adv gladly, willingly

liber libri m book

liber libera liberum free; **liberi** mpl children

librarium -i n bookshelf

licitator -oris m bidder

lilium -i n lily

linea -ae f line, stripe

Licinius -i m (*male name*) Licinius

lingua -ae f tongue; language

Livia -ae f (*female name*) Livia

loco -are -avi to place, put

locus -i m place; **loca** npl places

locutio -onis f phrase, expression

longe adv far

longus -a -um long

loquor loqui to speak; **loquere!** speak!

lorica -ae f breastplate

lucerna -ae f lamp

Lucius -i m (*male name*) Lucius

ludibundus -a -um playful

ludifico -are -avi to kid, fool

ludo ludere lusi to play

ludus -i m play, game; school

lumen luminis n light

luna -ae f moon

lupus -i m wolf

lutum -i n mud

M

macellum -i n produce market

macer -era -erum thin

magis adv more; **magis quam** more than

magister -tri m master, Mr.; (male) teacher; captain

magistra -ae f (female) teacher

magnificens; magnificentis magnificent

magnificus -a -um magnificent, fantastic

magnus -a -um big; loud

Maius -i m May

male adv badly, poorly

malum -i n apple

malus -a -um bad

malus -i m mast

mane adv in the morning; **mane, meridie, noctu** morning, noon, and night

maneo manere mansi to remain, stay

manus -us f hand; trunk

Marcella -ae f (*female name*) Marcella

Marcellus -i m (*male name*) Marcellus

mare -is n sea; **mare altum** high seas

margo -inis f edge

Marius -i m (*male name*) Marius

Mars -tis m Mars (*god of war*)

Martius -i m March

mater -tris f mother

maxime adv most, very much

maximus -a -um biggest, very big

Maximus -i m Maximus

medicina -ae f medicine

medicus -i m doctor

medius -a -um central, middle; **media nocte** in the middle of the night, at midnight

mel mellis n honey

melius adv better; **me melius habeo** I feel better

membrum -i n member

memorabilis -is -e memorable

memoria -ae f memory

mensa -ae f table; **mensa secunda** dessert

mensis -is m month

Mercurius -i m Mercury (*messenger of the gods*)

mereo merere merui to earn

meridies -ei m midday, noon; south

meus -a -um my

miles militis m soldier

militia -ae f military service

Minerva -ae f Minerva (*goddess of wisdom*)

minime adv no, not at all; **minime vero** not at all

minimus -a -um smallest, very small, very little

mille indecl one thousand; **constare mille denariis** to cost a thousand dollars

minor; minoris less, smaller; **minor natu quam** younger than

mirabilis -is -e wonderful

mirus -a -um strange

miser -era -erum poor; miserable

miserabilis -is -e miserable

mitis -is -e kind, mild

mitto mittere misi to send

modestus -a -um modest

modo . . . modo sometimes . . . sometimes

modus -i m way; **hoc modo** in this way

molestus -a -um annoying

mollis -is -e soft

monile -is n necklace

mons montis m mountain

monstrum -i n monster

monstruosus -a -um monstrous

mordeo mordere momordi to bite; to sting

mortuus -a -um dead; **mortui mpl** dead (people)

mos moris *m* custom

moveo movere movi to move

multus -a -um much; **est multo melius** it is much better; **multa poma** much fruit; **multi -ae -a** many

mundus -i *m* world

munio munire munivi to build

murmuro -are -avi to murmur

murus -i *m* wall

mus muris *m* mouse

musculus -i *m* muscle

musica -ae *f* (female) musician; music

musicus -i *m* (male) musician

muto -are -avi to change

N

nam *conj* for, since

narro -are -avi to tell, narrate

nasus -i *m* nose

natalis -is *m* birthday

nato -are -avi to swim

natura -ae *f* nature

natus -a -um born; . . . **annos natus** . . . years old

navicula -ae *f* boat

navigatio -onis *f* navigation

navis -is *f* ship; **navis oneraria** cargo ship

-ne *suffix* (*attached to the first word of a sentence, introducing a question expecting a "yes" or "no" answer*)

nebulosus -a -um misty

necessarius -a -um necessary

nectar -aris *n* nectar (*drink of the gods*)

neque *conj* nor

nemo -inis *m* no one

Neptunus -i *m* Neptune (*god of the sea*)

nescio nescire nescii not to know

nidus -i *m* nest

nimis *adv* too; **nimis remotus** too far away; **nimis valde** too hard

nihil *indecl* nothing; **nihil novi** nothing new

nix nivis *f* snow

nobilis -is -e noble

nobiliter *adv* nobly

noceo nocere nocui (+ *dat*) to harm, hurt

noctu *adv* at night

nolo nolle nolui to be unwilling, not to want; **noli (nolite) timere** do not fear

nomen -inis *n* name; noun; **mihi nomen est** . . . my name is . . .

nomino -are -avi to name

non *adv* not; (*in answer to a question*) no; **non jam** no longer; still not; **non solum . . . sed etiam** not only . . . but also

nonaginta *indecl* ninety

nondum *adv* not yet

nonne *adv introduces a question expecting a "yes" answer*

nonus -a -um ninth

novem *indecl* nine

novus -a -um new

noster -tra -trum our

November -bris *m* November

nox noctis *f* night; **hac nocte** tonight

nos *pron* we; (*direct object*) us

notus -a -um familiar

nubes -is *f* cloud

nudus -a -um nude, bare

num *adv introduces a question expecting a "no" answer*

nummus -i *m* cent

numerus -i *m* number

nuntius -i *m* messenger

O

obediens; obedientis obedient

obedienter *adv* obediently

obesus -a -um fat, obese

obscurus -a -um dark

obstinatus -a -um obstinate

obstinate *adv* obstinately

occidens -entis *m* West

occido occidere occidi to set

occupatus -a -um busy

oceanus -i *m* ocean

Octavia -ae *f* (*female name*) Octavia

octavus -a -um eighth

octo *indecl* eight

October -bris *m* October

octoginta *indecl* eighty

oculus -i *m* eye

offero offerre obtuli to bring to, present, offer; **offertis** you offer

officina -ae *f* workshop

oleum -i *n* oil

oliva -ae *f* olive

omnis -is -e each; **omnes** all

onus oneris *n* weight, load; cargo

oppidum -i *n* town

optime *adv* very well

optimus -a -um best, very good

opto -are -avi to want, wish

ora -ae *f* shore; **ora maritima** seashore

oratio -onis *f* speech; **orationem habere** to give a speech

oriens -entis *m* East

ornamentum -i *n* ornament

os oris *n* mouth

otiosus -a -um not busy

ovis -is *f* sheep

ovum -i *n* egg

P

paenitet paenitere paenituit it grieves; **me paenitet** I'm sorry, it grieves me

paenula -ae *f* (hooded) raincoat

panis -is *m* bread

paratus -a -um prepared, ready

parentes -ium *mpl* parents

pareo parere parui (+ *dat*) to obey

pario parere peperi to produce; to lay (*eggs*)

paro -are -avi to prepare

pars partis *f* part; quarter; **in omnes partes** in all directions

parvus -a -um small

pater -tris *m* father

patientia -ae f patience
patria -ae f country, native land
patrona -ae f patroness
paulatim adv little by little
paulo adv a little; **paulo post** a little later
Paulus -i (male name) Paul
pauper; pauperis poor
pavimentum -i n pavement; floor
pavo -onis m peacock
pax pacis f peace
pectus -oris n chest
pecunia -ae f money
pellis -is f fur
pendeo pendere pependi to hang
per prep (+ acc) through
per- pref completely; through
percipio -cipere -cepi to perceive; to notice; to understand
peregrinus -i m stranger, foreigner
perficio -ficere -feci to do completely; to perfect
pergula -ae f portico, porch
periculosus -a -um dangerous
peristylium -i n (colonnaded) garden, courtyard
peritus -a -um good, skillful
permulceo -mulcere -mulsi to pet, stroke
perna -ae f ham
persona -ae f person; character
personalis -is -e personal
perterritus -a -um very scared
pertineo -tinere -tinui (+ dat) to belong to
pervenio -venire -veni to arrive
pes pedis m foot
pessimus -a -um worst, very bad
petasus -i m (broad-brimmed) hat
peto petere petivi to chase after
physicus -i m scientist
pictor -oris m painter
pie adv piously
pila -ae f ball
pilum -i n javelin
pinguis -is -e fat

pirum -i n pear
pisa -orum npl peas
piscina -ae f swimming pool
piscis -is m fish
pistor -oris m baker
pistrina -ae f bakery
placenta -ae f cake
placeo placere placui (+ dat) to please
plaustrum -i n wagon
planeta -ae f planet
plenus -a -um full
pluit it is raining
pluma -ae f feather
plurimus -a -um most, very much; **plurimi -ae -a** pl very many, most
Pluto -onis m Pluto (god of the underworld)
politus -a -um polite
pluvia -ae f rain
pomarius -i m fruit vendor
pomeridianus -a -um (in the) afternoon
Pomponius -i m (male name) Pomponius
pomeridie adv in the afternoon
pono ponere posui to place (a bet)
pons pontis m bridge
popina -ae f restaurant
popularis -is -e popular
porcus -i m pig
porta -ae f gate
porto -are -avi to carry; **portabitis** you (pl) will carry
portus -us m harbor, port
possum posse potui to be able; **possumus** we can
post prep (+ acc) behind; after
post- pref behind, after
postquam conj after
poto -are -avi to drink
prae- pref before, ahead
praecedo -cedere -cessi to go before, precede
praecipio -cipere -cepi to take beforehand; to instruct, teach
praecipue adv especially
praeda -ae f prey
praefero praeferre praetuli to bring before; to prefer
praepositio -onis f preposition
praeter prep (+ acc) except

praeterea adv besides; **quid praeterea?** what else?
prandium -i n lunch
prasinus -a -um (dark) green
pratum -i n meadow
pretium -i n price
primum adv first; for the first time
primus -a -um first; **prima luce** at first light, at dawn
pristis -is f shark
pro prep (+ abl) for, before; **pro me** for me
pro- pref forward, forth
procedo -cedere -cessi to go forth, proceed
procul adv at a distance; **procul ab** (+ abl) far from
produco -ducere -duxi to lead forth; to produce
proelium -i n battle
professor -oris m professor
pronomen -inis n pronoun
prope prep (+ acc) near
propheticus -a -um prophetic
propinquus -a -um near
prosperus -a -um prosperous
protego -tegere -texi to protect
proximus -a -um nearby; next-door; next
prudens; prudentis prudent
prudenter adv prudently
prunum -i n plum
publicus -a -um public
Publius -i m (male name) Publius
puella -ae f girl
puer pueri m boy
pugil pugilis m boxer
pugno -are -avi to fight
pugnator -oris m fighter
pulso -are -avi to beat against; to knock at
Pupienus -i m (male name) Pupienus
purpureus -a -um crimson
purus -a -um pure

Q

quadraginta indecl forty
quaero quaerere quaesivi to ask; to look for
quaeso please

quaestio -onis f question
qualis -is -e what kind of, what a; **qualis tandem** just what kind of
quam adv how; what a
quamquam conj although
quando adv when
quantus -a -um how much; **quanti (constat)?** how much (does it cost)?; **quantum** how much
quartus -a -um fourth
quattuor indecl four
quattuordecim indecl fourteen
-que conj and
qui rel pron who
quia conj because
quid pron what; **quid agis?** how do you do?; **quid novi?** what's new?
quies -etis f quiet; rest, nap; **quietem capere** to take a nap
Quieta -ae f (female name) Quieta
quindecim indecl fifteen
quingenti -ae -a five hundred
quinquaginta indecl fifty
quinque indecl five
quintus -a -um fifth
Quintus -i m (male name) Quintus
quis pron who?
quisque pron each one
quo conj where (to)?
quoad conj as long as
quod pron which; **de quibus** from which; **quod nomen est tibi?** what's your name?
quod conj because
quomodo adv how
quoque adv too
quot indecl how many?
quotus -a -um how much; **quota hora est?** what time is it?

R

raeda -ae f carriage
rapio rapere repi to grab, seize
rapidus -a -um fast, rapid
rarus -a -um rare
re- pref back; again
recedo -cedere -cessi to go back, recede

recens; recentis fresh
recipio -cipere -cepi to get back; to receive
recte adv right; **recte dicis** you are right
reduco -ducere -duxi to lead back; to reduce
refero referre rettuli to bring back; to refer
reficio -ficere -feci to redo; to repair
refugio -fugere -fugi to flee back; to take refuge
regia -ae f palace
regina -ae f queen
regio -onis f region
regula -ae f ruler
religio -onis f religion
remigo -are -avi to row
remotus -a -um remote
remus -i m oar
reperio reperire repperi to find
repo repere repsi to creep
reporto -are -avi to bring back; to report
res rei f thing, matter, affair; **magna res non est** it is not important
respondeo respondere respondi to answer, respond
resto restare restiti to be left, remain
rex regis m king
rideo ridere risi to laugh
ridiculus -a -um ridiculous
ripa -ae f bank
rivus -i m brook, stream
robustus -a -um strong, robust
rogo -are -avi to ask
Roma -ae f Rome
Romanus -a -um Roman
rosa -ae f rose
rosarium -i n rose bed
roseus -a -um pink
rotundus -a -um round, rotund
ruber rubra rubrum red
rudo rudere to roar
Rufus -i m (male name) Rufus
ruo ruere rui to rush
rus ruris n country; **rus** to the country; **ruri** in the country
rusticus -a -um rustic, (of the) country; **rusticus** m peasant

S

saccarum -i n sugar
sacculum -i n wallet
sacer sacra sacrum holy, sacred
saepe adv often
sagitta -ae f arrow
salio salire salii to jump
saluto -are -avi to greet
salve interj hello! **salvete** (pl) hello!
sandalium -i n sandal
sane adv yes
sapientia -ae f wisdom
Saturnus -i m Saturn (father of Jupiter)
Sarmatae -arum mpl Sarmatians (Russians)
Sarmatia -ae f Sarmatia (Russia)
Sarmaticus -a -um Sarmatian (Russian)
sartor -oris m tailor
sartrix -tricis f dressmaker
satis indecl enough; **satis pecuniae** enough money
saxum -i n rock
schola -ae f school
scribo scribere scripsi to write
scrupulosus -a -um scrupulous
sculptor -oris m sculptor
scutum -i n shield
secludo secludere seclusi to seclude
secundum prep (+ acc) according to
secundus -a -um second
sed conj but
sedecim indecl sixteen
sedecimus -a -um sixteenth
sedeo sedere sedi to sit
sella -ae f chair; **sella tonsoria** barber chair
semel adv once
semihora -ae f half-hour
senator -oris m senator
Seneca -ae m (family name) Seneca
septem indecl seven
September -bris m September
septendecim indecl seventeen
septentriones -um mpl North
septimana -ae f week

Septimius -i m (male name) Septimius

septimus -a -um seventh

septuaginta indecl seventy

serva -ae f maid, servant

servo -are -avi to save

servus -i m servant

severe adv severely, sternly

severus -a -um severe, stern

servio servire servii (+ dat) to serve

sex indecl six

sexaginta indecl sixty

sextus -a -um sixth

Sextus -i m (male name) Sextus

si conj if

sic adv so; like this

Sicilia -ae f Sicily

Siculus -a -um Sicilian

signum -i n standard

sileo silere silui to be silent

silva -ae f forest

simia -ae f monkey

similis -is -e similar, like

simius -i m ape

simplex; simplicis simple

simplissimus -a -um very simple

simul ac, simul atque conj as soon as

sincere adv sincerely

sincerus -a -um sincere

sine prep (+ abl) without

sinister -tra -trum left

sitio sitire to be thirsty

situs -a -um located

societas -atis f partnership

socius -i m associate, assistant

sol solis m sun

solea -ae f sandal

solum adv only; **non solum ... sed etiam** not only ... but also

solus -a -um alone, only

somnum -i n sleep; **somnum pomeridianum** siesta

sordidus -a -um dirty, sordid

soror -oris f sister

spatiosus -a -um spacious

specto -are -avi to watch

speculum -i n mirror

specus -us m cave

spero -are -avi to hope

splendide splendidly

splendidus -a -um splendid

stabulum -i n stable

stadium -i n stadium

stagnum -i n pond

statim adv immediately

statua -ae f statue

stella -ae f star

stilus -i m stylus

sto stare steti to stand

stola -ae f (long) gown

stomachus -i m stomach

stramentum -i n straw

strepitus -us m noise

strideo stridere to howl

studeo studere studui to study

studiosus -a -um studious

stupidus -a -um stupid

suavis -is -e delicious

sub-, suc- pref under, beneath; from beneath, up

sub prep (+ abl or acc) under

subrideo -ridere -risi to smile

Subura -ae f Subura (a noisy district in Rome, near the forum)

subsellium -i n bench

subsido -sidere -sessi to subside, calm down

subterraneus -a -um below (the ground)

suburbium -i n suburb

succedo -cedere -cessi (+ dat) to go after, succeed

sudo -are -avi to sweat

suffero sufferre sustuli to bear up under, suffer

sum esse fui to be; **ero** I'll be; **es** you are; **sunt** they are

summus -a -um highest; **in summo monte** on the top of the mountain

sumo sumere sumpsi to take, eat

super prep (+ abl) above; (+ acc) over

superbus -a -um proud

surgo surgere surrexi to get up; to wake up

susurro -are -avi to whisper

suus -a -um his/her/its/their own

Syria -ae f Syria

Syrius -a -um Syrian

T

taberna -ae f shop; tavern;

taberna chartaria stationery store; **taberna crustularia** pastry shop; **taberna laniena** butcher shop; **taberna tignaria** carpenter shop; **taberna vestiaria** clothing store

tabula -ae f (wax) tablet

tablinum -i n living room

tacite adv quietly

tacitus -a -um quiet

talis -is -e such a; **talis ... qualis** such ... as

tam adv so

tamen conj still

tamquam conj just as, like, as

tandem adv at last

tantum adv only

tantummodo adv only

tardus -a -um late, tardy; slow

taurus -i m bull

tectum -i n roof

templum -i n temple

tempus temporis n time; **ad tempus** just in time; **tempus anni** season

te pron you

teneo tenere tenui to hold

Terentius -i m (male name) Terence

terreo terrere terrui to frighten

terribilis -is -e terrible

tertius -a -um third

Tiberia -ae f (female name) Tiberia

Tiberis -is m Tiber (River)

theatrum -i n theater

thermae -arum fpl (public) bath

tigris -is f tiger

timeo timere timui to be afraid (of)

timide adv timidly

timidus -a -um timid

Titus -i m (male name) Titus

toga -ae f toga

tollo tollere sustuli to raise, lift; to weigh

tomaclum -i n sausage

tondeo tondere totondi to cut

tonsor -oris m barber

tonstrina -ae f barbershop

tonstrix -icis f hairdresser

tonsura -ae f haircut

tot *indecl* so many

totus -a -um whole, total; **in toto** in all

trans *prep* (+ *acc*) across

transfero transferre transtuli to bring across; to transfer

transeo transire transii to move

transporto -are -avi to carry across; transport

tredecim *indecl* thirteen

tremendus -a -um tremendous

tres tres tria three

triclinium -i *n* dining room

tridens -entis *m* trident

triginta *indecl* thirty

tristis -is -e sad

triticum -i *n* wheat

tu *pron* you

tuber -eris *n* hump

tunc *adv* then; **tunc maxime** just then

tunica -ae *f* tunic

tuus -a -um your

U

ubi *adv* where

ubi *conj* when

ubique *adv* everywhere

ultra *adv* more

ultra *prep* (+ *acc*) on the other side of, beyond

una *adv* together; **una cum** together with

unde *adv* where (from)

undecim *indecl* eleven

undecimus -a -um eleventh

undequinquaginta *indecl* forty-nine

undetriginta *indecl* twenty-nine

undeviginti *indecl* nineteen

unus -a -um one

Uranus -i *m* Uranus (*god of the sky*)

urbanus -a -um city, from the city

urbs -is *f* city

ursus -i *m* bear

ut *conj* as, when; **ut . . . sic** as . . . so

utilis -is -e useful

utque *adv* at least

uva -ae *f* grape

uxor -oris *f* wife

V

vacca -ae *f* cow

vacuus -a -um empty

vado vadere vasi to go

valde *adv* a lot

valeo valere valui to be fine; **vale!** goodbye!; **valete!** (*pl*) goodbye!

Valeria -ae *f* (female name) Valeria

validus -a -um strong

valles -is *f* valley

varius -a -um various

vehiculum -i *n* vehicle

velifico -are -avi to operate the sails

vello vellere to tug at

velocissimus -a -um fastest

velocitas -atis *f* speed

velum -i *n* sail; veil; **vela ventis dare** to set sail

venator -oris *m* hunter

vendito -are -avi to sell

venditor -oris *m* vendor, seller

venditus -a -um sold

vendo vendere vendidi to sell

venio venire veni to come; **veni mecum** come with me

ventus -i *m* wind

Venus -eris *f* Venus

ver veris *n* spring

verbum -i *n* verb

vero *adv* really; **vero vado** I AM going

vero *conj* but

verto vertere verti to turn; **se vertens** turning

verus -a -um true

vespere *adv* in the evening

vestiarius -i *m* (clothing) salesman

vestibulum -i *n* entrance way

vestimentum -i *n* clothing

vetus; veteris old

vexillum -i flag

vicinus -i *m* neighbor

victor -oris *m* victor

vicus -i *m* street, block

video videre vidi to see

viginti *indecl* twenty; **viginti unus** twenty-one

villa -ae *f* villa, country house

villosus -a -um bushy

vinco vincere vici to conquer

vindico -are -avi to claim

vinum -i *n* wine

viola -ae *f* violet

vir viri *m* man

viridis -is -e (light) green

vis vis *f* charge; **vis electrica** electrical charge

visito -are -avi to visit

vivo vivere vixi to live

vocabulum -i *n* vocabulary word

volo -are -avi to fly; **volans; volantis** flying

volumen -inis *n* volume; scroll

vos *pron* you

vox vocis *f* voice; **una voce** with one voice

Vulcanus -i *m* Vulcan (*divine blacksmith*)

vulpes -is *f* fox

vultus -us *m* expression

Vocābula Anglica-Latīna

A

able: to be able possum posse potui

about (*approximately*) circa (+ *acc*); (*concerning*) de (+ *abl*)

above super (+ *acc or abl*)

accept accipio accipere accepi

according to secundum (+ *acc*)

ache dolor -*oris m*

ache doleo dolere dolui

across trans (+ *acc*)

actor actor -*oris m*

actress actrix -*icis f*

advice consilium -*i n*

afraid: to be afraid (of) timeo timere timui

Africa Africa -*ae f*

African Africanus -*a -um*

after (*conj*) postquam; (*prep*) post (+ *acc*)

against adversus (+ *acc*)

ago abhinc

all omnes -*es -ia*

alone solus -*a -um*

already jam

also etiam

altar ara -*ae f*

although quamquam

amphitheater amphitheatrum -*i n*

anchor ancora -*ae f*

ancient antiquus -*a -um*

and et; -que

animal animal animalis *n*

another alius -*a -ud*

answer respondeo respondere respondi

apartment cenaculum -*i n*

apartment building insula -*ae f*

ape simius -*i m*

apple malum -*i n*

Apollo Apollo -*inis m*

April Aprilis -*is m*

aqueduct aquaeductus -*us m*

arm bracchium -*i n*

arms arma -*orum npl*

army exercitus -*us m*

around circum (+ *acc*)

as ut

ask quaero quaerere quaesivi; rogo -*are -avi*

as long as dum; quoad

assistant, associate socius -*i m*

as soon as simul ac; simul atque; **as soon as possible** cum primum

astonished attonitus -*a -um*

athlete athleta -*ae m*

atrium atrium -*i n*

attend frequento -*are -avi*

August Augustus -*i m*

autumn autumnus -*i m*

B

baby infans infantis *mf*

Bacchus Bacchus -*i m*

back dorsum -*i n*

baker pistor -*oris m*

bakery pistrina -*ae f*

bald calvus -*a -um*

ball pila -*ae f*

banana ariena -*ae f*

bank ripa -*ae f*

barber tonsor -*oris m*

bark latro -*are -avi*

bath balneum -*i n*; (*public bath*) thermae -*arum fpl*

battle proelium -*i n*

be sum esse fui

bear ursus -*i m*

beard barba -*ae f*

beast bestia -*ae f*

because quia; quod

bed lectus -*i m*

bedroom cubiculum -*i n*

before antequam; (*prep*) ante (+ *acc*)

begin incipio incipere incepi

behind post (+ *acc*)

believe credo credere credidi

belt cingulum -*i n*

bench subsellium -*i n*

besides praeterea

best optimus -*a -um*

between inter (+ *acc*)

big magnus -*a -um*

bird avis -*is f*

birthday natalis -*is m*

bite mordeo mordere momordi

bitter amarus -*a -um*

black ater atra atrum

blacksmith faber -*bri* ferrarius -*i m*

block vicus -*i m*

blue caeruleus -*a -um*

boat navicula -*ae f*

body corpus corporis *n*

bold audax; audacis

book liber libri *m*

bookcase librarium -*i n*

boot caliga -*ae f*

bow arcus -*us m*

boxer pugil pugilis *m*

boy puer pueri *m*

bracelet armilla -*ae f*

break frango frangere fregi

breakfast jentaculum -*i n*

broad latus -*a -um*

bread panis -*is m*

breastplate lorica -*ae f*

bridge pons -*tis m*

bring fero ferre tuli; **bring together** confero conferre contuli

Britain Britannia -*ae f*

British Britannus -*a -um*

brother frater fratris *m*

brown fuscus -*a -um*

building aedificium -*i n*

bull taurus -*i m*

but sed

butcher lanius -*i m*

buy emo emere emi

by a, ab (+ *abl*)

C

cadaver cadaver -*eris n*

cake placenta -*ae f*

camel camelus -*i m*

camp castra -*orum npl*

cape lacerna -ae f
captain magister -tri m
cargo onus oneris n
carpenter faber -bri m
  tignarius -i
carriage raeda -ae f
carry porto -are -avi
cat feles -is f
catch capto -are -avi
cavalryman eques equitis m
celebrate celebro -are -avi
centurion centurio -onis m
Ceres Ceres Cereris f
certainly certe
chair cathedra -ae f; sella -ae f
change muto -are -avi
charge vis; vis f
chariot curriculum -i n
cheese caseus -i m
cherry cerasum -i n
chest pectus pectoris n
chicken gallina -ae f
children liberi -orum mpl
citizen civis -is m
city urbs -is f
class classis -is f
clear clarus -a -um
climb ascendo -ere -i; **climb
  aboard** conscendo -ere
  -i; **climb down** descendo
  -ere -i
close claudo claudere clausi

clothing vestimentum -i n
cloud nubes -is f
cold frigidus -a -um
color color -oris m
come venio venire veni
comfortable commodus -a
  -um
commander imperator -oris m
complete conficio conficere
  confeci
conquer vinco vincere vici
conversation conversatio
  -onis f
cook coqua -ae f; conquus -i m
cookie crustulum -i n
corpse cadaver -eris n
country patria -ae f; **in the
  country** ruri; **to the
  country** rus
cow vacca -ae f
cozy commodus -a -um

crude crudus -a -um
cucumber cucumis cucumeris
  m

Cupid Cupido -inis m
custom mos moris m
cut tondeo tondere totondi

D

daily cotidie
dangerous periculosus -a -um
dark obscurus -a -um
daughter filia -ae f
day dies -ei m
dead mortuus -a -um; the dead
  mortui -orum mpl
dear carus -a -um
deceive decipio decipere
  decepi
December December -bris m
defend defendo -ere -i
dessert mensa -ae secunda -ae
  f
destroy deleo -ere -evi
dialog colloqium -i n
Diana Diana -ae f
different varius -a -um
difficult difficilis -is -e
dining couch lectus -i m
dining room triclinium -i n
dinner cena -ae f
divide divido dividere divisi
dirty sordidus -a -um
do facio facere feci
doctor medicus -i m
dog canis -is m
domestic domesticus -a -um

donkey asinus -i m
door janua -ae f
dove columba -ae f
down from de (+ abl)
drink poto -are -avi

E

each omnis -is -e
eager (for) cupidus -a -um
eagerly cupide
eagle aquila -ae f
ear auris -is f
earn mereo merere merui
earrings inaures -ium fpl

easily facile
East oriens orientis m
easy facilis -is -e
eat edo edere (or esse) edi
egg ovum -i n
elegant elegans; elegantis
empty vacuus -a -um
enemy hostis -is m

enormous enormis -is -e
enough satis; **enough money**
  satis pecuniae
enter intro -are -avi
envy invideo invidere invidi
  (+ dat)
especially praecipue
Europe Europa -ae f
European Europaeus -a -um
even etiam
evening: in the evening
  vespere
everywhere ubique
except praeter (+ acc)
explain explico -are -avi
expression vultus -us m
eye oculus -i m

F

face facies faciei f
fair aequus -a -um
faithful fidelis -is -e
faithfully fideliter
fall cado cadere cecidi
fall autumnus -i m
false falsus -a -um
familiar notus -a -um
family familia -ae f
famous clarus -a -um
far longe; **far from** procul ab
  (+ abl)
farm fundus -i m
farmer agricola -ae m
fast rapidus -a -um
fat pinguis -is -e; obesus -a
  -um; crassus -a -um
father pater patris m
February Februarius -i m
fellow soldier commiles itis m
field ager agri m
fierce ferox; ferocis
fight pugno -are -avi
finally denique
find reperio reperire repperi
fine bene
finger digitus -i m
finish finio -ire -ivi
finish finis -is m; **finish line**
  finis -is m
firm firmus -a -um
first primus -a -um; (adv)
  primum
fish piscis -is m
flee fugio -ere -i
flower flos floris m
fly volo -are -avi

food cibus -i m
foot ped pedis m
for pro (+abl)
forces copiae -arum fpl
forest silva -ae f
fortunate fortunatus -a -um
forum forum -i n
fox vulpes -is f
free liber libera liberum
fresh recens; recentis
Friday dies -ei m Veneris
friend amicus, -i m; amica -ae f
friendly amicus -a -um
frighten terreo terrere terrui
fruit fructus -us m
full plenus -a -um

G

Gallic Gallicus -a -um
game ludus -i m
garden hortus -i m
gate porta -ae f
Gaul (France) Gallia -ae f; **Gauls** Galli -orum mpl
gem gemma -ae f
German Germanus -a -um; **Germans** Germani -orum mpl
Germany Germania -ae f
gift donum -i n
girl puella -ae f
gladiator gladiator -oris m
go eo ire ivi; cedo cedere cessi; vado vadere vasi
god deus -i m
goddess dea -ae f
golden aureus -a -um
good bonus -a -um
good-bye vale; (pl) valete
gown stola -ae f
grab rapio -ere -ui
grain frumentum -i n
grandfather avus -i m
grandmother avia -ae f
grape uva -ae f
grass herba -ae f
Greece Graecia -ae f
Greek Graecus -a -um; **Greeks** Graeci -orum mpl
green (light green) viridis -is -e; (dark green) prasinus -a -um
greet saluto -are -avi
grey canus -a -um
grown-up adultus -a -um

H

hair coma -ae f
hairy pilosus -a -um
hairdresser tonstrix tonstricis f
hand manus -us f
hang pendeo pendere pependi; **hang down** dependeo dependere dependi
happy felix; felicis; laetus -a -um
harbor portus -us m
harm noceo nocere nocui
hat petasus -i m
have habeo habere habui
he is
head caput capitis n
hear audio -ire -ivi
heart cor cordis n
heavy gravis -is -e
hello salve; (pl) salvete
helmet galea -ae f
help auxilium -i n
help adjuvo adjuvare adjuvi
here hic
hide lateo latere latui
high altus -a -um
hill collis -is m
his ejus; his own suus -a -um
hold teneo tenere tenui
hole cavum -i n; foramen -inis n
holiday dies -ei m festus -i
home domus -us f; **at home** domi; **home(ward)** domum
horse equus -i m
hot calidus -a -um
hour hora -ae f
house domus -us f; casa -ae f; **at the house of** apud (+ acc)
how quam, quomodo; **how many** quot
however autem
hungry: to be hungry esurio -ire
hurt doleo dolere dolui

I

I ego
if si
immediately statim
immortal immortalis -is -e
in in (+ abl)
incredible incredibilis -is -e

in front of ante (+ acc)
inhabit inhabito -are -avi
inhabitant incola -ae m
ink atramentum -i n
intelligent intellegens; intellegentis
into in (+ acc)
invite invito -are -avi
it id
Italic Italicus -a -um
Italy Italia -ae f

J

January Januarius -i m
Janus Janus -i m
javelin pilum -i n
joy gaudium -i n
July Julius -i m
jump salio salire salii
June Junius -i m
Juno Juno -onis f
Jupiter Juppiter Jovis m
just justus -a -um

K

kind benignus -a -um
king rex regis m
kitchen culina -ae f

L

lake lacus -us m
language lingua -ae f
late tardus -a -um
laugh rideo ridere risi
law jus juris n
lawyer advocatus -i m
lead duco ducere duxi
leaf folium -i n
leave discedo discedere discessi
learn disco discere didici
left sinister -tra -trum
leg crus cruris n
letter epistula -ae f
lettuce lactuca -ae f
library bibliotheca -ae f
lie: to lie down jaceo jacere jacui
lift tollo tollere sustuli
light lumen luminis n
lightning bolt fulmen fulminis n
like diligo diligere dilexi

lily lilium -i n
lion leo -onis m
lip labrum -i n
litter lectica -ae f
little by little paulatim
live vivo vivere vixi; **to live in**
 inhabito -are -avi
look for quaero quaerere
 quaesivi
lovable amabilis -is -e
love amo -are -avi
lunch prandium -i n

M

magnificent magnificus -a
 -um
make facio facere feci; fabrico
 -are -avi
man vir viri m; homo hominis
 m
many multi -ae -a
march iter facio
marketplace forum -i n
mast malus -i m
May Maius -i m
maybe fortasse
meat caro -nis f
medicine medicina -ae f
member membrum -i n
memorable memorabilis -is -e
memory memoria -ae f
Mercury Mercurius -i m
messenger nuntius -i m
military service militia -ae f
milk lac lactis n
mind animus -i m
Minerva Minerva -ae f
mirror speculum -i n
Miss domina -ae f
Monday dies -ei m Lunae
money pecunia -ae f
monkey simia -ae f
monster monstrum -i n
month mensis -is m
moon luna -ae f
more magis
morning mane
most maxime
mother mater matris f
mountain mons -tis m
mouse mus muris m
mouth os oris n
move moveo movere movi;
 (*from one home to another*)
 transeo -ire -ivi
muscle musculus -i m

music musica -ae f
musician musicus -i m;
 musica -ae f
my meus -a -um

N

name nomen nominis n
narrow angustus -a -um
nature natura -ae f
navigation navigatio -onis f
near prope (+ acc); (adj)
 propinquus -a -um
nearby proximus -a -um
neck collum -i n
necklace monile -is n
neighbor finitimus -i m;
 vicinus -i m
Neptune Neptunus -i m
new novus -a -um
next proximus -a -um
night nox noctis f; **at night**
 noctu; **in the middle of the**
 night media nocte
no non; minime; minime vero;
 no longer non jam
noble nobilis -is -e
noon meridies -ei f
no one nemo neminis m
nor neque
north septentriones -um mpl
nose nasus -i m
not non; **not at all** minime
 vero; **not only ... but also**
 non solum ... sed etiam;
 not yet nondum
nothing nihil
November November -bris m
number numerus -i m

O

obedient obediens; obedientis
obediently obedienter
obey pareo parere parui (+
 dat)
October October -bris m
often saepe
oil oleum -i n
old vetus; veteris; ... **years**
 old ... annos natus -a -um
olive oliva -ae f
on in (+ abl)
once semel
one unus -a -um
only solus -a -um; (adv)
 tantum, tantummodo; solum

open aperio aperire aperui
or aut; an
other alter altera alterum
our noster nostra nostrum
out of e, ex (+ abl)
outside extra (+ acc)
over super (+ abl or acc)
own: his (her, its, their) own
 suus -a -um

P

painter pictor -oris m
palace regia -ae f
pardon ignosco ignoscere
 ignovi (+ dat)
parents parentes -um mpl
park horti -orum mpl publici
 -orum
part pars -tis f
party convivium -i n
peace pax pacis f
pear pirum -i n
peas pisa -orum npl
pen calamus -i m
people homines -um mpl
pet permulceo permulcere
 permulsi
pick carpo carpere carpsi
pig porcus -i m
price pretium -i n
place locus -i m
plain campus -i m
play ludo ludere lusi
playground area -ae f
please quaeso; **to please**
 placeo placere placui (+ dat)
plough aro -are -avi
plum prunum -i n
Pluto Pluto -onis m
polite politus -a -um
popular popularis -is -e
poor pauper; pauperis;
 (*pitiable*) miser misera
 miserum
porch pergula -ae f
portico pergula -ae f
prepare paro -are -avi
prepared paratus -a -um
pretty bellus -a -um
prey praeda -ae f
produce market macellum -i
 n
prosperous prosperus -a -um
protect protego -tegere -texi
proud superbus -a -um

prudent prudens; prudentis
pupil (*schoolboy*) discipulus -i m; (*schoolgirl*) discipula -ae f
pure purus -a -um

Q

queen regina -ae f
quickly cito
quiet quies -etis f

R

rabbit cuniculus -i m
rain pluvia -ae f; **it is raining** pluit
rain basin impluvium -i n
raincoat paenula -ae f
read lego legere legi
ready paratus -a -um
really vero
receive accipio accipere accepi
red ruber rubra rubrum
region regio -onis f
religion religio -onis f
restaurant popina -ae f
rich dives; divitis
ring anulus -i m
river flumen fluminis n
rock saxum -i n
Roman Romanus -a -um
Rome Roma -ae f
roof tectum -i n
room conclave -is n
rooster gallus -i m
round rotundus -a -um
ruler regula -ae f
run curro currere cucurri; (*of a road*) duco ducere duxi
rush ruo ruere rui; **to rush about** festino -are -avi

S

sacred sacer sacra sacrum
sad tristis -is -e
safety pin fibula -ae f
sail velum -i n; **to sail** navigo -are -avi
salad acetaria -orum npl
sand (h)arena -ae f
sandal solea -ae f, sandalium -i n
Saturday dies -ei m Saturni
save servo -are -avi
say dico dicere dixi
school schola -ae f; ludus -i m

scroll volumen -inis n
sea mare -is n
seashore ora -ae f maritima -ae
secretly clam
see video videre vidi
seize rapio rapere rapui
sell vendo vendere vendidi
senate building curia -ae f
senator senator -oris m
send mitto mittere misi
servant serva -ae f; servus -i m
severe severus -a -um
sharp acer acris acre
sheep ovis -is f
sheet charta -ae f
shield scutum -i n
ship navis -is f
shoe calceus -i m
shop taberna -ae f
shore ora -ae f
short brevis -is -e
shout clamo -are -avi
shout clamor -oris m
Sicilian Siculus -a -um
Sicily Sicilia -ae f
sick aegrotus -a -um
silent: to be silent sileo silere silui
sincere sincerus -a -um
sing canto -are -avi
singer cantor -oris m; cantrix -icis f
sister soror -oris f
sit sedeo sedere sedi; **sit down** consido considere consedi
sky caelum -i n
skylight compluvium -i n
slave serva -ae f; servus -i m
sleep dormio dormire dormivi
sleep somnum -i n
slow tardus -a -um
small parvus -a -um
smile subrideo -ridere -risi
snow nix nivis f
so sic
soft mollis -is -e
soldier miles militis m
some aliquot
someday aliquando
something aliquid
sometimes interdum; **sometimes . . . sometimes . . .** modo . . . modo . . .
son filius -i m
song carmen carminis n

sordid sordidus -a -um
soup jus juris n
South meridies -ei m
spacious spatiosus -a -um
Spain Hispania -ae f
Spanish Hispanus -a -um; **the Spanish** Hispani -orum mpl
splendid splendidus -a -um
spring fons -tis m; (*season*) ver veris n
stable stabulum -i n
stadium stadium -i n
standard signum -i n
star astrum -i n; stella -ae f
stay maneo manere mansi
stern severus -a -um
still tamen
stomach stomachus -i m
story fabula -ae f
strange mirus -a -um
stranger peregrinus -i m
stroke permulceo -mulcere -mulsi
strong validus -a -um, robustus -a -um
stylus stilus -i m
summer aestas -atis f
sun sol solis m
Sunday dies -ei m Solis
sweet dulcis -is -e
swiftly celeriter
swim nato -are -avi
sword gladius -i m
sword belt balteus -i m

T

table mensa -ae f
tablet tabula -ae f
tailor sartor -oris m
take capio capere cepi; (*eat*) sumo sumere sumpsi
teach doceo docere docui
teacher magister -tri m; magistra -ae f
tell narro -are -avi
temple templum -i n
terrible terribilis -is -e
thanks gratias
that ille -a -ud
theater theatrum -i n
their eorum mpl; earum fpl; **their own** suus -a -um
then (*at that time*) tunc; (*next*) deinde
therefore itaque; igitur

they ei eae ea
thing res rei *f*
thirsty: to be thirsty sitio
  sitire
this hic haec hoc
through per (+ *acc*)
Thursday dies *-ei m* Jovis
Tiber Tiberis *-is m*
tiger tigris *-is f*
to ad (+ *acc*)
today hodie
toga toga *-ae f*
together with una cum (+
  abl)
tomorrow cras
tongue lingua *-ae f*
tonight hac nocte
too (*also*) quoque; (*excessively*)
  nimis
town oppidum *-i n*
tree arbor arboris *f*
trip iter itineris *n*; **take a trip**
  iter facere
troops copiae *-arum fpl*
true verus *-a -um*
Tuesday dies *-ei m* Martis
tunic tunica *-ae f*

U

ugly deformis *-is -e*
under sub (+ *abl or acc*)
until donec
Uranus Uranus *-i m*
useful utilis *-is -e*

V

valley valles *-is f*
vegetable holus holeris *n*
veil velum *-i n*
vendor venditor *-oris m*
Venus Venus Veneris *f*
victor victor *-oris m*
villa villa *-ae f*
vinegar acetum *-i n*
visit visito *-are -avi*
Vulcan Vulcanus *-i m*

W

wagon plaustrum *-i n*
wait for exspecto *-are -avi*
walk ambulo *-are -avi*
wall murus *-i m*
want opto *-are -avi*
war bellum *-i n*
wash lavo lavare lavi
water aqua *-ae f*
wave fluctus *-us m*
we nos
wear gero gerere gessi
Wednesday dies *-ei m*
  Mercurii
week septimana *-ae f*
weight onus oneris *n*
welcome excipio excipere
  excepi
West occidens *-entis m*
what quid; **what kind of**
  qualis *-is -e*
when ubi; quando
where ubi
while dum

white albus *-a -um*; (*shiny*
  white) candidus *-a -um*
who (*interrogative*) quis;
  (*relative*) qui, quae
whole totus *-a -um*
why cur
wide latus *-a -um*
wife uxor *-oris f*
wild ferus *-a -um*
wind ventus *-i m*
window fenestra *-ae f*
wine vinum *-i n*
wing ala *-ae f*
winter hiems hiemis *f*
wish opto *-are -avi*
with cum (+ *abl*)
without sine (+ *abl*)
wolf lupus *-i m*
woman femina *-ae f*
wonderful mirabilis *-is -e*;
  admirabilis *-is -e*
work laboro *-are -avi*
work labor *-oris m*
workshop officina *-ae f*
world mundus *-i m*
write scribo scribere scripsi

Y

yellow flavus *-a -um*
yes ita; sane
you tu
young parvus *-a -um;*
  younger than minor natu
  quam
young man adulescentulus *-i*
  m
your tuus *-a -um*

Grammatical Index

Topical Index